World Disasters Report

2003

Focus on ethics in aid

International Federation
of Red Cross and Red Crescent Societies

The *World Disasters Report 2003* was edited by Jonathan Walter.

Thanks to all those who assisted contributors during travel and research.

Baseline maps by Geoatlas® – ©GRAPHI-OGRE, Hendaye, France
Typesetting by Strategic Communications SA, Geneva, Switzerland
Printed by SADAG Imprimerie, Bellegarde/Valserine, France
Production manager: Sue Pfiffner   Research: Aradhna Duggal

Contact details:

International Federation of Red Cross and Red Crescent Societies
17, chemin des Crêts, P.O. Box 372
CH-1211 Geneva 19, Switzerland
Tel:. (41)(22) 730 4222 Fax: (41)(22) 733 0395
E-mail: secretariat@ifrc.org
Web: http://www.ifrc.org

To order the *World Disasters Report,* contact:

Kumarian Press Inc
1294 Blue Hills Ave
Bloomfield CT 06002, USA
Tel.: +1 860 243 2098
Fax: +1 860 243 2867
E-mail: kpbooks@aol.com
Web: http://www.kpbooks.com

Eurospan
3 Henrietta Street, Covent Garden
London WC2E 8LU, UK
Tel.: +44 20 7240 0856
Fax: +44 20 7379 0609
E-mail: orders@edspubs.co.uk
Web: http://www.eurospanonline.com

Contents

Section One Focus on ethics in aid

Section Two Tracking the system

Putting principles into practice – key to legitimacy

The humanitarian ethic is about saving the lives of those in greatest need. But, swamped as we are by the statistics of suffering, we must also respect the human dignity of every woman, man and child whose life is shattered by conflict, hunger, disease or disaster. Putting the two parts of this ethic into practice remains the greatest challenge facing not only humanitarian organizations, but all those with a stake in humanitarian crises.

The record, however, is very mixed. Humanitarian aid tends to favour high-profile emergencies at the expense of more invisible suffering far from the media or political spotlight. While countries targeted in the 'war on terror' have attracted unprecedented levels of humanitarian and reconstruction aid, other – arguably more pressing – crises languish in the shadows. Africa is besieged by droughts, floods, conflict, infectious diseases and – most deadly of all – the HIV/AIDS pandemic, which claimed an estimated 6,500 lives every day last year. Floods and snowstorms have wrecked hundreds of thousands of lives across the Russian Federation and Mongolia. Tens of millions of Asians, Africans and Latin Americans have been forced by violence, natural disasters or economic ruin to flee their homes in search of survival.

Humanitarian aid does not deal an equal hand to all those suffering under the shadow of conflict, disease or disaster. Within weeks of ousting Saddam Hussein, the US Department of Defense reported that it had raised US$ 1.7 billion in relief for the Iraqi people. While this will certainly be gratefully received, what about the 40 million people in 22 countries across the African continent on the verge of starvation? In Angola alone, more than 4 million people depend on aid to help them survive. In September 2002, the International Federation launched an emergency appeal for humanitarian assistance to 100,000 of the most vulnerable in the country. Four months later, the appeal was less than 4 per cent covered. Sadly, the story is repeated across West Africa, the Sahel and around the world.

New research into the connections between needs assessments and the allocation of relief aid suggests that the scale of humanitarian appeals is often slanted towards what the donor 'market' will bear – high-profile crises routinely attract higher appeals for aid, even if other forgotten disasters are more deserving. This trend must stop. There is an urgent priority to invest in credible, objective assessments of humanitarian needs across the globe, so that aid is allocated to those at greatest risk and need, not to those at the top of the strategic and media agenda.

Attracting sufficient resources to address the effects of disaster is only half the battle. We must also ensure those resources are properly used in a way that respects the dignity, capacity and aspirations of every person we seek to help. Again, the record is mixed. The recent history of humanitarian interventions is littered with examples of inappropriate aid, which reflect more the priorities and needs of donor agencies than the needs of those affected by crisis. The fledgling Afghan administration has complained that the billions donated in aid have been too focused on relief rather than reconstruction. Huge food imports have undermined local markets. Meanwhile the influx of hundreds of international aid organizations during 2002 has sent rents and salaries sky-high, driving local non-governmental organizations from their premises and sucking most skilled and experienced Afghans who remain in the country away from vital posts in government and civil society.

Getting the balance right between quick delivery of life-saving relief and a form of aid that supports local capacities and respects local participation is a complex task, calling for sound humanitarian judgement. This year's report analyses many of the moral dilemmas which arise in working with local organizations in disasters and complex emergencies. Should human rights abuses be exposed, at the risk of sacrificing access to those in greatest need? Do agencies that declare their intention to build local capacities risk promising more than they can deliver? There are no simple answers. We can only develop this essential art of humanitarian judgement through openly declaring the ethical principles we believe in, trying our best to put them into practice and being prepared to measure the effects and reassess our decisions on a continual basis.

The legitimacy of the entire humanitarian enterprise is based on how successfully we are seen to be putting our principles into practice. We need to create an environment in which the key humanitarian value of saving lives with dignity – according to need alone – is widely recognized, understood and prioritized. That means promoting our values with all those who have a stake in humanitarian crises – host authorities, donor governments, development agencies, civil society, military forces, private sector companies and the media.

But advocating adherence to humanitarian principles is only part of the story. Crucially, we must put our principles into practice – in partnership with those in need. Otherwise, we stand no hope of alleviating the suffering of millions beyond the political or media spotlight of the day.

Didier J. Cherpitel
Secretary General

Section One

Focus on ethics in aid

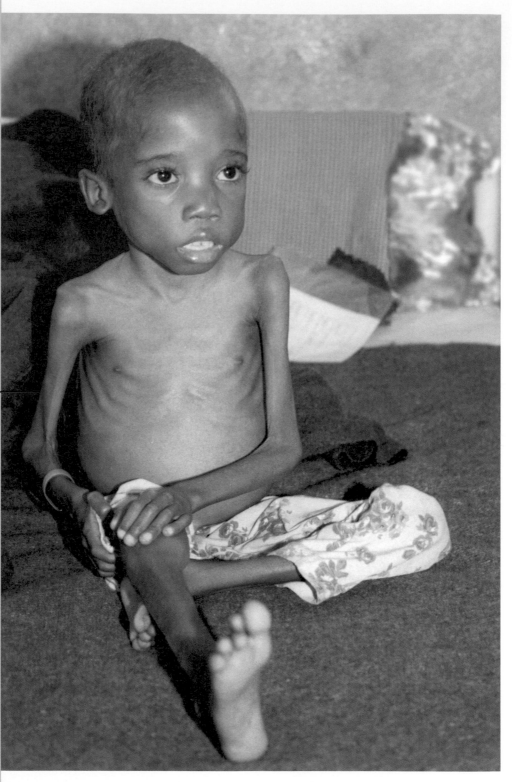

Humanitarian ethics in disaster and war

The humanitarian ethic is an ancient and resilient moral idea. In simple terms, it is the conviction that it is right to help someone when they are in grave danger. But its most distinctive feature is not the idea of help itself but the idea that this help is universal. The humanitarian ethic tells us not just to help some people – people we love, people we know, people like us, people who might help us in return – but to help anyone who needs it.

It is the universality of the humanitarian ethic that makes it so ambitious in scope and so challenging in practice. Its universality makes enormous demands on all of us – geographical, emotional, moral, creative, technical, financial, political and social demands. Yet, despite the enormity of these demands, the essential moral idea of helping anyone in need continues to resonate in the consciences of people around the world. The idea of helping others in desperate need is not just a rational moral proposition. It seems to be a very real feeling that exists in the vast majority of human beings – a sense of sympathy with the suffering of others whom we do not even know.

Common values in different disguises

As one might expect, this deeply held humanitarian value is found in every culture and expressed in many different forms. It appears as religious commandments of compassion, charity and obligation in all the great world faiths. In each of them, particular concern is to be shown for the weakest members of society, most notably the poor, widows, orphans and strangers.

Many of these faiths share the idea that all human beings are sacred because they are created by a god or supreme being and so are manifestations of that god in some way. This belief gives rise to the common religious idea of the 'sanctity of all human life' and the resulting duties to respect, protect and preserve it wherever it exists and whenever it is threatened. The same humanitarian idea is also to be found in more secular forms of belief like the notion that we all share a 'common humanity' – the conviction that we are all essentially the same and that what is common to us is felt palpably between us as if we were all physically related in a wider 'human family'.

These primarily spiritual or biological expressions of common obligations between all people have always been developed into more explicitly political manifestations of the humanitarian ethic. Perhaps the two most influential contemporary political ideologies of universal mutual human obligation are those of solidarity and rights.

Photo opposite page:
Twenty-seven years of civil war – combined with famine and disease – have devastated Angola and left at least 4 million people dependent on aid to survive. They are not getting enough. While the UN appeal for Afghanistan raised over US$ 300 per affected person in 2001, Angola attracted just US$ 50 per head.

Quintiliano des Santos/ International Federation, Angola.

The political idea of human solidarity suggests that what we have in common as human beings is not biologically or divinely *given* but has to be politically *made*. To help people, we have to become politically aware of the suffering of others and the part that we might play with others in the construction of such suffering. Only through this common political consciousness can we then actively work together and reach out in increased solidarity with one another in the struggle for a just and humane world.

In the ideology of human rights, many of these ideas tend to combine. The ideas of the 'right to life' and an essential 'human dignity' common to all people are coupled with a sense of universal and equal human relations that need to be continually worked for. This is seen as best done through an international political and legal project that formalizes a belief that we all share certain equal rights to the world's resources and to just treatment from one another.

These rights are then framed as law and as the particular duties of governments and individuals alike in the many international conventions and declarations of human rights law. In the special case of war, the obligations of the humanitarian ethic have been spelled out in the legal prohibitions and demands of the Geneva Conventions and their Additional Protocols – commonly referred to as international humanitarian law. For those people fleeing across state borders in fear of persecution, the protection and assistance to which they are entitled are embodied in the Refugee Convention and subsequent Protocol. For many millions more who are internally displaced, their legal protection depends on a range of human rights and humanitarian law as noted in the United Nations (UN) Guiding Principles on Internal Displacement.

Within the (secular) International Red Cross and Red Crescent Movement, the humanitarian ethic has traditionally been expressed by the principle of 'humanity'. As stated in the Movement's fundamental principles, this is the desire "to prevent and alleviate human suffering wherever it may be found... to protect life and health and to ensure respect for the human being". Humanity's sister principle of impartiality then affirms that aid will make "no discrimination as to nationality, race, religious beliefs, class or political opinions. It endeavours to relieve the suffering of individuals, being guided solely by their needs, and to give priority to the most urgent cases of distress".

In 1994, a wide range of humanitarian non-governmental organizations (NGOs) worked together with the Movement to spell out the humanitarian ethic still further in the Code of Conduct for the International Red Cross and Red Crescent Movement and NGOs in Disaster Relief. This uses the idea of 'the humanitarian imperative' to encapsulate the ethic of unconditional universal help. By March 2003, 227 aid organizations had signed up to the Code.

Meanwhile in 1998, the humanitarian charter of the Sphere project built on the Code and on human rights conventions, international humanitarian law and refugee law to affirm a belief in three foundational principles: the right to life with dignity, the distinction between combatants and non-combatants, and the commitment to non-refoulement (not returning anyone to a country where they risk being persecuted). In doing so, Sphere's humanitarian charter shows humanitarian agencies drawing, to an unprecedented degree, on the more legal and political idea of human rights and duties as additional support for the humanitarian ethic.

Practising the humanitarian ethic

Believing and expressing a universal ethic is one thing, but applying it during war and disaster is another. For while the great majority of human beings do share the humanitarian ethic, they may not do so all the time. Like most moral ideas, it is frequently contested within individuals and in the world at large and so is forced to compete with other values – some good and some bad. Although the humanitarian ethic is ever present in human affairs, it is by no means dominant.

Because of this, in the hatred of war and the social injustice of disaster, humanitarians have found it wise to declare an explicit disinterest in the particular arguments of human politics so that they can champion the more transcendent moral case of the humanitarian ethic. To be able to do this in practice, they have come to value two essential operating principles – neutrality and independence.

Principle 3 of the Code makes clear that "humanitarian aid will not be used to further a political or religious standpoint", while principle 4 states that humanitarian agencies "shall endeavour not to act as instruments of government foreign policy". The main purpose of these operational ethics is to gain access to those in need. By affirming their disinterest in the particular politics of a war or disaster, humanitarians can better argue the right to focus on the more universal value of the humanitarian ethic. To this end, the operational principles of neutrality and independence are essentially tactical, while those of the humanitarian imperative and impartiality express fundamental moral values.

But, while humanitarians – by virtue of their neutrality and independence – may sometimes gain access to many of those in need, they will still face profound moral contests to which war and disaster give rise. These contests, or 'value clashes', are essentially between humanitarian and anti-humanitarian values on one hand (i.e. 'good versus bad'), and between competing 'goods' on the other. These value clashes and moral dilemmas are as old as humanitarianism itself, yet recognizing them and judging the best course of action remains as urgent today as ever.

Clash of values can prove controversial

A first type of moral clash is when the humanitarian ethic confronts an explicitly anti-humanitarian set of values being determinedly pursued by sections of society. In war, such anti-humanitarian values might include the targeting or wilful neglect of civilians, a deliberate policy of sexual violence or the use of disproportionate force. In disasters, they might include the deliberate and politically motivated exclusion of some groups from humanitarian assistance, refusal to recognize the land rights of the most vulnerable communities or the prioritization of prestige development over basic health and education. In famines, starvation may be used as a weapon of war; or aid may be deliberately blocked to depopulate an area or leave its people destitute, as part of a particular war aim or political policy.

A second type of values clash is when the priorities of the humanitarian ethic confront the priorities of those seeking other moral 'goods' like democracy or a peace settlement. These goods are not essentially at odds with humanitarian values but – deliberately or not – may sideline vital humanitarian concerns. Such competing goods often turn on the perennial tension between order and justice in human society.

For example, politicians or powerbrokers pursuing a particular policy of peace or stability may not give equal emphasis to humanitarian protection, assistance or justice. They may deliberately shelve humanitarian concerns because to pursue them would involve challenging those factions they are politically courting in their primary strategy of stability. In Afghanistan since late 2001, for example, both western and Afghan analysts have expressed grave concern that violations of human rights (especially women's rights) have gone unpunished and unchecked in the interests of maintaining cordial relations with regional powerbrokers (see Chapter 4, Box 4.4). In the Democratic Republic of the Congo (DRC), international agencies have been criticized for promoting peace while virtually ignoring the plight of millions of victims of violence and disease (see Box 1.1).

Occasionally, as in Sierra Leone between 1997-98 or Iraq between 1991-2003, donors have decided to severely limit humanitarian aid as part of a wider political policy of pressure to undermine an inhumane government or non-state group. This approach has been widely criticized as making humanitarian aid 'conditional' on political outcomes, rather than prioritizing it as a universal right and end in itself.

The tensions between promoting peace and saving lives, and between order and justice are not the only clashes of moral goods involving the humanitarian ethic. An equally common problem arises when it seems impossible to realize two rights simultaneously without compromising one of them. One well-documented example is that of gender justice in Afghanistan when the Taliban government's oppressive

Box 1.1 Politics and peace building fail to save millions in DRC

Prioritizing the moral good of peace building may not be the right ethical choice at a time when the sheer volume of people's suffering dictates that more emphasis should be placed on simpler life-saving.

This is a criticism that has been powerfully made about international involvement in the Democratic Republic of the Congo (DRC) – "the world's worst humanitarian disaster of the last decade" – in a recent report by the Geneva-based Centre for Humanitarian Dialogue, entitled Politics and Humanitarianism: Coherence in Crisis? The report draws on mortality surveys carried out by the International Rescue Committee (IRC) from 1998-2001, which suggested that around 2.5 million people died in the east of the country from war-related causes, mainly disease and malnutrition. Yet, while peace operations attracted US$ 250 million in 2000, the humanitarian aid budget was just US$ 37 million. The report argues:

"The low funding of humanitarian assistance due to low political and strategic interest in DRC, compounded by an excessive fear caused by agencies' interpretation of the 'do no harm' doctrine led to what could be described as 'premature developmentalism' and 'humanitarianism as peacebuilding'. That is, humanitarian actors used their scarce funding to pursue projects that were developmental (or described as developmental) rather than life-saving, due to a desire to conform to the peacebuilding agenda preferred by donors and the UN system…Given the massive and urgent humanitarian situation in DRC – where some 2.5 million lives were lost from war-related causes – this deviation of humanitarian assistance may have failed to prevent significant loss of life."

In April 2003, IRC published the findings of a new nationwide mortality survey, which concluded that by November last year, at least 3.3 million people had died as a result of war in DRC. This massive death toll – equivalent to the entire population of Ireland – makes the conflict in DRC the deadliest since the Second World War. The latest survey – which measured mortality among over 40 million people across 20 districts in both the east and west of the country, found that the vast majority of deaths were from easily treatable diseases and malnutrition rather than from violence. The IRC supported the UN's peacekeeping mission but argued that donors must also provide relief and reconstruction aid proportional to the level of need.

Michael Despines – IRC-New York's senior policy and programme advisor and one of the report's authors – asks why the war and suffering in DRC are not more of a priority for international policy-makers. In the face of a country where 1,000 people die every day, he asks: "Where is the outrage?" Throwing down the challenge to aid workers and politicians alike, he argues: "In Iraq a coalition of 30 countries sent armies and lost lives and will spend at least 100 billion dollars on its military and reconstruction efforts. Yet the entire Iraq conflict has produced a death toll equivalent to a few days in the Democratic Republic of Congo. Who are the greater hypocrites, the politicians or the humanitarians? Do we not need to rethink how humanitarian agencies do business and reassess how we use our scarce resources?" ■

policies prevented women from participating fully in the humanitarian assistance to which they were entitled. Does an agency make a stand for gender justice at the risk of being expelled from the country, thereby losing the chance to deliver humanitarian aid of any kind? The dilemma that Oxfam faced in Kabul under the Taliban is described in Chapter 2.

Five humanitarian dilemmas

In the last few years, as agencies have worked together to share their insights into operational dilemmas, five particular areas of moral hazard have emerged:

- **Risk of humanitarian complicity in facilitating abuses** is perhaps the most excruciating dilemma. During the 1990s in Bosnia, agencies that felt bound to evacuate people from invaded or violent areas were also deeply worried that they were facilitating extremist policies of deportation and 'ethnic cleansing'. In the large Rwandan refugee camps in eastern Zaire between 1994-96, several agencies felt trapped by an impossible choice between inevitably feeding the perpetrators of the genocide (thereby helping them re-group and re-arm) or withdrawing from the camps and abandoning the hundreds of thousands of men, women and children whom they saw as innocent and exploited by their leaders. In her recent book, *Condemned to Repeat*, Fiona Terry, of *Médecins sans Frontières* (MSF), has explored the many other occasions when 'refugee warriors' and their backers have posed difficult operational choices for humanitarian agencies.

- **Risk of legitimizing violations.** In Colombia, the International Committee of the Red Cross (ICRC) has been deeply challenged by the possibility that its attempts to help victims of kidnappers may have somehow legitimized or normalized the practice. Elsewhere, the need to prioritize humanitarian aid over investigating and securing convictions for human rights violations may have contributed to a culture of impunity. Most recently, many humanitarian agencies found it difficult to prepare for a possible military invasion of Iraq without being seen to give credibility or 'humanitarian cover' to such a policy.

- **Potential for aid to have a negative effect** has become a constant moral and programmatic preoccupation in the last decade. Agencies may over-supply an area with food aid, thereby undermining local markets. Well-resourced international agencies often attract skilled locals away from essential public sector posts, undermining recovery (see Chapter 4, Box 4.3). Violent factions might steal aid, tax it or kill for it. Aid's 'magnetic' ability to attract large populations into one place can be deeply detrimental. In many famines, mortality has increased not from starvation but from contagious diseases spreading where people congregate to receive food. During war, violent factions have exploited aid's magnetic qualities as a means of depopulating enemy areas or providing occasion to raid vulnerable communities. Aid's ability to become counter-protective as well as protective is a constant concern.

- **Targeting and triage,** its medical equivalent, pose frequent dilemmas. In situations of extreme need, when time and resources are short, triage can be excruciating. Patients are divided into three categories: those well enough to wait for treatment, those who will recover with immediate treatment, and those so ill they may have to be left to die. So, although impartiality prioritizes the 'most urgent cases of distress', these may often not be those who can be most effectively helped. Difficult choices between what needs doing and what agencies are best able to do pervade much humanitarian decision-making in the most desperate phases of a crisis. Even more routine humanitarian targeting involves significant ethical decisions. Some agencies only have mandates and expertise to focus on children, refugees or the elderly. Is it morally acceptable to limit aid to these groups when needs are experienced by everyone? Is it fair to provide high-quality health care only to destitute refugees, when the communities hosting them are equally in need? Most agencies find common-sense ways of resolving these problems. Children's agencies know that it helps children most to work with their families as a whole. Refugee agencies can make their services available to the host community. But these are still important moral problems and decisions that can be overlooked in the heat of war and disaster. They need to be anticipated.
- **Choice between advocacy or access** is a fifth dilemma regularly faced by humanitarian workers, particularly when navigating the politics of armed conflict. Humanitarians have long realized that saying things can be as effective as giving things in certain situations. But they also know that speaking out can spell the end for material aid, because agencies may be expelled or frustrated by indignant authorities.

Advocacy – speaking out for humanitarian principles

Attracting urgent attention to particular disasters or lobbying for specific action to help protect civilians (and aid workers) in war are key aspects of humanitarian advocacy. So too are longer-term campaigns like those to ban landmines, control the small arms trade, combat climate change or reduce the risk of disasters.

For operational agencies, humanitarian advocacy is preferably carried out alongside aid programmes. But in some extreme situations, NGOs have considered it right to prioritize advocacy over deeply compromised programming options and have withdrawn their aid. Others have decided to prioritize their humanitarian access to victims and have remained publicly silent to do so. In Angola, from 2000-02, MSF – which had pulled out of the Democratic People's Republic of Korea (DPRK) over concerns that aid was becoming irrevocably politicized – was able to maintain a balance between speaking out against human rights abuses while maintaining access to those in need (see Box 1.2).

Box 1.2 Struggling to do right in Angola – stay, leave or speak out?

Humanitarian action is based on a moral imperative: it is simply right to assist people who suffer. But the very powers that create suffering are often those controlling humanitarian access to victims. Should agencies provide assistance when they are denied access to the majority of people and when authorities deliberately abuse civilians under their control? How can agencies ensure their aid is not manipulated to oppress the very people it aims to help? MSF faced these challenges in Angola. While there are no simple answers, humanitarian action must be constantly analysed within a coherent ethical framework, leading to transparent reasons for action or withdrawal.

Angolans have suffered through one of the most barbaric wars of the 20th century. MSF has poured more resources into Angola than any other conflict, despite the oil and diamond wealth of both warring parties. After the collapse of the international peace process in 1998, significant oil interests led western powers to choose sides, supporting the MPLA government in all-out war against UNITA rebels. As the MPLA refused humanitarian access to UNITA areas (claiming it politically legitimized UNITA), the UN and international powers minimized efforts to negotiate humanitarian access to UNITA territory. UNITA concluded that the relief effort was politically biased and also denied access to humanitarian agencies.

As UNITA began to lose the war, they battled for control of people, initiating a terror campaign – raping, killing and enslaving, while horrifically punishing 'betrayal' (people were killed for the 'crime' of having salt in their food). Government troops behaved little better – raping, looting and herding rural people into cities, where they starved. Humanitarian agencies were allowed intermittent access to some of these populations, but struggled to reduce terrible suffering in the face of corruption and indifference.

Some NGOs simply left conflict areas. MSF teams became so frustrated with problems of access, obstruction and manipulation of aid that we too debated whether to stay. Our teams believed we were being used to mop up the worst excesses of an inhumane war, sanctioning the barbarism perpetrated by the authorities. Worse still, the denial of access to victims under UNITA control prevented us from helping the neediest.

In Goma or DPRK, MSF was not able to access the people freely, nor could we genuinely improve the lives of those we did access. Our assistance simply enhanced the legitimacy and capacity of the very political forces responsible for the suffering of those we were trying to help. So we withdrew amidst public protest. But in Angola, we were able to access many people suffering acutely; we could make a difference to their lives and dignity; and we were not a significant contributor to MPLA or UNITA war machines. True, we were substituting for the MPLA's responsibility to look after its people. But we did not believe that by leaving, the government would be forced to alter its actions. After all, there were other populations 'cleaned' into camps, where NGOs were denied access and the MPLA did nothing. Angolans were being left to die; our leaving would simply have abandoned more to certain death.

Yet staying without protest was to risk becoming co-opted into a dirty war that the MPLA and international governments had no appetite to expose to scrutiny. NGOs were tolerated, but there was no international will to enforce protection of civilians or expand humanitarian action. MSF launched a risky public campaign, collecting medical data and testimonies from victims of war and releasing a report in November 2000. The report denounced the battle tactics of both sides, demanded that all parties respect civilians in conflict, and urged the government and UN to increase significantly humanitarian access and assistance.

The reaction was sharp. The Angolan government warned MSF they could be expelled for criticizing them. International complacency about the humanitarian situation changed and there were greater efforts to access populations in danger. But the effort was insufficient. So we released a second report in June 2001, exposing displaced populations under government control suffering starvation without any assistance. Despite increased obstruction to our operations, MSF followed up the report by testifying, with other NGOs, to the UN Security Council and releasing further accounts demonstrating the suffering of those abandoned in Angola's war zones. Donors said we were doing a good job assisting people but we should keep quiet. The UN was furious with the criticism. The government privately interrogated each MSF head of mission, again threatening programme closures and expulsion.

By early 2002, it was evident that UNITA had collapsed and the humanitarian crisis beyond our reach was catastrophic. Huge numbers of starving and wounded poured out of the former UNITA-controlled zones towards aid centres. In April, following the death of the UNITA leader, a peace agreement was signed. With new prospects for peace, the UN coordinated the humanitarian sector to unite and enforce governmental responsibility. The UN demanded the government sign a memorandum of understanding (MoU), detailing various humanitarian, peacekeeping and disarmament roles for the UN. Until then, there would be no relief for hundreds of thousands of people gathering in UNITA areas.

While MSF was convinced the government must be forced to shoulder its responsibilities, we disagreed with making humanitarian aid conditional on a political deal. It meant that negotiations for immediate humanitarian access were tied to lengthier, contradictory agendas. Meanwhile, MSF surveys showed disastrous mortality and malnutrition rates from starvation and violence. We lobbied WFP to launch an emergency appeal to avert the most serious famine crisis in years. WFP claimed their annual programme was sufficient, unwilling to appear active while confronting the MPLA over the MoU.

MSF responded with a large medico-nutritional programme, despite condemnation from the UN and many NGOs, who claimed we were letting the government off the hook. We reasoned that whereas taking action would not contribute to furthering oppression, failing to act would condemn thousands to certain death. The government had neither the capacity nor the will to react effectively to this crisis, so no act of defiance could force them to do so. Playing poker when the lives of people are the chips is not effective when the other side doesn't care if they lose. Would holding the government to account be worth the wait? Making such calculations are not the responsibility or the expertise of humanitarian agencies. The agreement was finally signed in June 2002, two months after the peace accord. By delaying an emergency appeal, refusing to act without an agreement and restricting direct NGO action, we believe the relief effort was delayed by many months and missed the peak of the calamity. Humanitarian actors failed to save thousands of lives.

It is critical to be able to appreciate in real time whether our action (or inaction) assists people in desperate need. While aid during conflict may appear to fuel inhumane war strategies and undermine a sense of official responsibility, the question remains: what would happen without aid? Humanitarian action that attempts to create good political behaviour before addressing immediate suffering loses its moral currency – which is based on caring for human beings in crisis. ■

Advocacy can take several forms: relatively 'quiet', face-to-face discussion in private (humanitarian negotiation or persuasion); or much 'louder' public comment, which may extend to outright criticism or denunciation. Advocacy may be directed at both 'host' and donor governments. In February 2003, for example, the president of InterAction, the largest alliance of American NGOs, wrote an open letter to US president, George Bush, urging him to put any future aid and reconstruction efforts in a post-war Iraq under civilian command. The letter stated: "The American nongovernmental organizations which provide humanitarian assistance, like their counterparts throughout the world, are bound to respect principles of impartiality and independence. Violation of these principles would jeopardize their access to those suffering the consequences of future conflicts. Fidelity to these principles would be compromised by working in Iraq under the direction of American military authorities."

Advocacy may be pursued more vigorously by local and national organizations than by international agencies – Zimbabwean and Malawian NGOs, for example, have been far more outspoken than their foreign counterparts about the structural causes of the ongoing famine and the need to respect humanitarian principles (see Chapter 2, Box 2.1 and Chapter 3, Box 3.4).

Advocacy of all kinds is now recognized as a vital part of humanitarian work that serves to remind states, non-state actors, corporations and individuals of their humanitarian obligations. But while speaking out on matters of principle is clearly regarded as a moral responsibility for humanitarian agencies, it is not without its moral risks, which include:

- **Getting it wrong** – essentially a risk of technical inaccuracy. In a fast-moving and complex emergency, it is not easy to be sure of the facts. But equally, what agencies say can influence international response and affect the lives of those they seek to help. This gives agencies a particular responsibility to take all reasonable care in gathering and interpreting information and in the subsequent statements they make. Being seen to 'cry wolf' about a famine or to misinform people about the context of violations in a war can lose an agency and the wider humanitarian community valuable credibility for years to come.
- **Creating a backlash** – which may come about because an agency's information is all too accurate. Going public about atrocities in war or government failure during disaster can put humanitarian staff and the people they are trying to protect in even greater danger of a vicious backlash. This might mean expulsion for an agency and its international staff, so jeopardizing aid and protection to those in need. Worse still, it could mean intimidation, imprisonment or death for local staff, community leaders or witnesses. Following the creation of a documentary film alleging human rights abuses committed against Taliban prisoners in northern Afghanistan in late 2001, several witnesses to the atrocities were reported to have disappeared or been tortured.

■ **Violating humanitarian principles** – affecting an agency's humanitarian integrity. On occasion, agencies have taken to heart the particular suffering of one party to a conflict or a particular group's experience of a disaster and spoken out disproportionately on their account. Equally common is the pressure agencies can feel to be fair and find some moral equivalence between the atrocities committed by different sides, which they then emphasize in their advocacy. Getting too close to one group's experience or over-compensating to represent all sides as equal violators can lead an agency to lose, or be perceived as losing, its impartiality, neutrality and independence.

As Chapter 3 on the food security crisis in southern Africa shows, these risks mean that a special duty of care comes with humanitarian advocacy, as agencies weigh up the relative advantages of advocacy, operational programming and security. To know the facts, agencies need to be extremely good at their research. To know the legal implications of the facts (for states and for those organizations with legal mandates), agencies must know humanitarian, human rights and refugee law. To know the risks run by the people they are trying to help and their own staff, they must have genuine relationships with affected communities and a clear sense of what they think the risks are. To achieve the best results, agencies must be proficient in different forms of 'loud' and 'soft' advocacy so that they can choose when persuasion, denunciation or even silence might be best.

Finally, agencies must have a keen sense of the best local, national and international targets for their advocacy or the best channels through which to pass their information on to others better placed to reach these targets. One success story of well-targeted advocacy based on sound empirical research is the case of British NGO Save the Children, which sounded several warnings to both donor and host governments and UN agencies during late 2001 and early 2002 that much of Malawi faced imminent famine (see Chapter 3, Part 1).

Global aid tracks political priorities

There is a still more strategic moral problem that faces the application of the humanitarian ethic globally: global impartiality and the obvious selectivity of emergency aid worldwide.

International financing for humanitarian action comes mainly from Organisation for Economic Co-operation and Development (OECD) governments. Humanitarian aid (at 1999 prices) rose from US$ 2.1 billion in 1990 to an all-time high of US$ 5.9 billion in 2000, according to *The new humanitarianisms: a review of trends in global humanitarian action*, published by the London-based Overseas Development Institute (ODI). To put this figure in perspective, official development assistance from OECD countries totalled US$ 53.7 billion in 2000. Breaking down the humanitarian part of this budget by individual donor governments reveals, according to the ODI, that "a handful of donors account for the bulk of humanitarian assistance. In most years, the US is the largest donor by a factor of three or four".

These figures show that humanitarian expenditure and therefore humanitarian policy are mainly in the control of a few powerful states. But is the allocation of these funds made according to the ethic of universal and impartial help? Does humanitarian aid follow a predictable moral geography based on need alone? Unfortunately not. The global distribution of humanitarian expenditure reveals a distinct *political* geography that is highly selective and concentrated. Some regions, some conflicts and some disasters are obvious priorities.

The ODI reports that between 1993-2000, some 47 per cent of the humanitarian funds of the European Community Humanitarian Office (ECHO) were spent in central and eastern Europe. Reports on the UN's consolidated appeals for 2000 reveal enormous discrepancies: the northern Caucasus received 89 per cent of its appeal, DRC received 64 per cent and Somalia only 22 per cent. Emergency aid allocated per head from UN appeals in 2000 varied wildly from less than US$ 10 for DPRK or Uganda to as much as US$ 185 per person in south-eastern Europe (see Figure 1.1).

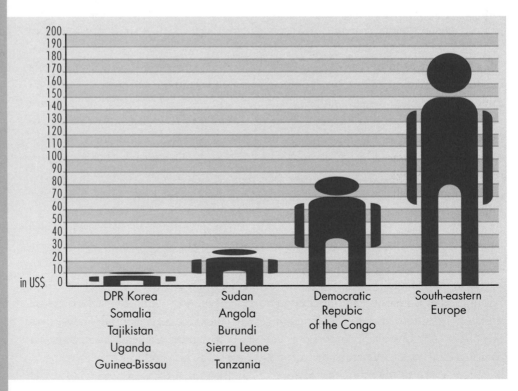

Figure 1.1
Global humanitarian equity? Humanitarian aid received per affected person from UN consolidated appeals, 2000.

Source: ODI, 2002.

The tendency for aid to favour high-profile crises continues to raise serious concerns. On 7 April 2003, James Morris, executive director of the World Food Programme (WFP) addressed the UN Security Council and contrasted the generous provisions being made to meet the needs of people in post-war Iraq with the plight of 40 million Africans in 22 countries facing the "greater peril" of starvation. Referring to the scale of suffering as "unprecedented", he noted that WFP's US$ 1.8 billion appeal for emergency food needs in Africa was nearly 1 billion dollars short. He said: "As much as I don't like it, I cannot escape the thought that we have a double standard. How is it we routinely accept a level of suffering and hopelessness in Africa we would never accept in any other part of the world? We simply cannot let this stand." Then, on 22 April 2003 – just one month after the US began its war on Iraq – the *New York Times* reported that the US Department of Defense had raised "about US$ 1.7 billion in financial assistance, food, medicine and other relief products" for Iraq, following the ousting of Saddam Hussein's regime.

Many humanitarians see the selectivity and concentration of humanitarian funding by OECD governments towards politically strategic conflicts in particular as evidence that humanitarian action is losing its impartiality and becoming increasingly politicized. They argue that humanitarian aid seems not so much to track individual needs in war, disaster and chronic emergencies but the geo-strategic logic of western policy. Humanitarian relief is thought to be invested mostly in conflicts where it can make an important contribution to a wider and more 'coherent' policy which aims to achieve peace settlements, spread neo-liberal democracy and support the war against terrorism.

This selectivity of humanitarian aid allocations reveals a deep partiality and inequity in global humanitarian action. Many of the world's wars and disasters – and the millions of people affected by them – are now known as 'forgotten emergencies', relatively neglected by international donors. Chapter 5 details the forgotten disaster of the millions of migrants forced from their homes by conflict, violence, environmental disaster or economic ruin. Whether displaced within their own countries or smuggled across frontiers, their clandestine and illegal movements make forced migrants all but invisible to aid organizations, beyond the protection of international law and therefore highly vulnerable.

The ODI, meanwhile, is one of a number of research organizations collaborating on a major donor-driven analysis – due to be published in mid-2003 – of global humanitarian financing and the factors influencing aid allocations. One disturbing finding is that humanitarian organizations seem to base their funding requests less on evidence of objective need than according to what they think certain donors are prepared to pay for certain emergencies (see Box 1.3). Accurate, credible and impartial data on the humanitarian needs generated by all wars and disasters is a basic prerequisite for the success of humanitarian aid as a global ethic (see Chapter 7).

Box 1.3 Meeting whose needs?

It is accepted wisdom that donor governments allocate more funding to some disasters and give less to others, often for political reasons. Much less recognized is the way that aid agencies themselves often reinforce this pattern of inequitable resource allocation. In other words, it is not just donors who are failing to ensure a needs-based approach to humanitarian action.

The Humanitarian Financing Working Group is an initiative supported by a number of donors and humanitarian organizations concerned to ensure that humanitarian response is driven by the principle of impartiality, in other words, is proportionate to need. As part of this initiative, the London-based Overseas Development Institute has conducted a year-long study into how humanitarian needs assessments influence allocations of aid. The study, to be published in mid-2003, is based on field research in southern Africa, Somalia and Sudan. The team has conducted over 150 interviews with a wide range of staff from UN agencies, international NGOs and governmental aid departments in the US and UK.

One of the study's important findings is that at present, there are few incentives for operational agencies to conduct rigorous needs assessments. Instead, their assessments and funding requests tend to reflect what agencies think donors are prepared to pay for. In other words, there is no robust, independent assessment of 'real' levels of global need, but rather, fluctuating estimates of what the 'market' can bear.

Donors encourage this tendency by often deciding on the level of their responses 'in advance' and by placing insufficient value on both initial and continuing assessment. While quick, initial decisions about the level of disaster response may have to be based on estimates rather than detailed needs assessment, these decisions are rarely revised in the light of later evidence. Assessment, concludes the ODI study, is constrained by lack of funds and tends to be a one-off process.

What also emerges from the study is that there is no system that enables global need to be 'triaged' – with the most urgent and life-threatening emergencies automatically jumping to the top of the queue. Instead, there is a much more ad hoc and fragmented set of decisions by donors and agencies alike, so it is very difficult to make sure that resources go where they are most needed.

Collectively, therefore, donors and agencies are in a weak position in terms of their ambition to uphold the principle of impartial humanitarian aid based on need alone. There is a sense, which pervades organizations, of weary acceptance that some crises will attract more funds than others. This has fatal consequences: the people of southern Sudan, for example, are suffering global acute malnutrition rates as high as 20 per cent, double the level considered 'acceptable'. Yet this extremely serious situation has somehow become 'normalized', accepted as inevitable.

It is this sense of fatalism that the ODI study calls on all relief workers to reject. Humanitarian organizations bear a special responsibility as the world's conscience. If they fail to apply consistent moral standards to their work, then the pressure on politicians to care for those in greatest need will lessen. And, in the scramble for profile and prestige, the voices and needs of the most vulnerable will be lost. ∎

HIV/AIDS – equivalent to 15 air crashes a day

Meanwhile, an increasingly permanent disaster – the HIV/AIDS pandemic – is not yet attracting the serious levels of aid it requires. According to UNAIDS, sub-Saharan Africa – the world's worst-affected region – is now home to 29.4 million people living with HIV/AIDS. Last year alone, an estimated 2.4 million Africans – most of them in the prime of their lives – died of the disease. That death toll is equivalent to more than 15 fully loaded 747-aircraft crashing every day of the year.

Funding from private, national and international sources to cope with HIV/AIDS in all low- and middle-income countries totalled an estimated US$ 3 billion in 2002. This is less than half the amount needed to fight the epidemic in 2003 and just 20 per cent of the funds needed every year from 2007 for at least the next decade.

The emergence of HIV/AIDS as a major structural factor fuelling the vulnerability of southern African societies to famine has become cruelly clear in recent years. HIV/AIDS attacks the most productive members of society, shattering livelihoods at frightening speed (see Chapter 3, Part 2). Meanwhile, the terrible transmission power of HIV/AIDS by marauding armies and paramilitaries, with their strategies of sexual violence and trafficking, makes HIV/AIDS a structural aspect of contemporary armed conflict as well as of famine.

Since prevention is the only cure for most societies too poor to afford western drugs, the HIV/AIDS pandemic is breaking down the barriers between short-term relief and long-term development. Saving lives becomes more about slowly strengthening livelihoods and changing attitudes than about quick medical interventions. But how far should humanitarianism go in supporting long-term strategies? Equally, how far should long-term development go in embracing humanitarian principles? The relationship between humanitarian and development ethics remains largely unexplored (see Box 1.4).

Saving life with dignity

Just as there are questions about how far governments should go in linking humanitarian action with wider political and economic goals, similar questions are also faced by humanitarian agencies. Should humanitarian action stop at saving lives? Or does it have a moral responsibility to go further, to secure wider economic and social goods like healthier livelihoods, fairer distribution of resources, greater participation, gender justice, stronger social institutions and peace building?

Box 1.4 Humanitarian and development ethics – common ground?

How should humanitarian action relate to the ethics of development? The issue is crucial if humanitarians are to work effectively in places where development agencies are major actors. A growing proportion of aid in post-conflict situations is being channelled through development agencies. The World Bank's trust funds in Afghanistan support both large infrastructural investment and health services, where NGOs (including humanitarians) are the main 'subcontractors'. UN coordination structures are often designed primarily to support development, even if many resources still support relief.

Development cooperation has traditionally been seen as rather a value-free pursuit, led by economists and technicians. It was assumed that economic growth would lead naturally to poverty alleviation and other public goods. Chronic poverty, however, has not disappeared even where sustainable economic growth has been achieved – Central America is one example. There is now a consensus that good development needs a firmer ethical framework than mere econometric statistics.

The Millennium Development Goals are one attempt to embrace a wider ethical perspective. The UN Development Programme is promoting 'human development' that emphasizes fundamental security and the freedom to pursue livelihoods with dignity. A large World Bank research project introduced the 'voices of the poor' into the debate. The Inter-American Development Bank has established an ethics and development initiative. There is even an International Development Ethics Association, which highlights values underpinning development efforts. But, the operational implications of these ethical commitments are different. Whereas humanitarians have a direct duty to 'save lives', development planners merely nudge national processes towards enhancing quality of life. This nudging is now less about project-based aid and more about influencing wider policy – for example through poverty reduction strategy papers.

Development planners are also more willing to look at 'safety nets' (e.g., social insurance, pensions, microfinance, public works). Once shunned as relics of phantom welfare states, safety nets are now recognized as crucial to support those vulnerable to conflict, disaster, economic collapse and a general decline of social security in many transitional states. There is a growing recognition that the humanitarian imperative may actually have a place in development. After disaster, the most vulnerable are those least able to re-establish their livelihoods. They risk being left behind when over-ambitious recovery efforts attempt to rapidly link relief, rehabilitation and development. This is an ethical dilemma for development actors that humanitarians should ensure they face up to.

Areas of mutual interest include the HIV/AIDS pandemic, which defies efforts to make simple divisions between relief and development. Chronic food insecurity is another grey area. Famine in Malawi was partly caused by discontinuing a development project which distributed subsidized seeds and fertilizer to farmers. The poorest simply couldn't afford the inputs and production sank. The project had been stopped because it was financially unsustainable. But there is no sustainable solution in sight for dealing with chronic food insecurity in Malawi. Before the famine, many agricultural economists considered the plight of desperately poor farmers to be 'somebody else's problem'. With ethical hindsight, most agree it is everyone's problem. The World Bank is now making major loans available for food security support. The medicine of reducing subsidies to ensure economic stability in Malawi's public finances was clearly not ethically appropriate if the patients ended up dying.

Will the 'lessons' from southern Africa prompt humanitarian and development players to look beyond what divides them, towards their common commitments to basic survival? Failure to do so would be nothing short of unethical. ■

For humanitarians, these questions are not new. They are essentially about the moral limits of the humanitarian ethic and the extent of an agency's obligations to help people in grave danger. This is the tussle between giving a fish or a fishing rod, of the superior morality of helping or enabling self-help. It is the old debate between the relief-development 'continuum' with its idea of developmental relief or the 'back-to-basics' conception of humanitarian action that is essentially about saving life. For human rights advocates, it is the question about the non-hierarchical and indivisible nature of rights. Are all human rights of equal value, or should certain 'basic' rights take precedence in particular situations?

Current humanitarian ideology tends towards a clear hierarchy of objectives. The Code of Conduct's characterization of the humanitarian imperative clearly indicates that saving life is always the priority for humanitarian workers. Immediate relief of human suffering (principle 1 of the Code) has moral primacy. It is, therefore, something of a 'trump card', while the subsequent principles of impartiality, non-political action and independence (principles 2-4) are ways of ensuring the trump can be played fairly in highly contested political environments.

However, the second part of the Code (principles 5-10) makes clear that the humanitarian ethic demands more complicated moral obligations than simply saving lives in any way possible. The Code commits its signatories to respect culture and custom (principle 5), to build disaster response on local capacities and actively involve people's participation (principles 6 and 7), to reduce people's long-term vulnerabilities to disaster by creating sustainable lifestyles (principle 8) and to represent people respectfully in their publicity material (principle 10). The Code also demands that agencies must be fully accountable for all that they do, which should include appropriate monitoring and assessment of aid and its impact (principle 9).

This is a much more ambitious moral project than simply alleviating suffering. It is about promoting mutual respect, personal dignity and important social and economic rights. It is as much about a responsibility to prevent future disaster as to relieve the present one. If the humanitarian ethic asserts that it is right to help *anyone*, it also makes clear that it would be wrong to help them *anyhow*. Many years of agency experience are crystallized in the Code to reveal that humanitarian morality in war and disaster is a universal ethic with particular obligations to work with people in a certain way and to aim at far more than their basic needs. To do otherwise would be unethical and degrading.

Anyone who has done any humanitarian work will recognize the reality of these wider obligations of respect, inclusion and economic rights. In the Franco-Prussian War of 1870, Clara Barton, the founder of the American Red Cross, felt bound to develop her initial relief handouts to wounded soldiers into what was probably the first Red Cross micro-enterprise development intervention. She gave them sewing machines from which to earn a living and regain their personal autonomy and self-respect. The more recent emphasis in disaster response on 'the right to life with dignity' and 'saving lives and livelihoods' is motivated by the same irresistible moral logic that one encounters when faced with the needs of real people which do not stop when they are saved.

Risks of getting too involved

While this deeper engagement with people's lives is morally responsible, it brings with it certain moral risks for humanitarianism's primary concern to save life and its commitment to political disinterest. During ongoing conflicts, encouraging people's participation can mean confronting political and armed groups that seek to control people rather than empower them. This may expose those local people who cooperate with international agencies to vicious retribution. Reducing people's vulnerability to violence might lead humanitarian agencies into peace building, which could then prompt suspicions from one or more parties to the conflict. Tackling such structural issues can put an agency's impartiality and independence at risk.

As agencies have become increasingly involved in humanitarian work in armed conflicts in the last ten years, so too they have become more interested in conflict prevention and active peace building. The moral logic on the ground seems irresistible. Although not specifically mentioned in the Code of Conduct, many agencies have followed Mary Anderson's *Do No Harm* theory to interpret the idea of reducing vulnerabilities and increasing local capacities as inevitably combining aid and peace work of some kind. Some agencies have attempted to resolve conflict by trying to transform relationships between opposing groups. Others have incorporated discreetly peaceful objectives into traditional humanitarian programmes in health, water, livelihoods, food aid and shelter.

In addition, humanitarian agencies have been repeatedly criticized – for example, in Sudan and Afghanistan during the 1990s – for introducing resources, which might then free up belligerents to invest more of their own resources in war. However, the idea that warring parties would – in the absence of aid – have naturally spent more money on humanitarian work is highly speculative.

In the context of 'natural' disasters, addressing the reasons for people's vulnerability can mean engaging in questions of land rights and political exclusion – again, putting organizational neutrality at risk. And, as Chapter 2 on building capacity shows so clearly, a humanitarian agency's relationship with local institutions also requires important moral judgements. While it is morally right to save people's lives, it is immoral to do so in a neo-colonial fashion that undermines local institutions and shows no respect for individuals. Moreover, agencies which promise to build capacities and tackle root causes of disaster may shatter the hopes of local people if they pull out their resources prematurely.

Finding a balance – humanitarian pluralism

These deeper forms of engagement with local needs and institutions risk agencies being perceived as in violation of their core principles of impartiality and independence. Worse still – as the experience in DRC suggests – prioritizing peace or development before saving lives could have catastrophic results. Because of the extremely difficult situations in which agencies operate, there is an operational tension in the Code itself between humanitarianism's range of immediate and more developmental moral ambitions. Trying to make sense of this tension, many humanitarian actors and analysts have tried to resolve it by veering headlong across the spectrum of humanitarian obligations to one end or the other. They become either 'humanitarian minimalists', who prioritize life-saving over everything else, or 'humanitarian maximalists', who continually embrace developmental relief and local peace dividends.

This approach to humanitarianism's moral tension is overly dualistic. As a psychoanalyst might observe, it has attempted to end the tension by 'splitting' it. But

Respecting the dignity of disaster-affected people is central to the humanitarian ethic – and it makes practical sense too. An evaluation of responses to the Gujarat earthquake in 2001 found that foreign agencies which adopted a 'top-down' style of intervention were less efficient in delivering relief than agencies which worked with local groups.

Patrick Fuller/ International Federation, India.

instead, this approach simply leaves one part of humanitarian morality constantly in search of the other. It seems wiser, therefore, to accept the natural tension in humanitarian morality and to work with it as a 'humanitarian pluralist' – someone who embraces the fact that the obligations of the humanitarian ethic are many. A pluralist would accept the full spectrum of humanitarian obligations (principles 1-10 of the Code) and make constant judgements about how much of it can wisely, safely and usefully be done in a given place at a given time.

In this respect, conflicts often make different demands from 'natural' disasters. Eva von Oelreich, head of disaster preparedness and policy for the International Federation, points out: "Many organizations see opportunities to be more pluralist in natural disasters but remain more minimalist in conflict." While engaging with local organizations may be complicated by the politics of war, 'natural' disasters should pose fewer problems. Chapter 2 describes how international relief agencies which intervened in a 'top-down' (minimalist) fashion after the Gujarat earthquake in 2001 were less effective than those which participated with local NGOs – a more pluralist approach. Significantly, the evaluation of humanitarian responses to the earthquake – conducted by the Disasters Emergency Committee, an alliance of British NGOs – measured agencies' performance against the ten principles of the Code of Conduct and found that a major local women's NGO performed much better than the collective response of British agencies (see Chapter 6, Box 6.1).

It seems sensible to agree that the importance of saving lives and relieving suffering has a definite primacy in humanitarian morality. But it is also important that any life should be one of dignity – so a second humanitarian ethic of respect, inclusion and empowerment is also fundamental as an end in itself. It can never be ignored. And it is not only as an end but also as a means that it is morally important, because there is no doubt that working *with* people is a far more effective way to save their lives and relieve their suffering than a more detached and authoritarian approach. So principles 5-10 of the Code are good in themselves, but they are also good as a means to achieving principle 1.

How this second ethic (of respect, inclusion and empowerment) is pursued is a matter of judgement, determined by considerations that moral philosophers describe as 'prudential'. How far and how fast one goes in capacity building, participation and peace work depends on how prudent such activities are alongside the primary aim of saving lives. If such broader ways of working risk threatening security in conflict situations, compromise an agency's ability to save life or result in humanitarian aid having significant negative effects, then they should be treated with caution and different ways of showing respect must be found. But there can also come a point where the inverse is true. If an agency's top-down method of saving life unnecessarily undermines people's dignity and future livelihoods, then different more inclusive ways of saving lives must be found.

Legitimacy – proving moral values through performance

Morally responsible humanitarian programming is more than a matter of making judgements on difficult dilemmas or deciding the range of moral obligations with which to engage. Good humanitarian work is not only about *what* you intend to do but *how well* you do it and *to whom* you are responsible. Intentions are critical to ethical behaviour but they are not everything. The behaviour itself is of great importance. So too is an essential honesty in openly reflecting upon one's intentions and behaviour when they affect the lives of others. It is here that the moral obligation of humanitarian agencies to be accountable for what they do and say comes into play.

At heart, the humanitarian idea is about expanding relationships of help. Humanitarian agencies are required by their mandates and by those that support them to extend a range of practical provisions which help to realize people's rights and meet their needs in war and disaster. As the go-between in such relationships, a humanitarian organization is responsible to all parties concerned: to the people it seeks to help, to its private supporters and to its governmental donors. Beyond this web of personal relations, an agency is usually subject to various national and international legal obligations, as well as being bound by the principles and standards it signs up to as the touchstones of its profession.

Humanitarian agencies have made much progress in trying to meet their accountability obligations in recent years. But it is widely agreed that most of this progress has been descriptive. The humanitarian community has described to whom, for what and how it should be accountable. Some organizations, through guidelines and standards, have begun to define their roles in relation to human rights conventions, international humanitarian law and refugee law. A Humanitarian Accountability Project has been launched and a Humanitarian Accountability Partnership is being created as a self-regulating membership organization to improve accountability towards those in need. Yet, despite a couple of major evaluations, the actual process of accountability in the field remains under-developed and under-resourced (see Chapter 6, Box 6.2).

Organizations do not yet routinely use their own principles and operational standards as a measure of self-evaluation – although the Disasters Emergency Committee, which pioneered the use of the Code of Conduct during its Gujarat evaluation, now aims to develop this approach further (see Box 1.5). Really operationalizing

Box 1.5 Using the Code of Conduct as an evaluation tool

The devastating earthquake which rocked the Indian state of Gujarat in January 2001 provided the context within which the Code of Conduct for the International Red Cross and Red Crescent Movement and NGOs in Disaster Relief was first pioneered as a tool for programme evaluations. In the process, Tony Vaux, one of the consultants who carried out the evaluation on behalf of DEC, made some interesting discoveries:

■ In practice the Code is widely acknowledged but scarcely used – no aid agency staff were actively using the Code in the Gujarat response.

■ Using the Code as a set of values against which to measure the performance of a range of different agencies reduced the subjective nature of the evaluation and provided a transparent assessment for the donating public.

■ The principles do not entirely eliminate the subjective role of the evaluators. In Gujarat, this was resolved by using a formal opinion survey of over 2,300 disaster-affected people.

■ The Code emphasizes developmental aspects of disaster response, such as capacity building and reducing future vulnerability. This may lead to agencies with a purely short-term perspective being criticized in any evaluation.

■ Using the Code to evaluate collective rather than individual agency response can reduce its developmental bias. This in turn implies that agencies must be more aware of what others are doing.

■ Far from being rigid and outdated, the Code was surprisingly flexible and 'modern'.

■ Some principles appear contradictory. In Gujarat, respect for local customs (supported under principle 5) might involve toleration of discrimination against women (prohibited under principle 2).

■ After discussion, DEC members considered it best to affirm the primacy of principle 1 ("the humanitarian imperative comes first") and not distinguish further between the remaining principles.

■ The Code may not be sufficiently conflict-focused – but better use of the annexes (particularly annex 1 which outlines the legal responsibilities of host governments) in future evaluations may help address this.

■ The apparent contradictions within the Code help bring out the real dilemmas facing managers in the field. The Code is helpful precisely because it offers a way of analysing conflicting principles.

■ Evaluation needs to be a longer and more continuous process that more directly feeds into decision-making.

■ The experience of using the Code as an evaluation tool suggests that it is useful because it stretches agencies towards ideals that they might otherwise forget.

■ The Code is the best available tool for DEC evaluation. Sphere's humanitarian charter builds on it, especially in relation to conflict, and adds the concept of minimum standards. The Code and Sphere can be used together.

■ Up to now the Code has not been fully used, possibly because it lacks precise indicators and questions. Indicators, based on key issues outlined in the table below, have now been developed.

Key issues raised in DEC evaluations against Code of Conduct principles

Principle	Issue 1	Issue 2	Issue 3
1. Humanitarian imperative	Self-interest of agencies v. needs	Publicity-driven actions	Individual v. collective functioning
2. Non-discrimination	Quality of needs assessment	Targeting (geographical cover, rich and poor)	Gender issues
3. Religion and politics	Impartiality	Relation to national government	Bias in religious-based agencies
4. Foreign policy	Identify strategic interests of aid actors	Neutrality in conflict	Funding from governmental donors
5. Culture and custom	Respectful manner	Imposition of western solutions	Local knowledge
6. Build on local capacity	Use of local organizations	Training and local staff development	Awareness of political implications
7. Involve beneficiaries	Procedures for formal consultation	Beneficiaries represented in programme planning	Transparency
8. Reduce future vulnerability	Long-term time scale for involvement	Advocacy strategy related to disaster preparedness plan	Structures designed to resist disaster
9. Accountable to donors	Efficiency	Financial accountability	Agency evaluation (as well as DEC)
10. Dignity in images	Positive images	Increase public understanding	

Sources: The DEC and the Red Cross Code – a policy proposal, Tony Vaux, Humanitarian Initiatives, July 2002; The Red Cross/NGO Code as a Management and Evaluation Tool, DEC, 2003.

accountability in this way is a major moral challenge for the foreseeable future, if humanitarian agencies are not to fall victim of the same criticisms that they so often level at states and corporations – that of signing up to and then shelving the codes and standards on which they agree. As discussed in Chapter 6, much of this practical accountability involves improving assessments of the *impact* of humanitarian work. Simply quantifying 'outputs' of humanitarian resources such as cash or blankets fails to capture the actual effects such aid has on alleviating suffering. For humanitarian practice to improve, tracking the impacts of aid has to become part of all programme monitoring and evaluation.

Practical accountability of organizational performance is important not just for a transparent report of what humanitarian agencies do and how they do it. Being accountable – publicly demonstrating that you are practising your principles – is critical to that other valuable moral asset: an agency's *legitimacy*. To be recognized as a legitimate humanitarian agency is much more than simply operating correctly under the national or international laws that apply. It is about being able to prove your essential moral values through your practical performance, expertise and tangible networks of supporters. Legitimacy is about being trusted. It is about giving people confidence that an agency is what it says it is. Legitimacy is about humanitarian integrity in thought and word and deed.

A great deal of what is discussed as accountability and legitimacy may be best understood as being professional in the best sense of the word. It is about professing a set of values and having the right expertise, knowledge, resources, codes, standards, self-criticism – and ultimately the right judgement – to try and put these values into action to best effect. To be anything less might be unethical.

Yet there is a concern, especially amongst some French agencies, that current ideas of humanitarian accountability and professionalism are excessively technocratic. These agencies see the plethora of new technical standards as inhibiting personal judgement and expertise in a given situation, rendering humanitarian response too homogenous and inflexible. Worse still, there is a fear that by becoming mesmerized with professional standards, humanitarian workers may never look up from their manuals to read and understand the politics of a situation. Meanwhile, there is a danger, analysed in Chapter 6, that measuring impact against specific standards may encourage agencies only to intervene in situations where their impact is easily measurable, rather than where the need is greatest.

Such fears have an important element of truth. They serve as a valuable warning to safeguard the essential pragmatic skill of judging how best to operationalize humanitarian principles and standards in different contexts.

Who can be humanitarian?

If professionalism is morally responsible, it can also be exclusive. There is little doubt that humanitarianism is institutionalizing as never before. Academic institutes around the world are providing ever-more comprehensive humanitarian and disaster management courses. This raises moral questions about whether increasingly professional agencies are transforming a universal ethic that can be enacted by everyone into a particular expertise that is the preserve of those powerful enough to write its codes and rich enough to implement them.

Every human being should be trying to help their neighbour, particularly when they are in trouble. Yet, there is a legitimate distinction between humanitarian desire and expertise. At one level, it makes practical sense to suggest that while everyone is right to *feel* humanitarian, it would be wrong for everyone to *be* an operational humanitarian. As local, national and global institutions, professional agencies provide important networks where people can express global humanitarian sentiments through donations and campaigning. As mediating institutions, they play an important role by putting people in touch with one another, channelling humanitarian energy and targeting resources.

But professionalism is not everything. Voluntary and spontaneous humanitarian solidarity is still perhaps the most vital aspect of the humanitarian ethic as it operates in the world. Professional agencies can easily exaggerate their own importance in a crisis. More often than not, it is affected people's personal and social support to one another that gets them through disaster or war. In the aftermath of 1999's devastating Marmara earthquakes in Turkey, 98 per cent of the 50,000 people pulled alive from the rubble were rescued by locals. According to Chapter 5, following El Salvador's twin earthquakes in 2001, their president successfully persuaded the US to grant legal work permits to migrant workers, after calculating that such status would increase remittances by US\$ 250 million per year – a far greater sum than could be expected in foreign aid. The humanitarian profession always needs to value both personal and professional humanitarianism – individual activism and organizational expertise. It needs both. And both can save lives.

The growing debate about standards has raised the issue of humanitarian professionalism. The question of which NGOs should qualify as good enough was raised directly in the highly influential evaluation of the international response to the Rwandan genocide, which suggested the idea of accreditation. Since then, the debate has moved beyond the NGO sector to assess the humanitarian credentials of two other types of organization – private sector companies and military forces.

Private sector and soldiers muscle in

Private sector companies have become increasingly involved in bidding for and winning donor tenders for humanitarian contracts – particularly in post-conflict situations such as Afghanistan and Iraq. This may be the beginning of a much greater private sector role in the more infrastructural and logistical aspects of humanitarian work. But can such companies honestly sign up to the humanitarian principles and standards that values-based agencies are championing? This is still contested territory.

Where a private sector role can be more easily agreed is on the question of corporate social responsibility around war economies. The need for responsible trading in resources like diamonds, oil and timber – so often at the heart of contemporary wars – is now recognized by the great majority of companies.

Military forces, meanwhile, have been questioned on practical issues of technical competence: images of soldiers during the recent war in Iraq throwing aid parcels out of the back of a truck, or of yellow food packages falling on Afghanistan from US military aircraft only encourage the perception that soldiers are poor at targeting aid to those in greatest need.

But the more strategic objection to a military role in humanitarian aid is one of principle. The concerns of humanitarians are rooted in two main fears. First, that soldiers may use humanitarian aid as an instrument of their war aims – to pacify a population or to foster their own 'force protection' – rather than to alleviate suffering on the basis of need alone. This fear has risen to particular prominence in Afghanistan, where both armed soldiers and joint civil-military teams operate with mixed mandates to maintain political stability and gather intelligence while supporting aid and reconstruction.

The second, related fear is that blurring the distinction between soldiers and civilians will compromise the neutrality and security of humanitarian workers. In March 2003, an international aid worker was killed in Afghanistan, while visiting a water project near the southern city of Kandahar. He was forced to leave his vehicle and shot dead, while his two Afghan colleagues were spared. When reporting on this incident in its monthly review, the British Agencies Afghanistan Group said: "This incident has further undermined the confidence of humanitarian agencies that their neutrality and impartiality will be respected by those bearing arms in conflict areas."

Raymond C. Offenheiser, president of Oxfam America, has voiced concerns about the leading role taken by the US Department of Defense in controlling relief and reconstruction in Iraq, following the fall of Saddam Hussein in April 2003. He was recently reported as saying that a new template of assistance was emerging, "in which the American military plays a significant role early on and marginalizes the roles of the nongovernmental organizations and the United Nations. It reduces them to subcontractors."

In a number of formal and informal statements, most notably the recent policy of the Steering Committee for Humanitarian Response, aid agencies have generally stated that military forces – because of their status as actual or perceived belligerents – should always give priority in aid operations to civilian humanitarian agencies. Furthermore, it is argued, soldiers should only get involved in humanitarian action in very exceptional circumstances, where a civilian option is not possible (see Box 1.6). In response to the war in Iraq, the UN issued its own particular guidelines on civil-military relations and activities.

Box 1.6 Principles guiding humanitarian-military relations

The following is a summary of the position paper on humanitarian-military relations in the provision of humanitarian assistance, published in 2002 by the Geneva-based Steering Committee for Humanitarian Response (SCHR):

This position paper endorses the primacy of humanitarian organizations in humanitarian work while respecting that the main aims of international military support are to establish and maintain order and security, to protect civilians, and to facilitate a comprehensive settlement to a conflict.

The four main positions agreed by the SCHR agencies are:

1. It is never appropriate for the military to directly implement humanitarian activities in general circumstances.
2. Only in exceptional circumstances, and very rarely, is it appropriate for the military to directly implement humanitarian activities, for which there must be specific criteria, such as:

- The military are a last resort and there is no other humanitarian option
- There is a significant level of need as determined by civilian agencies
- If possible, humanitarian assets and interventions should remain under civilian control to ensure humanitarian independence
- Any such intervention is clearly time-bound.

3. Humanitarian agencies will only use military armed protection as a last resort in extreme circumstances.
4. Certain types of information can and should be shared between humanitarian agencies and the military. This should be confined to information on:

- Security conditions
- Conditions in shared logistical space (airfields, aid movements, transport)
- General estimates about the scope of the emergency. ■

This humanitarian agency position is usually respected by military forces, which have no desire to become humanitarian agencies. Yet, aid agency discussion of the subject has been felt by some soldiers to project a note of moral superiority that tends to deny the military the opportunity for important gestures of human sympathy.

This mixed message from humanitarian organizations is unfortunate because it is vital that all military forces are humanitarian in the deepest sense of the word. International humanitarian law demands serious humanitarian obligations on all military forces as belligerents, occupiers or peacekeepers. Although aid agencies are wise to be alert to a possible conflict of interests in any military humanitarian programming, they should also be very keen to sustain a sense of humanitarian responsibility in military forces and to encourage the personal ethic of help, restraint and compassion in all military people. This is vital if the principles of civilian protection and proportional force are to be valued and respected by armies around the world.

Humanitarian judgement to analyse context

Bringing an ethic of impartial help and kindness into the hatred and ravages of war and disaster appears morally simple but is practically complicated. There will always be difficult decisions to make that require an astute assessment of people's conditions and considered ethical analysis by humanitarian agencies. Perhaps the best way to understand these decisions is as humanitarian *judgement*, which analyses the situation from three different perspectives:

- **Field analysis** – the 'real'context of disaster-affected people's needs (for assistance and protection), vulnerabilities, capacities and preferences, as well as local actors who may seek to help or hinder the situation.
- **Ethical/legal analysis** – the 'ideal' context of laws, conventions, principles, codes and standards designed to safeguard people's lives and dignity.
- **Humanitarian analysis** – the context of what is 'possible', what can realistically be achieved, given the political will, cooperation and funding of donor and host governments, as well as the expertise and capacities of specific humanitarian organizations (see Figure 1.2).

Critically, any humanitarian judgement must balance an accurate people-centred assessment of conditions with an ethical and legal analysis of humanitarian responsibility. Not all responsibility lies with humanitarian agencies. Most of it lies with governments, belligerent forces and individuals who choose to pursue strategies of violence, exploitation and oppression – or who may lack the means or the will to reduce the risks from disasters. A good assessment should be based on the rights, needs, vulnerabilities and desires of those most affected and an effective understanding of the political, social and economic conditions in which they are living and suffering.

In all their work, humanitarian agencies have a duty of care to ensure that they apply the humanitarian principle of saving life with dignity as ethically as possible. This means thinking hard – and thinking together with the people they are trying to help and other agencies whose actions can be complementary to their own. Ultimately, it also means making decisions, being ready to justify them, putting them consistently into action and then changing them if necessary.

Conclusion: put principles into practice

The flow of humanitarian resources towards strategically significant crises in the Balkans, Afghanistan and Iraq suggests that aid is becoming dangerously politicized. Millions of the world's most vulnerable – whether suffering from the effects of HIV/AIDS, malnutrition, disease, natural disaster or forced migration – remain beyond the reach of humanitarian assistance and protection. The overriding

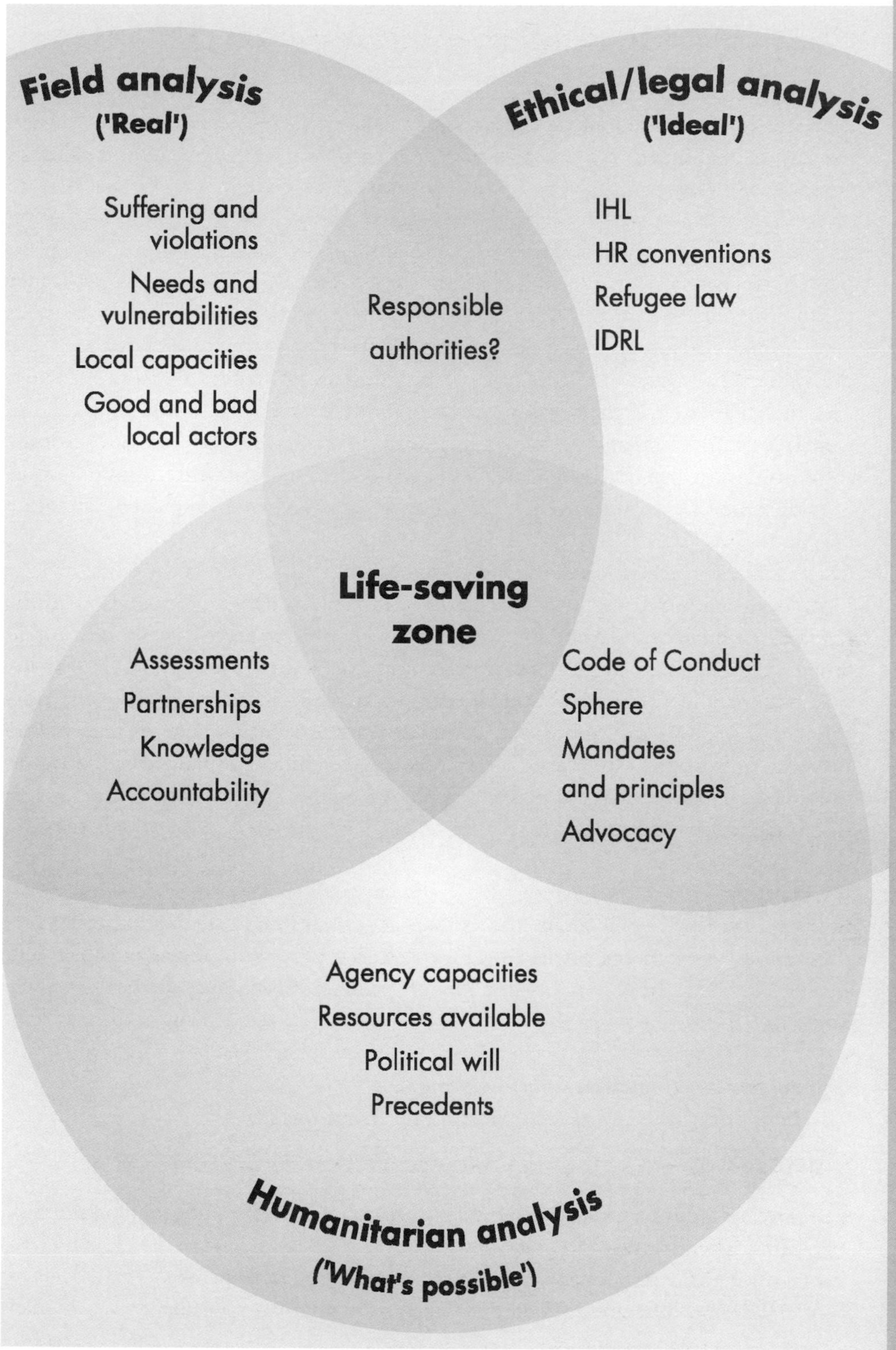

chapter 1

Field analysis
('Real')

Suffering and
violations

Needs and
vulnerabilities

Local capacities

Good and bad
local actors

Ethical/legal analysis
('Ideal')

IHL

HR conventions

Refugee law

IDRL

Responsible
authorities?

Life-saving
zone

Assessments
Partnerships
Knowledge
Accountability

Code of Conduct

Sphere

Mandates
and principles

Advocacy

Agency capacities

Resources available

Political will

Precedents

Humanitarian analysis
('What's possible')

Figure 1.2
Making the right
ethical decisions
during complex crises
is never simple.
Weighing up
programming options
involves humanitarian
judgement, which
balances the
'ideal' context of
humanitarian laws
and principles on one
side, the 'real' context
of the field situation
on the other, and
assesses what kinds of
humanitarian action
are possible with the
resources available.

Source: J. Walter, 2003.

humanitarian principle of alleviating suffering according to need alone – present in all the world's cultures and formalized in international law ever since the first Geneva Convention of 1864 – is still very unevenly applied. But how complicit are humanitarian organizations themselves in following the trajectory of the political-media spotlight, rather than campaigning for the most vulnerable people, hidden from view?

As the following chapters illustrate, some authorities, which preside over crisis, may manipulate aid for political reasons. Some seek to prioritize peace and order before impartial aid and justice. Meanwhile, many actors that come into contact with humanitarian needs – development agencies, private sector companies and the military – may not subscribe to humanitarian principles at all. And those agencies that have signed the Code of Conduct may not translate all those principles into practice, nor assess their impacts against the ethics to which they subscribe. Is the gap between principles and practice, rhetoric and reality in danger of widening?

While many of the world's neediest receive no aid at all, others are swamped by too much of the wrong kind of aid. Saving lives alone is not sufficient. Respecting people's dignity – which translates into listening to their preferences, supporting their capacities and taking steps to be held accountable – is equally important. Yet too often, humanitarian aid risks undermining local markets and capacities, imposing supply-led solutions and retarding recovery. Partnerships between agencies and those they seek to serve are often unequal and the resourcefulness of people caught up in disaster is routinely underestimated. Sadly none of this is new – but can we accept that it never changes?

Humanitarian organizations bear two special responsibilities: to practise the values they espouse and to promote these values to others implicated in suffering and disaster. Humanitarian agencies could start to close the gap between principles and practice by pursuing a twin strategy of principled action and humanitarian advocacy:

Operationalize humanitarian principles
- Build principles into all assessments of need and impact.
- Conduct 'real-time' impact assessments and accountability monitoring to inform ethical decision-making.
- Develop indicators to help field actors and evaluators put principles (and not only technical standards) into practice.
- Communicate principles with field actors and vulnerable people.
- Analyse and disseminate good practice in humanitarian judgement.

Advocate principles to other actors

- Support (rather than neglect) local NGOs which make a stand for principles.
- Build consensus among actors in the field to operationalize principles.
- Hold donor aid budgets to account on the basis of global humanitarian impartiality.
- Invite donor agencies, UN organizations and host governments to sign up to the Code of Conduct.
- Prepare new annexes to the Code of Conduct for development actors, private sector contractors and civil-military units to sign up to.

From sudden impact disasters through to complex emergencies, the world's crises need the principled engagement of a whole range of state and non-state actors. Humanitarian organizations can claim legitimacy only by practising as well as preaching the universal value of alleviating suffering wherever it is found. Saving lives remains the priority, but not in a way which undermines the dignity of those receiving aid or their capacity to recover. Getting the right balance between top-down interventions and more participatory programming, between prevention and cure is a matter of humanitarian moral judgement – an art which must be cultivated alongside the technical skills of relief and development aid.

Principal contributor to this chapter and Box 1.6 was Hugo Slim, Reader in International Humanitarianism at Oxford Brookes University and recently appointed as Chief Scholar at the Centre for Humanitarian Dialogue in Geneva. Austen Davis, general director of MSF-Holland for the last four years, contributed Box 1.2. Ian Christoplos, a researcher and consultant working with humanitarian and rural development issues, contributed Box 1.4. Boxes 1.1 and 1.5 were contributed by Jonathan Walter, editor of the World Disasters Report. *He also worte Box 1.3 with ODI's James Darcy and Joanna Macrae.*

Sources and further information

Anderson, M. *Do No Harm: How Aid Can Support Peace or War*. Boulder, CO: Lynne Reiner, 1999.

Centre for Humanitarian Dialogue. *Politics and Humanitarianism: Coherence in Crisis?* Geneva: Centre for Humanitarian Dialogue, 2003.

de Waal, A. 'Aids, Aid and Famine: New-Variant Famine in Southern Africa' in *Index on Censorship*, Volume 32(1) 2003.

ICRC. *Protection: Towards Professional Standards*. Geneva: ICRC, 1998.

ICRC. *Strengthening Protection in War: A Search for Professional Standards*. Geneva: ICRC, 2001.

International Federation. *Code of Conduct for the International Red Cross and Red Crescent Movement and NGOs in Disaster Relief*. Geneva: International Federation, 1994.

International Rescue Committee. *Mortality in the Democratic Republic of Congo: Results from a Nationwide Survey*. New York: IRC, 2003.

Juma, M. and Suhrke, A. *Eroding Local Capacity – International Humanitarian Action in Africa*. Uppsala: Nordiska Afrikainstitutet and Transaction, 2002.

ODI. *The New Humanitarianisms: A Review of trends in Global Humanitarian Action*. London: ODI Humanitarian Policy Group, 2002.

Oxfam. *Iraq: Humanitarian-Military Relations*. Oxfam Briefing Paper 41, 2003.

Oxfam. *An End to Forgotten Emergencies*. Oxford: Oxfam Publishing, 2000.

Slim, H. 'Claiming a Humanitarian Imperative: NGOs and the Cultivation of Humanitarian Duty' in *Refugee Survey Quarterly* 21(3), 2002.

Slim, H. 'Doing the Right Thing: Relief Agencies, Moral Dilemmas and Moral Responsibility in Political Emergency and War' in *Disasters* 21(3), Blackwells, Oxford, 1997.

Sphere Project. *The Humanitarian Charter and Minimum Standards in Disaster Response*. Oxford: Oxfam Publishing, 2000.

Steering Committee for Humanitarian Response. *Position Paper on Humanitarian-Military Relations in the Provision of Humanitarian Assistance*. Geneva: SCHR, 2003.

Studer, M. 'The ICRC and Civil-Military Relations in Armed Conflict' in *International Review of the Red Cross,* June 2001.

Terry, F. *Condemned to Repeat: The Paradox of Humanitarian Action*. Ithaca, NY: Cornell University Press, 2002.

United Nations. *General Guidance for Interaction Between United Nations Personnel and Military Actors in the Context of the Crisis in Iraq*. New York: UN, 21 March 2003.

Web sites

AlertNet **http://www.alertnet.org**
ICRC **http://www.icrc.org**
International Development Ethics Association **http://www.development-ethics.org**
International Federation (Code of Conduct) **http://www.ifrc.org/publicat/conduct/**
International Rescue Committee **http://www.intrescom.org/**
ODI **http://www.odi.org.uk**
Sphere Project **http://www.sphereproject.org**

chapter 2

Section One

**Focus on
ethics
in aid**

Building capacity – the ethical dimensions

> *Women and men, however poor or marginalised, always have many capacities, which may not be obvious to outsiders, and which even they themselves may not recognise. It may take time to discover these capacities and potential. But to intervene without doing so is not only disrespectful; it also wastes an opportunity to build on these existing capacities, and – even more importantly – risks undermining them, and so leaving people even more vulnerable than they were before.*

Deborah Eade, *Capacity-Building:*
An Approach to People-Centred
Development

Why build capacity? In the minutes, hours, days and weeks after disaster strikes, the spontaneous responses of loosely knit, informal groups created within communities play a crucial role. By the time outside support arrives, these 'emergent groups', as they are called, have often undertaken the largest and most critical aspects of the response effort by themselves, such as search and rescue, damage assessment, handling the dead, distributing relief supplies and presenting survivors' grievances to the authorities.

During the first three days after the Mexico City earthquake in 1985, the response was dominated by actions of this kind. A decade later, when a massive earthquake devastated Kobe, Japan, a strong contingent of volunteers emerged to respond even though there was little tradition of voluntary organization or community self-help in the city. One woman remembered "the noise of all the plates and glass in the kitchen falling down and the walls came in all around me… I yelled for help and a neighbour heard me but it took five hours to dig us out… We managed to get into the local kindergarten for shelter. It was locked and dark but I had found a flashlight somewhere and we got in through a window and took shelter. Other people followed us and it sort of became an unofficial shelter. We were there for three months" (see the *World Disasters Report 1996).*

When the Indian state of Orissa was hit by a cyclone in October 1999, the disruption to power supplies, transport and communications was severe, contributing to a breakdown in the state government's systems for the first two weeks after the disaster. Nor were many non-governmental organizations (NGOs) outside the state able to

Photo opposite page:
Capacity cannot be built through a simple transfer of information or skill, it requires generating a fertile environment within which the seeds of training have a chance to grow.

International Federation, Tajikistan.

respond quickly: it was weeks before some of the international agencies got their relief supplies in, and by then local organizations had already begun to move on to rehabilitation.

Likewise, in slow-onset disasters such as famines – which don't generate such urgent media headlines and donor attention as more sudden disasters – local organizations are often the first to raise the alarm. And even after the emergency response has died down, local agencies remain highly motivated to start reducing the risk of future disasters (see Box 2.1).

Box 2.1 Malawian NGOs jumpstart disaster response and rights debate

"Those deaths should not have happened," says Collins Magalasi, pointing to a grey metal filing cabinet in his office in Lilongwe. It holds medical reports, death certificates, affidavits and newspaper clippings confirming the death by starvation of 398 people between December 2001 and March 2002. Magalasi is coordinator of the Malawi Economic Justice Network (MEJN), comprising 45 church, development and human rights groups. Its campaign to prevent more such deaths jumpstarted a humanitarian operation for Malawi's starving people, pressing donors and government into action.

The first warnings of famine flashed in September 2001, when the British charity Save the Children (SCF-UK) reported rising malnutrition rates and lack of food in two districts. Prices for maize, the staple food, tripled after floods and a dry spell devastated the harvest. When the alarm was raised, donors were arguing with the government over corruption and mismanagement, conflicting reports on the size of the food deficit and the non-transparent sale of the entire national strategic grain reserve. This dispute delayed the humanitarian response until the grim evidence of deaths and rising malnutrition rates piled up.

As hunger spread across Malawi, MEJN and others mobilized activists and local media. Armed with mortality and malnutrition data and fired with indignation, civil society groups lobbied donors and confronted the government until they recognized, at the end of February 2002, that Malawi was facing a famine. In terms of casualties, this was Malawi's worst famine ever. In the big hunger of 1949, about 200 people starved to death. In 1991-92, during the worst drought in living memory, a few dozen people died of cholera. In 2001-02, estimates of deaths from both hunger and hunger-related cholera accepted by most observers range between 1,000 and 2,000.

The tragedy marked a watershed for Malawi's young civil society. Having emerged from the repressive three-decade dictatorship of President Banda in 1994, Malawi has a short experience of democracy, public debate and citizen empowerment. Yet the campaign around the famine showed how organized citizens can act as advocates for the poor and watchdogs over government and donors. Civil society emerged strengthened. NGOs now figure prominently in the relief operation, from chairing a number of key subcommittees to implementing food distribution.

Initially, the 'soft data' supplied by NGOs, traditional leaders and churches failed to convince donors, who waited for 'hard data' from the official famine early warning systems (FEWS) and the United Nations. But FEWS got its estimation of the food gap wrong, and the UN was slow to react. The shortcomings of FEWS data, based more on crop yields and weather patterns and less on people's access to food, became evident. On-the-ground data supplied by locally-based NGOs has acquired more credibility.

"In a crisis, one should listen more to people and organizations which are close to the actual situation and problems than to general statistics and macro analysis," says Asbjorn Eidhammer, Norway's ambassador to Malawi.

The famine revealed a serious omission. Malawi – a country that historically suffers from high malnutrition rates – lacks a proper, well-developed food security policy. "We have statements that pass as policy," says Richard Kachule, a researcher with the Food Security Unit at Bunda College of Agriculture. "We need a clear broad policy, with strategies and a plan of action, with household food security at its heart." One is on the way. Chaired by the international NGO ActionAid, one of the five subcommittees of the Joint Emergency Task Force is developing a draft policy for nation-wide consultation. "Food security is the first step out of poverty and into empowerment," says Humphreys Shumba, programme manager with SCF-UK in Lilongwe.

Another positive post-famine development is a new focus in Malawi on the right to food and other economic rights as a basic underpinning of human rights. "People here wait for assistance instead of demanding their rights," says Magalasi. "We must increase awareness of the right to food." MEJN is developing an economic literacy programme to bolster the capacity of NGO, church, trade union and community leaders to engage in policy dialogue through a better understanding of the economy with a rights-based approach.

A wide debate on food security should be coupled with strong advocacy with government, politicians and donors on the right to food and on policy reform in the areas of land and food security, says Ollen Mwalabunju, director of the Centre for Human Rights and Rehabilitation. "We need to put our heads together because 90 per cent of the solutions to our problems lies with us Malawians." ■

Given that local individuals, groups, communities and organizations are invariably in the front line of any disaster and become the key actors in disaster response and recovery, few would disagree that building their capacity to do that job as effectively as possible is vitally important. What's more, even if external organizations *could* arrive in timely fashion, local actors – survivors' families, neighbours, community groups, NGOs and local authorities – should *still* be the key players in decision-making and response. Not only are locals far more knowledgeable about local needs and capabilities than external organizations, but they should also be the directors of their own rehabilitation and recovery. If external agencies take any role at all, it should be one of improving the capacity of local actors to take control over the decisions which affect their lives in the short, medium and long term.

Capacity building: worthy but vague

Although capacity building has gained in importance since the 1980s – driven largely by the emergence of civil society participation in development programmes – its precise meaning remains vague. Definitions range from 'helping people to help themselves' to fostering democratization and accountable government. The United Nations Development Programme (UNDP), for example, defines capacity building as "the process by which individuals, organizations, institutions and societies develop abilities (individually and collectively) to perform functions, solve problems and set and achieve objectives".

Nor is there a universally accepted model of capacity building: the term is used to describe activities such as awareness-raising poster campaigns, technical training for tradespeople, community association development, classroom exercises with children, leadership workshops for local authorities, literacy campaigns, trigger-funding projects and rotating loan schemes. Any identifiable activity that should, in theory at least, 'help people help themselves' can and does fall into the capacity-building category.

Despite this lack of clarity, good capacity building is easy to spot when it appears. A now classic and widely cited example is the reconstruction project spearheaded by the Intermediate Technology Development Group (ITDG) in the Alto Mayo region of Peru, in 1990. After an earthquake destroyed most of the homes and public buildings in the town of Soritor, ITDG worked with local craftsmen and homeowners to design an earthquake-resistant building technique appropriate to their culture, traditional building skills, natural environment and economic constraints. Nearly a year after the first disaster, a second earthquake hit the region. The vast majority of homes reconstructed using the new technique remained unscathed during the second event. The new design had passed the acid test and, because it had been developed to suit the local context, the homeowners who had chosen not to participate in the reconstruction project the previous year were still able to learn and apply those techniques in the reconstruction of their houses.

More to capacity than skills alone

Experience has shown, however, that capacity building is not always as triumphant as the case of Alto Mayo suggests. Although awareness-raising campaigns, workshops or community development programmes might yield impressive initial results, sometimes the success story ends there. Acquired knowledge is often not systematically applied to new risk reduction activities as time passes. Despite their training in appropriate construction techniques, builders often return to using old methods once the primary (i.e., supervised) reconstruction phase is over. Community groups, newly organized and animated for a specific purpose, sometimes fragment upon the completion of the original project and do not develop their social cohesion further.

Why is this the case? Often, it is because external organizations design and carry out capacity-building activities without giving adequate consideration to the other, equally important inputs required to make the change they desire both realistic and sustainable. Sometimes those inputs are financial or material resources, which might arrive with the capacity builders for the training exercise but become inaccessible once training is over. As wonderful as a new flood-resistant housing design might be, if the cost of building was subsidized by the implementing organization, or if important materials were brought in from another region, families might struggle to use those designs again, despite their newly strengthened skills. The same can be said for disaster preparedness capacity building. As one Red Crescent volunteer in the Sudan stressed: "Our biggest problem is that without sandbags, digging tools, jerrycans and water purification tablets, not to mention temporary shelter material like plastic sheeting and tents, the training itself does not reduce risk or realistically prepare us."

Very often, the other inputs required are not material but social or political in nature, making them harder to deal with but no less vital. These requirements may include access to resources, a voice in government, freedom from marginalization and discrimination, or the protection of basic human rights.

In major cities across the developing world, one of the most elusive of these inputs is land tenure. Many construction workers in Mumbai, India speak of the frustrations they face because of this problem. Although skilled in techniques for reducing the risk of flooding in slums, they almost invariably find themselves without a market for those services, as informal settlers choose not to invest precious resources in a home from which they might be evicted at any moment. In the face of these fundamental problems, simply training builders in risk reduction techniques has a very limited impact on their real capacity to reduce risk in the community.

The 'landmine harvesters' of Afghanistan provide a more life-threatening example of this. Despite receiving excellent training on the lethal dangers posed by landmines, some of the poorest Afghans still risk injury or death by digging up and selling landmines as scrap metal. So, until they find a more lucrative livelihood option, mine-awareness training will not translate into genuine change. Real capacity for change will not have been built.

In short, it seldom happens that real capacity can be built through a simple transfer of information or skill alone. Yet it is common for organizations to focus on strengthening the *ability* of communities to organize in a certain way or perform a certain task, without paying adequate attention to the *capacity* of those groups to realize the new skills in their daily life. To build genuine capacity requires generating a fertile environment within which the seeds of training have a chance to grow.

Even once the issue of 'capacity versus ability' has been understood, there is a dangerous and common misconception that capacity building is something that can be accomplished through any number of specific, fundable activities. Yet a community's capacities don't exist in a vacuum, influenced by nothing other than the activities specifically designed to build them. Virtually every aspect of an external intervention – including the kinds of aid offered, activities undertaken, methodologies employed and relationships built (or not built) – can affect local capacities, often in ways far broader and deeper than any number of workshops could achieve.

Ethical challenges of building capacity

Capacity building is far more complex than is often assumed. Rather than limiting our scope to the misleading concept of capacity building as a set of specific activities, we must consider it within a broader context, in which the entire intervention is accountable for the capacity-building process. This will bring us face to face with a range of ethical challenges, including:

- the risk that the presence of international agencies will undermine local organizational capacities;
- failure to match external aid supply systems to people's needs;
- unequal partnerships between outsiders and local organizations;
- how to work with government institutions in an effective and politically neutral manner;
- imposition of outsiders' predetermined aid agendas;
- how far agencies can and should go in addressing the root causes of vulnerability to disasters;
- what constitutes success and how to measure it; and
- the unintended and sometimes damaging consequences of interventions.

As we shall see, many of these issues arise out of the conflict between what aid agencies want to supply or achieve and what vulnerable people on the ground actually need.

Capacity-sapping presence of international agencies

The simple presence of international organizations in a region suffering from disaster can have serious consequences for local capacity, before activities are even initiated. Many local organizations find that the position they have enjoyed in local communities is undermined by the real or perceived resources and prestige that the newcomers bring with them and the expectations they generate. They may face eviction to make way for bigger, wealthier tenants, or find their drivers and social outreach workers enticed by the higher wage offers of external actors.

Experiences in Afghanistan, Bosnia and Herzegovina, and Kosovo have shown that when hundreds of international agencies rush into an area, rents and wages are driven up steeply, seriously undermining the capacity of local organizations to compete for workspace and staff. In Afghanistan, for example, Aschiana, one of the most effective local childcare charities which had run 'drop-in' centres for street-working children since 1995, was forced out of its Kabul premises during 2002 by rents which sky-rocketed from US$ 100 to US$ 4,000 per month when international organizations arrived after the fall of the Taliban (see Chapter 4, Box 4.3).

In such situations, local organizations, which are being offered training workshops to 'build their capacity', may find that, at the same time, their actual capacity to bring about change in their community is severely curtailed. Real capacity for effective action in the face of crisis is then lost.

As well as weakening the position of local organizations, the presence of international agencies may discourage local residents from investing their own resources into recovery. They may be tempted to sit back and wait for the outsiders to offer material assistance, however inappropriate. In situations where many agencies compete to offer aid, this disempowering effect can be very strong. Rahul Pathak, a journalist from the news magazine *India Today*, visiting villages in the Himalayan foothills of Uttarkashi two years after an earthquake in 1991 flattened 30,000 houses, wrote: "An excess of largesse has spawned an insatiable yearning for more and no one thinks he's got enough. There is greed and corruption and everyone waits for others to carry his burden." He found villagers refusing to rebuild their own homes when they knew outside agencies would do it for them.

How should an agency intent on increasing local capacities deal with these dilemmas? Many do not consider them at all.

Supply-driven aid and delivery systems

In a supply-driven intervention, programme decision-making is based less on what the actual needs on the ground are and more on what the intervening agency has to offer. Ethical problems begin to appear when supply and demand do not match. The most common (or most visible) supply-driven assistance occurs in the form of goods; for example, food aid that donor countries produce or can acquire cheaply, or tents, blankets or other supplies already stockpiled by the agency, to be flown immediately into the crisis zone. A second form of supply-driven humanitarian aid occurs through services, such as medical support based on procedures in which the intervening agency specializes.

Supply-driven interventions are often defended on the grounds that in the wake of disaster, speed is of the essence, or that 'something is better than nothing'. However, bringing food and material aid into an area where residents could provide at least some of those goods through local economic avenues can easily destroy an already precarious local market. This in turn will undermine the recovery of individual producers, merchants and the local economy as a whole.

Local methods of organization can easily be destabilized if external agencies force the creation of new structures instead of working with already established or naturally emergent groups. Some misguided food-for-work programmes have fallen into this kind of trap. If aid agencies establish domination over the food supply of a certain group of people over time, those people may lose vital economic and social connections necessary for renewed local food security once the external intervention ends.

In the very worst humanitarian emergencies, in which basic human requirements simply cannot be met locally, external agencies may have no choice but to dominate short-term supplies of food, water, shelter or health care. Even so, most groups of disaster victims will have a system of organizing such supplies that should be respected. Yet cases have been documented of international agencies rushing into a region where they had not previously worked with not only a predetermined form of aid, but a predetermined system for delivering that aid. In some refugee camps, food distribution was organized through the male heads of household, even though women traditionally held power over food resources and allocation. Not only did it unnecessarily upset a well-functioning system, but it also undermined the women's position of strength in family decision-making. Such supply-driven responses undermine the capacity of vulnerable communities to recover and to reduce their exposure to future disasters.

So, questions of ethical responsibility towards local capacity become important to resolve when some capacity does remain, with strong potential to be supported and even enhanced. The justification often given for not tapping into these resources is that urgently needed disaster relief would be significantly slowed by the process of understanding local capacities and integrating them into an effective response. This assumption, however, goes against the grain of experiences ranging from Mexico City and sub-Saharan Africa to Orissa and Kobe, which show that local people and structures are the first line of disaster response.

Local organizations – partners or porters?

It should come as no surprise that the most effective disaster relief agencies are those with local connections. An evaluation of the response to the 1999 Orissa cyclone by the Disasters Emergency Committee (DEC), a consortium of British relief NGOs, found that "the DEC agencies able to make the best initial response to the cyclone already had either local staff and infrastructure in Orissa or strong, active partnerships with NGOs in areas affected by the cyclone".

Unfortunately, the absence of such connections does not stop foreign agencies from rushing in blindly after a disaster, ignoring the existence of local capacity that could deliver relief more quickly and efficiently to those in the greatest need. This happens despite the fact that the Code of Conduct for the International Red Cross and Red Crescent Movement and NGOs in Disaster Response – a globally accepted benchmark for good practice that over 200 relief agencies have signed up to – states firmly: "We shall attempt to build disaster response on local capacities" (see Box 2.2). In times of crisis, outsiders are tempted to intervene without waiting to find out if they are really needed – or even wanted – by the community.

Another DEC evaluation, this time of responses to the Gujarat earthquake in 2001, found that the relief operation "could have achieved more if agencies had engaged more effectively with local NGOs. Gujarat has a strong tradition of NGOs, yet several DEC members – even those with strong connections in the area – operated through their own staff and relied unnecessarily and inefficiently on expatriates. In some cases local partners were ignored, and in others a climate of suspicion and distrust developed". The evaluation polled several thousand Gujaratis in order to measure the performance of aid agencies against the Code of Conduct's ten principles. While the foreign DEC agencies scored an average of 59 out of 100, a leading local NGO scored 86 (see Chapter 6, Box 6.1).

The Gujarat experience shows that the existence of international 'partnerships' with local NGOs does not automatically mean that community capacities will be recognized and supported, or even that the capacity of the partner NGO will be enriched. International agencies, particularly NGOs, often speak of their 'partnerships' with local organizations and communities. But how equal can such partnerships be when the balance of resources is weighed so heavily in favour of the outsiders? The possession of resources, especially funding, conveys great power. In many instances, local capacity building is used simply to enable foreign agencies to deliver externally designed aid projects more efficiently. Local institutions (whether governmental or non-governmental) or community groups are thus the instruments by which certain goals can be reached.

Northern agencies may be able to convince themselves that their relationships with southern partners are equal, but the local partners may see it quite differently. For instance, researchers reviewing the results of Canadian NGOs' support for reconstruction and rehabilitation projects in southern Africa during the 1991-92 drought were struck by the number of times staff in local NGOs in Mozambique, Namibia and Zimbabwe referred to Canadian NGOs as 'donors' rather than

Box 2.2 Code of Conduct

In 1994, the International Federation, along with seven other humanitarian agencies (Caritas Internationalis, Catholic Relief Services, International Committee of the Red Cross, International Save the Children Alliance, Lutheran World Federation, Oxfam and World Council of Churches), developed the Code of Conduct for the International Red Cross and Red Crescent Movement and Non-Governmental Organizations in Disaster Relief.

As at March 2003, the Code had 227 signatories. The voluntary code sets out universal basic standards to govern the way signatory relief agencies should work in disaster assistance. To sign up to the Code of Conduct or for more information, contact the International Federation's disaster preparedness and response department (maya.schaerer@ifrc.org) or visit the web site at http://www.ifrc.org/publicat/conduct/

The Code of Conduct devotes four of its ten principles to issues directly related to capacity building:

5. We shall respect culture and custom

We will endeavour to respect the culture, structures and customs of the communities and countries we are working in.

6. We shall attempt to build disaster response on local capacities

All people and communities – even in disaster – possess capacities as well as vulnerabilities. Where possible, we will strengthen these capacities by employing local staff, purchasing local materials and trading with local companies. Where possible, we will work through local NGHAs [non-governmental humanitarian agencies] as partners in planning and implementation, and co-operate with local government structures where appropriate. We will place a high priority on the proper co-ordination of our emergency responses. This is best done within the countries concerned by those most directly involved in the relief operations, and should include representatives of the relevant UN bodies.

7. Ways shall be found to involve programme beneficiaries in the management of relief aid

Disaster response assistance should never be imposed upon the beneficiaries. Effective relief and lasting rehabilitation can best be achieved where the intended beneficiaries are involved in the design, management and implementation of the assistance programme. We will strive to achieve full community participation in our relief and rehabilitation programmes.

8. Relief aid must strive to reduce future vulnerabilities to disaster as well as meeting basic needs

All relief actions affect the prospects for long-term development, either in a positive or a negative fashion. Recognising this, we will strive to implement relief programmes which actively reduce the beneficiaries' vulnerability to future disasters and help create sustainable lifestyles. We will pay particular attention to environmental concerns in the design and management of relief programmes. We will also endeavour to minimise the negative impact of humanitarian assistance, seeking to avoid long-term beneficiary dependence upon external aid. ■

'partners'. Zimbabwean NGOs expressed their frustration at having to deal with outsiders who arrived at the start of a project to decide what was to be done and reappeared only at the end to evaluate the work.

To whom are humanitarian agencies accountable? On the one hand, they are accountable downwards to beneficiaries, local partner agencies, their staff and supporters. But they are also accountable upwards to boards of management, donor agencies and host governments; the pull of this upward accountability is often stronger.

Control over defining objectives and outcomes makes it easier for international agencies to account for their actions to the managers and donors looking over their shoulders. Often, interveners do not seek out local participation or strive for equality in partnerships because they have a preconceived idea of what they want to achieve and how they want to achieve it. Local partners, however, might challenge these ideas, putting the intervening agency in an awkward situation. As a result, many interventions – perhaps more than we may like to recognize – are supply-driven instead of demand-driven.

National institutions – bypass or bolster them?

Just as international agencies can undermine local capacity and structures, so too can they undermine national capacity. Foreign aid agencies unwilling or unable to build a relationship with local governments often end up weakening them by effectively taking over their responsibilities, instead of helping them to do the job themselves. Should external aid-givers, however, bypass the institutions of national governments and work through other agencies, such as national NGOs or fellow international aid organizations, when governments are the legitimate authority in a country, with the principal responsibility for disaster response and reduction? Bypassing government institutions may be an attractive option in terms of cost-effectiveness. It may also be morally justifiable if governments manipulate the distribution of relief and reconstruction aid in favour of their own supporters and goals. However, bypassing legitimate authorities can also be seen as a form of political interference by weakening them in relation to other actors.

This ethical issue is not as clear-cut as it may appear. Should external players seek to build capacity in government organizations that are vulnerable to political forces? Is this a cost-effective use of aid resources? Reflecting on the World Bank's experience of risk reduction in La Paz, Bolivia in the 1980s, Alcira Kreimer and Martha Preece observed what many others have found: "Prevention and mitigation efforts often take longer than a policymaker's term of office, and projects that address risk prevention do not always produce short-term political or economic gains. They must compete with and often lose out to more visible or politically rewarding projects."

National politicians may bypass or politicize their own institutions in times of crisis. During the El Niño event which hit Bolivia, Ecuador and Peru in 1997-98, the crisis response was heavily influenced by party and presidential politics. In each country, the nominal emergency management systems (civil defence) were marginalized by new, temporary, government organizations, which took over management of the crisis. As a result, institutional roles were duplicated and confused, while civil defence organizations suffered a serious loss of credibility and morale. The justification given for the changes was lack of capacity in existing civil defence organizations and their response-focused attitudes. But the prime motive was to put allies of the countries' presidents in charge of dealing with El Niño as it rapidly became a national, political crisis. In other words, a short-term, politically expedient approach was preferred to the strategic development of disaster management capacity and even to more effective disaster response.

In some countries, the Philippines for example, national authorities have delegated responsibility for disaster reduction to local government levels, without always providing adequate training or resources to perform these functions. Such decentralized structures, however, may provide a less politically-loaded opportunity for international donors and domestic NGOs alike to invest in community-level disaster management (see Box 2.3).

Predetermined aid agenda

The politicization of crisis response is part of a broader, yet intangible trend for those agencies intervening in disaster to promote an external agenda. Of all forms of supply-driven intervention, this presents the greatest ethical challenges in relation to community and organizational capacity building.

Faith-based NGOs are usually among the first to be accused – often unjustly – of imposing their own agenda on communities. As we have seen, political parties intervene in emergency situations; some, undoubtedly, from a belief in social justice and compassion, others in an attempt to boost their own popularity.

Indeed, the majority of organizations (including the most apolitical and secular) have some sort of agenda that they bring to an intervention. Very often this agenda is not based on self-interest but on a clear mission statement reflecting that agency's vision of a better world. For example, many organizations, which believe in the inherent right of women to enjoy the same rights and opportunities as men, work on gender issues as a part or even the whole of their intervention efforts. This, in effect, becomes their agenda: it is the form of capacity that they would most like to build in their host community. Yet at some times and in some places, this may not necessarily be the top priority for the men or women living in the host communities.

An example from Afghanistan – described in *The Selfish Altruist*, a recent book by Tony Vaux, Oxfam's global emergencies coordinator during the 1990s – illustrates this ethical challenge. In late 1996, soon after the Taliban took control of Kabul, Oxfam decided to suspend work on renovating a major section of the capital's water supply. According to Vaux, the reason was the Taliban's ban on women going to work. In January 1997, however, at a special regional conference on assistance to Afghanistan, Afghan women made a joint statement saying: "Denial of female opportunities should not be used as a justification to stop aid." Nevertheless, Oxfam's country director at the time, Sue Emmott, defended the suspension by arguing that "a water programme could not succeed without the participation of women". Oxfam's aim, says Vaux, was to persuade other agencies to suspend their projects as well and pressure the Taliban into changing their policy towards women. This didn't happen. Instead, the suspension of the project left 400,000 Afghans with little alternative but to collect water from a polluted riverbed. Reflecting on the episode, Vaux writes: "It was not so much a question of what was appropriate policy for Afghanistan as whether Oxfam's gender policy would be applied or undermined."

In complex, ongoing political emergencies – such as Afghanistan or Africa's Great Lakes region during the 1990s – the ethical dilemma of whether to concentrate on saving lives or to invest in building long-term capacities to help resolve those emergencies becomes particularly acute. In the introduction to his book, *Patronage or Partnership: Local Capacity Building in Humanitarian Crises*, Ian Smillie refers to the 1998 case of a refugee camp for 4,000 Hutus in Burundi, where conditions were desperate. Despite the fact that the refugees' immediate survival was at stake, one British NGO was running a series of conflict resolution workshops nearby and attracted critical attention in the British press as a result. More recently in the Democratic Republic of the Congo, several hundred million dollars of aid were spent from 1998 to 2002 on trying to build a lasting peace. Meanwhile, according to mortality surveys conducted by the International Rescue Committee in the east of the country an estimated 3.3 million excess deaths occurred over the same period, mostly from malnutrition and disease. The ethical challenge is to judge where the balance lies between investing scarce aid resources in meeting critical immediate needs or delivering important but intangible future benefits.

Root causes and realistic expectations

The issue of how far to push an external agenda is particularly acute when it comes to considering how to overcome the complex web of socio-economic forces that make people vulnerable to 'natural' and man-made disasters in the first place. Resolving the root causes of conflict and how this should be balanced against the immediate imperative to save lives is a notoriously difficult ethical challenge. However, in the case of 'natural' disasters, many will argue that outside agencies have a moral responsibility

Box 2.3 Decentralized disaster management – a mixed blessing

Exhausted, still wet, and without food for the past 30 hours, two family leaders went to a government office for any kind of assistance they could get. They had spent the previous day and night on the roof of their house after a devastating seven-metre-deep *lahar* [volcanic mudslide] hit their village. But a government officer told them to get a certificate from the village head stating that they were indeed victims of the *lahar*. Indignant, they asked, "How can we get a note from our village head when the whole village was engulfed? We do not even know where they are now. Are our testimonies and physical appearance not sufficient evidence that we are victims?" They never received any support, except a few litres of water for their group of 30 families sheltering in a temporary refuge. The disaster happened in October 1995, after a week of heavy rain burst a section of the huge dyke constructed by the national government to protect villagers from landslides down the slopes of Mount Pinatubo in the Philippines.

The collapse and subsequent response raised a number of questions. How prepared are communities and local authorities to handle disasters like these? Who should take responsibility for disaster reduction and response? Is it reasonable to expect local organizations to cope on their own? Were the local government workers responsible for disaster management trained to handle such tasks?

A nation comprising 7,100 islands and almost 80 million people, the Philippines is committed to "a system of decentralization whereby local government units shall be given more powers, authority, responsibilities and resources". As early as 1978, a presidential decree established the national programme of community disaster preparedness, which oversaw the creation of disaster coordinating councils (DCCs) from national to village levels. Local DCCs are mandated to plan for dis-

asters; train their members, community leaders and residents; practise emergency drills; stockpile relief supplies; conduct emergency response and rehabilitation; and carry out public information programmes. There are now over 42,000 local government units (LGUs) across the country faced with these tasks. But, while decentralizing disaster management is a step in the right direction, experiences such as that beneath Mount Pinatubo suggest that it isn't having the desired effect.

While the national government has delegated responsibility for disaster management to local authorities, the necessary training and resources are inadequately provided. In many cases, NGOs take this as an opportunity to fill the gap. But this raises difficult ethical questions: should NGOs take on the role of government in training local officials? Does this let the government off the hook? And if NGOs play a greater role in disaster management, does this make them morally responsible for the impacts of future disasters?

Self-reliant communities sound good in theory. But the practice is different. In June 2002, for example, LGU officials in one frequently flooded municipality attended a workshop on community-based disaster management sponsored by an NGO. The officials admitted that their DCC was very inactive – one member didn't even realize he was on the disaster council. They acknowledged that no training had taken place and for almost all of the officials, the workshop was the first they had ever attended. This situation is repeated in LGUs across the country. At best, they may react to disasters by doling out relief. But disaster reduction measures are almost unheard of.

According to Rudencio C. Eduate, a programme officer with the league of *punong barangay* (village heads): "More than 90 per cent of the devolved functions of the national government are now on the shoulders of the *barangay*." Yet, despite this responsibility, "most of the *barangay* chairs have no knowledge of basic disaster management concepts," he says. "Generally, the LGU cannot determine what kind of mitigation projects to undertake... Most do not know the mechanism or the tools." The national agency mandated to supervise and train LGUs – the Department of the Interior and Local Government (DILG) – does not appear to be fulfilling its mandate.

Coupled with a lack of official training is the shortage of resources allocated for local disaster reduction. LGUs receive an annual revenue from the national government. But of this, only 5 per cent may be used "for relief, rehabilitation, reconstruction and other works or services in connection with calamities during the budget year". None of this money can be used for disaster preparedness or reduction. Even the national disaster coordinating council (NDCC) admits that it "does not have a budget of its own and operates only though its member-agencies under the principle of coordination, complementation of resources and agency participation".

Major General Melchor P. Rosales, head of the civil defence and NDCC, defends the role of the LGUs in disaster management on the basis of the 'golden hour' principle. In the first hour of a disaster, "the national government cannot be relied upon to save lives," he argues, because only LGUs can respond in time. He adds, "The NDCC cannot interfere with the LGUs because they are autonomous... The LGUs are supposed to legislate ordinances for the safety of the communities." But he admits, "Not all LGUs are at the same level of awareness and development."

Conscious of the problem, Rosales has asked the Local Government Academy to add a module on disaster management in their 40-hour training for LGUs. He says the NDCC will produce a *barangay* disaster management manual to be given to all local officials.

But some NGOs have already leapt into the gap and directly assist LGUs in developing community-based disaster awareness and reduction. According to one NGO worker: "The people in the communities we serve will be the ones to suffer if we will not collaborate with the government in providing alternative approaches."

The Philippine National Red Cross (PNRC) agrees. According to Danny Atienza, coordinator of their integrated community disaster planning programme (ICDPP), "because of the increasing population of the country, the government cannot fully do their responsibilities. It is part of the PNRC's role to respond in times of disaster. Through the ICDPP, we have trained LGU officials in disaster management".

Recently, a network of NGOs known as the Philippines Disaster Management Forum collaborated with the NDCC to organize the first national conference on community-based disaster management. NGOs saw this as an opportunity to influence government decision-making and resource allocation. General Rosales also seemed keen on collaboration, saying, "It is important for the NDCC to keep in touch with the NGOs in community-based disaster management to find out where we are still weak and to jointly come out with programmes." This is a far cry from the days when Filipino people-power ousted two of their presidents. Democracy has now created a more collaborative mood between the government and NGOs.

But mutual understanding is only the start. With the national budget billions of pesos in debt, effective national disaster reduction and response remain a distant dream. In the absence of such measures, the traditional Filipino value of *bayanihan* – voluntary community self-help – remains the best hope for most exposed communities. ∎

to use disasters as a vehicle for social transformation by addressing the root causes of people's vulnerability. Providing purely technical support, be it in building safer houses or preparing emergency response, does not tackle the factors that expose poor people to risk in the first place. Ultimately, attacking the root causes of vulnerability is the truest way of building capacity.

Vulnerability has many root causes. They include poverty; marginalization through age, gender and ethnicity; population growth; rapid and unplanned urbanization; inappropriate development models; weaknesses in governance; poor land management and environmental degradation. Addressing these problems is not a neutral issue, for it inevitably involves challenging local and even national structures of social, economic and political power. Here, the moral responsibilities of outside agencies – and the limits of those responsibilities – are ill-defined.

Take the example of gender. Women's position in many societies is weaker than that of men, and this has been shown to reduce their resilience to disasters. Yet the chaos and shared suffering that disasters cause sometimes break down established social and institutional relationships, and is widely believed to create a window of opportunity to improve the position of marginalized groups, such as women, in society. Should this opportunity be exploited by aid agencies and if so, how?

Post-disaster interventions can have a very positive impact, as in the World Bank/ Maharashtra government reconstruction programme after the 1993 Latur earthquake in India. This worked in 300 villages with local women's organizations (*mahila mandals*) which took on the role of rebuilding safer houses. The women – many of whom had little experience in community initiatives of this kind – were trained to build houses and offer technical advice to householders in design and construction. They met government officials and village committees to plan the rebuilding work and promote good practice. Within a few years, as a result of the skills and experience they gained, the *mahila mandals* were becoming more active in other development initiatives and more vocal in village assemblies.

But the morality of outside agents interfering with indigenous structures is problematic. In Maharashtra, a diplomatic approach was used to overcome male resistance to women's empowerment. A more forceful approach was tried in the Punjab in Pakistan after severe flooding in 1992. A local NGO, PATTAN, sought to use the disaster to liberate village women. Food distribution was entrusted to local women, new women's village organizations were created, women were involved in designing (and sometimes building) new houses to replace those lost to the floods, and PATTAN introduced joint ownership by husband and wife of these new homes. Some measures were uncontroversial: for example, the women's fair and efficient distribution of food gained them respect from the men. However, the creation of women's organizations would have been resisted in normal circumstances – since women were barred from joining traditional village committees. Yet because the villages were dependent on PATTAN for relief and rehabilitation support, the men felt that they could not oppose the initiative.

Another critical issue for organizations seeking social change is the question of what can be achieved during the time frame of the intervention. Lasting social change often takes years – sometimes generations – to bring about. Attempts to use disasters as 'windows of opportunity' for addressing root causes or transforming society are particularly risky. Once the external aid givers have gone, traditional elites will seek to reimpose their authority – a process famously documented by Peter Winchester during two decades of research in India's Krishna delta, after a cyclone devastated the area in 1977.

When faced with complex levels of need but armed with limited resources, agencies involved in risk reduction through social change need to be level-headed about such long-term requirements and the implications this has for their own commitments. They should be honest with communities and themselves about what they can achieve within a given time, with given inputs and within the context of wider trends. In many cases projects will only be able to tackle some of the immediate causes of vulnerability, not its root causes. Investing resources in an intervention that cannot be seen through to its end, or that may not survive once external support is withdrawn, is probably not the best use of those resources or the best way to build local capacity.

The largest and most critical aspects of the response effort in the wake of any disaster are undertaken by loosely knit, informal groups created within the affected communities.

International Federation, Peru 2001.

Likewise, it can take several years before community technical and managerial capacity and the ability to negotiate more effectively with other external agencies really take root. Some analysts estimate that a realistic time frame for organizational strengthening is over ten years. Yet most project cycles last from two to five years, while emergency interventions might only exist for weeks or months. Moreover, the impact of, for example, seven consecutive one-year interventions is likely to be far less than the results that could be achieved by planning a seven-year programme from day one. Securing the right kind of funding is therefore a key challenge for capacity-building agencies, especially since long-term funding is so rarely available.

Too few disaster mitigation and preparedness projects progress beyond the pilot phase. After Hurricane Mitch, the *Comite de Emergencia Garifuna de Honduras* (a community-based organization) complained that the disaster mitigation training programme of a major international NGO "existed here for a few months, but made no provision for follow up, provided no ongoing funds for replication to expand the number of people trained beyond the initial group, and left no materials or resources for implementation of what people had learned".

In some cases, external inputs will always be required. The Cyclone Preparedness Programme in Bangladesh, which has been running for 30 years, may be based on a 30,000-strong volunteer army but depends equally on ongoing funding from the government of Bangladesh and international donors for its professional staff, equipment, construction of shelters and other operational costs. In a recent study of local-level mitigation in Pampanga and Quezon provinces in the Philippines, it was shown that 'community organizers' (local people employed by NGOs) played an essential role in community-level training, planning and ensuring that risk reduction measures were maintained. Members of community disaster response committees acknowledged that their motivation dropped significantly when the community organizers were away; meetings were not held and activities were not carried out.

The lesson to be learned from these examples is that it's not ethical to start something that cannot be finished or for which no exit strategy can be developed which stands a good chance of being sustainable. When locals invest time and resources in a project, they are gambling livelihood assets that could be used in other ways. It is the intervening agency's ethical duty to make as certain as possible that the individuals or communities will not lose their bet.

How to measure success?

Related to the issue of when external agencies may judge it acceptable to cease capacity building is the challenge of how to measure the success of any given programme. Unfortunately, evaluation of capacity-building work is bound to be difficult, not just because of its multifaceted nature but also because of the length of time needed for the capacity-building process to achieve an impact and the often intangible nature of change, which is difficult to 'capture' with conventional monitoring indicators. This adds up to a big challenge for aid agencies seeking to support local capacities. How do they measure their achievements? Can capacity building ever be assessed adequately? And if not, how can project planners and managers make sensible decisions about whose capacity to support, how to go about it and where to allocate their resources?

In the disaster reduction context this is a point of vital importance, particularly for agencies that depend on public and private funds and are accountable (both legally and morally) for using them in the most effective way. In such circumstances it is clearly much easier to support tangible actions to help disaster victims and reduce vulnerability – such as giving out relief materials and building safer houses – than it is to engage in a long and complex capacity-building process whose results may never be fully apparent. In disaster relief, the pressure to deliver goods rather than build long-term resilience is even more intense.

But how should the benefits accruing from the short-term delivery of relief goods be weighed against the benefits of building the long-term capacity of communities to fend for themselves? Should agencies be encouraging donors to adopt more sophisticated kinds of impact assessment than the simplistic measures of material outputs currently used? (See Chapter 6.)

Unintended consequences

While some ground-breaking capacity building can be achieved, as we have seen, not all experiments result in success. When external agencies push for change, it is the communities and civil society groups that are thrown into the front line and shoulder the greatest risk. And if things go wrong, they have the most to lose. The possibility that negative consequences might ensue, and what those consequences might be, should be seriously weighed before innovative capacity building is attempted.

In countries with authoritarian or repressive governments, for example, civil society organizations may be at risk if they are seen to be challenging the legitimacy of the state in disaster response. The aftermath of the 1976 Guatemala earthquake provided a frightening picture of this. Some 22,000 people died and more than 90,000 were made homeless. The disaster had the greatest impact on the poor – slum dwellers in Guatemala City and Mayan Indians in the rural highlands – rather than the rich, leading one American journalist to call the event a 'class-quake'. Popular protest led to illegal invasions of safer land in the capital city by slum dwellers. With so many foreign journalists present, the authorities had to turn a blind eye. But two weeks later, a city official was shot after suggesting that homeless people should be encouraged to build on unoccupied private land, and in the following two months a wave of terror attacks claimed 40 lives. In the highlands, it was much worse. NGO aid projects sought to build up community capacity through reconstruction programmes. But community leaders were prime targets in the military repression of the early 1980s that claimed tens of thousands of lives.

Of course not all cases are so extreme, but well-meaning, naive capacity building can still backfire in unforeseen ways. In Turkey after the 1999 earthquakes, for example, it became apparent that the devastation from building collapse was largely due to a failure to enforce building codes. So, significant efforts were instigated to educate the public in the importance of structural stability and the different options for retrofitting buildings. Although empowering in one sense, the awareness-raising campaign also had a negative upshot; the landlords of previously retrofitted buildings, and those who chose to retrofit after the earthquakes, exploited people's escalated expectations and drove up rents, further marginalizing the poor and increasing the vulnerability gap.

Clearly, organizations must analyse the possible negative as well as positive outcomes of their capacity-building work and identify which other conditions may have to be in place for real change to occur.

Towards a more ethical approach: asking the right questions

There is nothing simple about the questions posed here. These are complex issues. The moral challenges are often acute and there are certainly no easy answers. Yet the way we deal with them can have huge ramifications on communities and local organizations.

Where does one begin to sort out these points and translate them into effective programming? The solution lies more in the process followed than in the individual actions taken. It lies in asking the right questions rather than expecting to know the right answers.

The issues can be distilled down to two very simple but fundamental questions:
- First, what do vulnerable people and disaster victims really want and need?
- Second, do our actions contribute to meeting those needs in any real way?

Asking the questions in this order forces us to ask at the outset why we are intervening. Only then should we move on to asking how we are undertaking our interventions, if we are able to accomplish our goal – given the conditions and inputs required and the time afforded us – and what the secondary consequences of our actions may be.

From these fundamental questions, a host of specific questions arise. Do the anticipated benefits of our decisions outweigh any potential drawbacks or negative consequences? Do we stand a realistic chance of achieving our aims?

What do we believe capacity building to be? In our 'capacity-building' programming, are we really building capacity or are we simply transferring ability or knowledge? Is this enough to achieve the desired aim or does it have to be combined with other inputs? In the context of multifaceted, deep-rooted vulnerability, where no one agency can address all the relevant problems, who should provide particular inputs and how can programmes be designed to make the most appropriate use of all relevant capacities?

If knowledge and ability transfer were the capacity-building approaches chosen, why was this? Were those decisions made because that's what the organization is good at, or because, after having done an assessment of the larger equation, it was determined that this would be the best way to contribute?

Are there other needs that are more important or more immediate to serve, given our limited time and money and the realistic chance of achieving our aim? What is, in fact, the best input we could offer in order to achieve the overall end goal?

How do our other actions impact upon local community and organizational capacity? Can we see that impact right away or will it be a slow or hidden impact? What can we do to ensure that every action taken and every decision made have as positive an impact as possible on local capacity? Sometimes asking the simple questions is what is needed most.

Principal contributors to this chapter were Jennifer Rowell, Urban Technical Adviser at CARE International (UK), and John Twigg, Honorary Research Fellow at the Benfield Greig Hazard Research Centre, University College London. Box 2.1 was written by Mercedes Sayagues, a freelance writer based in South Africa and box 2.3 by Emmanuel M. Luna, Associate Professor of Community Development, University of the Philippines.

Sources and further information

Bari, Farzana. 'Turning Crisis into Capacity. Pakistan: working with riverine communities', in Fernando, Priyanthi and Fernando, Vijitha (eds.). *South Asian Women: Facing Disasters, Securing Life*. Colombo: ITDG/Duryog Nivaran, 1997.

Blaikie, Piers et al. *At risk: natural hazards, people's vulnerability, and disasters*. London: Routledge, 1994.

Buchanan, Anne, 'Partnerships and accountability', in *Appropriate Technology*, 22(4): 6-8, 1996.

Comfort, Louise K. *Self Organization in Disaster Response: the great Hanshin, Japan, earthquake of January 17, 1995*. Quick Response Report 78. Boulder: Natural Hazards Research and Information Center, 1996. Available at http://www.colorado.edu/hazards/qr/qr78.html

Comité de Emergencia Garifuna de Honduras. *Lessons and experiences from the Garifuna coast after Mitch*. UN Secretariat for the International Strategy for Disaster Reduction (UN/ISDR) and Stakeholder Forum for Our Common Future, Earth Summit 2002 debate, contribution 11 May 2002. Available at http://earthsummit2002.dyndns.org/pages/

Eade, Deborah. *Capacity-Building: An Approach to People-Centred Development* Oxford: Oxfam, 1997.

Gopalan, Prema, *Cementing a Future: Women's Leadership in a Reconstruction Program*. Mumbai: Swayam Shiksam Prayog, 1997. Available at http://www.sspindia.org/

Humanitarian Initiatives, Disaster Mitigation Institute, MANGO, Independent Evaluation. *The DEC Response to the Earthquake in Gujarat, January-October 2001*. Oxford: Humanitarian Initiatives, Disaster Mitigation Institute, MANGO, 2001. Available at http://www.dec.org.uk

INTRAC. *Independent Evaluation of DEC India Cyclone Appeal Funds*. Oxford: INTRAC, 2000. Available at http://www.dec.org.uk

Jain, Dolly. *Practising disaster mitigation: Capacity building of southern NGOs for managing natural disasters*. MSc dissertation, Oxford Brookes University, 2002.

Olson, Richard S. et al. *The Marginalisation of Disaster Response Institutions: The 1997-1998 El Niño Experience in Peru, Bolivia, and Ecuador*. Special Publication 36. Boulder: Natural Hazards Research Center, 2000. Available at http://www.colorado.edu/hazards/sp/sp36/SP36.pdf

Olson, Richard S. et al. *The Storms of '98: Hurricanes Georges and Mitch. Impacts, Institutions' Response, and Disaster Politics in Three Countries*. Special Publication 38. Boulder: Natural Hazards Research and Applications Information Center, 2001. Available at http://www.colorado.edu/hazards/sp/sp38/sp38.html

Quarantelli, Enrico L. 'Organizational Response to the Mexico City Earthquake of 1985: Characteristics and Implications', in *Natural Hazards*, 8: 19-38, 1993.

Smillie, Ian (ed.). 'Patronage or Partnership', in *Local Capacity Building in Humanitarian Crises*. Bloomfield: Kumarian Press, 2001.

Twigg, John. *Capacity Building and its Challenges: A Review of the Baring Foundation's International Grants Programme 1997-1999*. London: Baring Foundation, 2001. Available at http://www.baringfoundation.org.uk/publications.htm#intreview

Winchester, Peter. *Power, Choice and Vulnerability. A Case Study of Disaster Mismanagement in South India*. London: James and James, 1992.

Winchester, Peter, 'Cyclone Mitigation, Resource Allocation and Post-disaster Reconstruction on South India: Lessons from Two Decades of Research', in *Disasters*, 24(1): 18-37, 2000.

Web sites

Aschiana Center for Street Working Children, Kabul
http://www.tdhafghanistan.org/projects6.htm
Disasters Emergency Committee (DEC) **http://www.dec.org.uk**
Intermediate Technology Development Group (ITDG) **http://www.itdg.org**
Oxfam **http://www.oxfam.org**
United Nations Development Programme **http://www.undp.org**
World Bank **http://www.worldbank.org**

chapter 3

Section One

**Focus on
ethics
in aid**

Famine stalks southern Africa

By the end of 2002, 15 million people were threatened with starvation across southern Africa. Yet this was no sudden or unpredictable disaster – the first evidence of a looming food security crisis emerged in mid-2001. Despite disaster warnings from non-governmental organizations (NGOs) a few months later, the region's governments initially denied the emergency existed and for nine months donors delayed conducting detailed analysis and providing sufficient funding. In early July 2002, the World Food Programme (WFP) launched a long-overdue international appeal to feed 10 million people. Donors finally paid up, and on 29 January 2003, WFP announced: "The international community has so far succeeded in averting a humanitarian catastrophe in southern Africa."

However, over 1,000 people in Malawi alone had already died from starvation and cholera – aggravated by hunger – without counting the impact of HIV/AIDS. These deaths were predictable and could, arguably, have been averted. Following a far worse drought in 1992, early warning systems were put in place to prevent future catastrophes. Were the warnings provided by these systems ignored or just wrong? Is it morally defensible to wait for dead bodies to pile up before taking action? In a highly politicized environment, where even the definition of need is open to manipulation, the role of evidence-based vulnerability analysis is crucial in providing a platform for impartial aid programmes. In Part 1 of this chapter, **Anna Jefferys**, emergency policy officer with Save the Children-UK (SCF-UK), analyses how different regional early warning systems first postponed then triggered the international response.

In late January 2003, James Morris, the head of WFP and the United Nations (UN) Secretary-General's Special Envoy for Humanitarian Needs in Southern Africa, said: "While responding to the severe food crisis in Southern Africa, an even greater disaster has been unearthed. The HIV/AIDS pandemic is compounding the premature death of thousands of productive people." While the connection between food insecurity and HIV/AIDS is of crucial importance, it is hardly a revelation. The HIV/AIDS pandemic has gripped sub-Saharan Africa for well over a decade – yet despite the region's food security crisis dragging on into a third year, the political and financial will necessary to reduce the impact of this compound crisis appears to be absent. Is it morally tenable to deal with this disaster without addressing its causes? HIV/AIDS is both a cause and an effect of disaster, collapsing the old barriers between emergencies and development. By attacking men and women of working age, HIV/AIDS has destroyed the traditional means by which Africa's agrarian societies could cope with

Photo opposite page:
Sihle Nhlanze stands in her unploughed maize field. She's waiting for the rains to come but there are no signs of them. Even if they do come, she doesn't know where she'll get the money from to buy seeds – the last harvest only yielded three bags of maize and her family's resources are been spent.

Nadine Hutton/ International Federation, Swaziland.

chapter 3

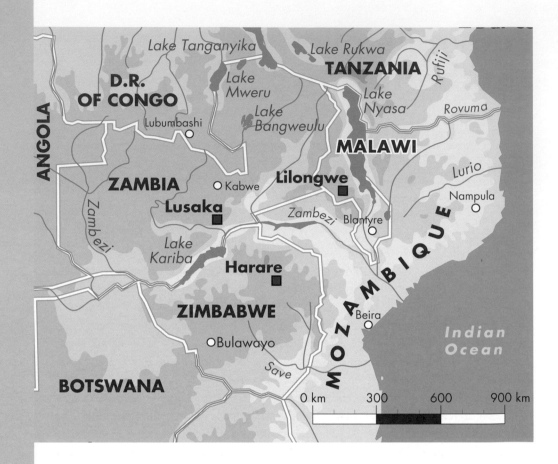

drought and famine. In Part 2, freelance reporter **Mercedes Sayagues** reports from Malawi's front line on the combined effects of hunger and HIV/AIDS.

Meanwhile, most international aid agencies have been circumspect in their criticism of the region's politicians and how their policies have, in part, driven the disaster. In Malawi, the government's sale of the entire strategic grain reserve, shortly before the famine took hold, remains a contentious issue, with the cash proceeds of the sale still unaccounted for. In Zimbabwe, the government has been accused by both international and domestic observers of starving its political opponents and feeding its supporters. In an operating environment where the impartial distribution of aid to the most needy is compromised, how far can and should aid agencies go in insisting on universal humanitarian principles? From a moral point of view, is it more important to show solidarity with those suffering and condemn those who manipulate aid? Or is it better to negotiate and maintain operational access? These questions are addressed in Parts 3 and 4 contributed, respectively, by **Mercedes Sayagues** and by **Chris McIvor**, programme director for SCF-UK in Zimbabwe.

Famine is never simply a 'natural' disaster. While drought may reduce crop yields, there are always man-made factors which govern who gains access to food and who doesn't. Addressing these factors presents numerous ethical challenges on which different agencies take different angles. Despite the differences, the need to debate these issues and how to approach them – before entrenched positions are taken – remains more urgent than ever.

Part 1 Early warning systems trigger donor response

In mid-2001 evidence emerged of a looming food security crisis in southern Africa. Despite the first NGO reports of an impending disaster emerging in September-October 2001, for a period of nine months the severity of the crisis was not acknowledged and no in-depth analysis was undertaken by donors. Eventually, after concerted NGO pressure, donors slowly started to respond. In early July 2002, WFP launched a long-overdue international appeal worth US\$ 507 million to provide nearly 1 million tonnes of food aid to 10 million people. By October the appeal – increased to around US\$ 600 million – was only 33 per cent covered. As at December 2002, the United States Agency for International Development (USAID) had committed US\$ 276 million, the United Kingdom's Department for International Development (DFID) GB£ 81 million, and the European Union (EU) 310 million euro.

While donor responses have been imperfect, the exploitation of good early warning data and analysis by NGOs operational in the crisis played a direct catalysing role in triggering their response, albeit belated. Here we set out to explore the different kinds of early warning analysis that were available to donors in the region, why they didn't trigger a more prompt donor response and how NGOs coordinated data to force action.

Regional famine early warnings

There are a number different vulnerability mapping and analysis systems currently in use in the southern African region, principally USAID's Famine Early Warning System Network (FEWSNET), Food and Agriculture Organization (FAO)/WFP assessments and Save the Children's Household Economy Analysis (HEA). A key factor in developing timely, well-targeted donor responses in the future will be to coordinate these approaches.

FEWSNET focuses primarily on remote satellite sensing and secondary sources to analyse an area's vulnerability to external shocks. FAO/WFP food security assessments often work in collaboration with FEWSNET and through agricultural ministries. They focus primarily on production and availability of food within an area's general socio-economic context, but do not focus on access at the household level. SCF's HEA is the only methodology to analyse food security vulnerability in terms of people's access to food, as opposed to assessing available levels overall. HEA was developed following disasters during the mid-1980s when it became clear there were no poverty-focused mechanisms in place to predict famines and assess which groups could or could not cope with such a crisis.

HEA methodology aims to provide an understanding of household economy and its relationship to markets and employment opportunities. This information is used to estimate the effect of an external shock on household income and food supply and the likely ability of the household to compensate for this by implementing the various coping strategies available to it. These may include the consumption of wild roots, sale of livestock or migration to find work. At the heart of these investigations is the attempt to understand the relative importance that families place on different sources of food and cash income. HEA has been used to predict and analyse needs in a number of crises, including Afghanistan, Burundi and Sudan. SCF's emergency livelihood support in Matebeland, Zimbabwe is a good example of HEA's predictive capacity and its ability to target the most vulnerable populations. In May 2001, it predicted that much of the Binga district was likely to suffer food insecurity prior to the harvest in April 2002 (see Part 4).

The data from HEA research areas, called 'food economy zones', can be processed through RiskMap, a computer programme that analyses data sets over large geographical areas. Over the past few years, national governments, often in collaboration with NGO partners, have conducted HEA baseline surveys in most of the countries implicated in the current food security crisis, including Lesotho, Malawi, Mozambique, Swaziland and Zimbabwe. These have provided information on the livelihood patterns of a substantial portion of rural populations, covering sources of food, cash income, expenditure patterns and socio-economic profile. After potential household coping strategies have been taken into account, HEA can produce a figure for the number of people in food deficit and the percentage of deficit that can be translated into tonnes of food required. While international donors currently have little capacity to undertake HEA assessments themselves, national capacity to carry out HEA is being bolstered.

Across the region, HEA findings revealed that the pernicious effects of poverty, a declining agriculture production and soil fertility, the impact of HIV/AIDS and eradication of 'asset buffers', and poor macroeconomic policies had all contributed to a rapid deterioration of livelihoods. While overall HEA analyses corresponded with FEWSNET and FAO/WFP food crop surveys, they differed in three key areas:

- Because HEA takes a livelihood approach, it identified the most vulnerable populations in given geographical areas, which FAO/WFP analysis could not do.

- HEA incorporates a socio-economic dimension, so it identified who the most vulnerable groups were, where they lived and what level of support they required.
- HEA analysis questioned the size of food aid rations, which were initially set below internationally accepted levels because access to other food sources was assumed. The HEA results, however, uncovered a dearth of food sources.

Results of vulnerability monitoring in Malawi

In July 2001, a monthly FEWSNET report estimated that Malawi's national maize production would drop by 32 per cent in comparison to 1999 and 2000. However, FEWSNET predicted that the deficit would be offset when other cereal crops, in particular tubers, were taken into consideration. This over-optimistic estimate played into delays of donor response and at this time the major donors refused to recognize the severity of the crisis. In August 2001, WFP's maize production figures were lowered, but experts still predicted that other foods would fill the gap. An SCF study examining the availability of roots and tubers in Malawi indicated that the majority of poor households (65 per cent of the population) had limited access to tubers and that they were not cultivated on a national scale, contradicting the FEWSNET results. Meanwhile, risk mapping from three food economy zones noted that maize prices had soared 180 per cent in Salima and Kasungue districts. National and regional early warning systems initially failed to predict the onset of this crisis. Existing food security and livelihood monitoring systems were inadequate and poorly integrated with effective national, regional and international policy response mechanisms.

In September 2001, SCF and FEWSNET jointly facilitated vulnerability assessment training, hosted by the Southern African Development Community (SADC) vulnerability assessment committee (see Box 3.1). At around this time, reports emerged that the Malawian grain marketing parastatal, the Agricultural Development and Marketing Corporation (ADMARC) had raised consumer maize prices by as much as 240 per cent, and that the government of Malawi had sold off most of its 165,000 tonne strategic grain reserve, leaving the country with next to no emergency stocks. In October 2001, SCF conducted a household economy analysis in Mchinji district, which revealed that maize prices had risen by 340 per cent, production had fallen by 40 per cent, the cost of agricultural inputs had risen by approximately 30 per cent and the poorest households were already out of food.

In view of these findings, SCF-Malawi commissioned a second HEA in November 2001 across three geographical areas to ascertain how widespread the problems were. The results showed the crisis had national implications. The organization started to prepare, presenting its findings to other agencies, the UN, donors and the Malawian government, which accused it of exaggeration. SCF conducted further surveys in December 2001 and March 2002 in collaboration with the Ministry of Health. These

Box 3.1 Regional vulnerability assessments – an opportunity for consensus

The Southern African Development Community (SADC) is a regional initiative, one of whose aims is to "encourage coordinated development in the field of vulnerability assessments". Each member nation undertakes food security assessments, which are coordinated through SADC's vulnerability assessment committee (VAC). This regional approach was adopted in response to the current food crisis – the worst for a decade – in order to monitor changing needs and estimate food aid requirements. Members of the VAC include regional governments, UN agencies, NGOs and the International Federation. But has the regional VAC delivered on its aim?

The VAC has successfully developed a methodology which draws on a livelihoods-based vulnerability assessment, linking nutritional surveys with different questionnaires at district, community and household levels. Repeat assessments in each country allow for comparisons and help operational decision-making. While national VACs lead the process, coordination and technical support is provided by the regional VAC. Overall, the assessment process has helped build the capacity of local and regional structures, boosted cooperation between governments, UN and humanitarian organizations, promoted a single assessment methodology and enabled sharing of resources.

At a time when information is sensitive and open to political manipulation, the VAC has developed a process that harnesses different organizational priorities to a common goal. The range of humanitarian organizations and regional governments involved increases the credibility and ownership of the results. Organizational biases are balanced and the assessment process is transparent and accountable. Most importantly, the process enables consensus-building between governments, donors, the UN and NGOs.

However, significant weaknesses remain. Standardizing the methodology across the region and its different livelihood patterns is problematic. More controversially, the process appears to have had little influence over the targeting of food aid to the most vulnerable. And, while encouraging consensus among diverse groups, the process allows little room for dissent. On a practical level, it has been cumbersome, requiring heavy investment from partners and stretching their capacities. Furthermore, the assessment process has failed to account for the unique and complex way in which HIV/AIDS has increased the people's vulnerability in the region. Often, continued emphasis is placed on food relief activities which address short-term crop failures, rather than on the chronic deterioration of livelihoods resulting from the HIV/AIDS pandemic. Similarly, once the present crisis subsides, there is a risk that the continuous investment needed to strengthen the assessment of and response to long-term vulnerability will dry up.

Despite these challenges, joint vulnerability assessments do provide opportunities to address issues of crucial importance to the region. The VAC offers a forum to engage governments in dialogue about not only the technical tools of vulnerability assessment, but also the humanitarian principles – such as impartiality and neutrality – which inform the entire process. VAC's strength lies in the joint ownership of the assessments' results by a group consisting of governments, UN and civil society actors. This could enable the committee to challenge problems in targeting and diversion of food assistance, based on the principle of impartiality, without the threat of sanction against any one organization. In other words, there is strength in unity. It remains to be seen if this strength is put to the test. ■

showed that malnutrition rates in Salima had risen from 9.3 per cent to 19 per cent and in Mchinji from 11.8 per cent to 12.5 per cent. These alarming results confirmed earlier predictions and led SCF to intensify its appeals to donors, the national government and the UN that a concerted international effort was needed to address the unravelling crisis in Malawi and the region.

FEWSNET, meanwhile, acknowledged that their previous assertions about the level of food availability were overestimated. The Malawian government finally declared a national state of emergency on 27 February 2002, estimating that 70 per cent of the population was affected. In March, SCF (on behalf of the policy working group of the Steering Committee for Humanitarian Response) made a formal presentation to the UN, highlighting the severity of the crisis across the region. Following this meeting, FAO/WFP and SCF carried out a series of inter-agency vulnerability assessments in the six most affected countries, to develop a shared analysis.

Because of the strength and the accuracy of HEA's early warning data, NGOs were able to lobby donors vigorously with a strong degree of confidence in their positioning. While this led at times to a strained relationship, the issues were at least forced into the public domain. Although DFID responded in February 2002, others were slower to react. On 26 March 2002, WFP warned: "Donor response to repeated WFP appeals has been sluggish." Despite the number of assessments and early warning systems in place, the EU continued to prevaricate until July 2002.

Preventing future famine

Current food security results in Malawi suggest that donors and agencies, despite numerous obstacles, appear to have averted immediate widescale disaster – although the future remains very precarious. Integral to averting future famine will be establishing and strengthening national food security and livelihood surveillance systems. Plans for a collaborative effort between SADC, national governments and international partners are now under way.

Meanwhile, building up a shared early warning analysis database is crucial in order to promote a more coordinated donor strategy. At present there's very little collaboration between the EU, DFID and USAID. It is vital that donors have a stake in this so that they believe in the results. A good start would be to find out exactly what donors are looking for in early warning analysis, so that different methodologies can be pieced together to fulfil their criteria. FEWSNET, WFP and SCF are developing ways of sharing data through SADC. However, these early warnings will only be sustainable if they also analyse wider issues of poverty, rather than focusing narrowly on food security.

chapter 3

Part 2 Hunger/poverty/AIDS – an apocalyptic combination

"I'm hungry as I talk to you," says Mpoverani Mkaka. Her wrinkled, weathered face says she is old enough to recall Malawi's 'big hunger' of 1949. Her frail, emaciated body says she nearly starved during the famine of 2002. "This hunger was the worst ever," says Mkaka.

Roughly 400 deaths by starvation were documented by the Malawi Economic Justice Network in early 2002. Malawi's worst-ever cholera epidemic – aggravated by hunger and HIV/AIDS – claimed 1,000 more lives. According to Ben Wisner, hazards specialist at Oberlin College, Ohio: "Piecing reports from agencies working in rural areas together, as many as 10,000 people, mostly the weak – children, the aged, people living with AIDS – may already have died by May 2002."

On average, Malawi and its southern African neighbours suffer a serious drought and food shortage once every ten years. In 1992, the crop failure due to 'the worst drought in living memory' was far more severe, but the region and its people coped. The latest famine, which by early 2003 had put around 15 million people at risk of starvation, has developed after a decade of HIV/AIDS and acute impoverishment. People's coping strategies and safety nets are exhausted.

Just look at Mrs. Mkaka. Her five ragged, swollen-bellied grandchildren orphaned by AIDS scour the ground for leftover kernels at the village mill. Neighbours give them maize husks that the 12-year-old girl pounds into a flour of little nutritional value. The soil on the family's tiny plot is moist with rain. Mrs. Mkaka owns a hoe but she has no seeds, fertilizer or labour to grow a crop. Nor can she replace the reed roof that caved in during a storm in 2001. A couple of years ago, the village chief would have organized a collective repair. But life is now too hard for age-old traditions to keep up. Neighbours are busy foraging for wild food, looking for odd jobs and just trying to survive.

Mrs. Mkaka lives in Malwenda village, 80 kilometres east of Lilongwe, Malawi's capital. Her story of poverty and vulnerability is multiplied across the ravaged region. Southern Africa has the world's highest HIV-prevalence rates, ranging from 15 per cent in Malawi to 33.7 per cent in Zimbabwe. The continent is home to three-quarters of the world's 42 million people living with HIV/AIDS. Hunger fuels the AIDS pandemic. Nutritious food helps people with HIV live longer and healthier lives; lack of it quickens the pace of disease. Destitution and desperation lead to high-risk behaviour, such as exchanging sex for food or money.

"The extent of AIDS only hit the agencies when coupled with hunger," says Ethel Kaimila, of the Malawi Red Cross. As AIDS kills mostly young adults, families lose the labour, income and skills of their most productive members. One AIDS-related adult death in a Zimbabwean farming household reduces the maize crop by 60 per cent, according to UNAIDS. Meanwhile in Malawi, HIV/AIDS has reduced life expectancy from 46 to 36 years.

To pay for health care and funeral expenses, families sell assets. The Mkaka hut is bare: a straw mat, a pot, a hoe and a few tattered clothes. This is not unusual in Malwenda. Children drop out of school to do domestic chores, nurse the sick and earn money in any way they can, from begging to gold-panning or selling sex. Orphans are so numerous – 800,000 in Zimbabwe, 470,000 in Malawi – that the extended family cannot care for them any longer.

The social fabric is stretched to breaking point. One external shock like food shortage, manageable just a decade ago, turns into a disaster. So evolves a famine "characterized by heightened vulnerability, a breakdown in coping strategies, rapid descent into starvation and inability to recover", says Alex de Waal in his paper, *New Variant Famine in Southern Africa*.

HIV/AIDS and the weather are not the only famine-making factors. Zimbabwe's 'land reform' destroyed a buoyant agricultural sector. Malawi's high birth rate means farming plots get smaller and smaller. Low world prices for commodities, reckless management of national grain reserves, misguided market reforms, corruption and political instability have all contributed to the crisis. And a regional dispute over the acceptability of genetically modified maize delayed the delivery of United States food aid (see Box 3.2).

Meanwhile, the region's poorest have been cut off from health and education by cost-recovery user fees, required by the International Monetary Fund's (IMF) structural adjustment programmes to sustain clinics and schools. In Malawi, budget cuts have brought the collapse of health and agricultural extension services. Subsidized seed and fertilizer packages for smallholders were cut back, compromising household food security. Today, the lethal combination of AIDS, poverty and hunger is forcing aid agencies into an extreme learning curve, demolishing the artificial compartments of emergency, recovery and development. AIDS is both a root cause of poverty and its consequence. Is it morally tenable any longer for relief agencies to deal with this humanitarian disaster without addressing its causes?

This crisis won't go away with the next good rains. It's a crisis of rural livelihoods, of widespread impoverishment, of the poor becoming invisible to economic planners, development agencies and politicians. "It's an ethical issue for donors and governments to prioritize people, especially poor people, and especially the rural poor,

Box 3.2 Genetically modified food aid fuels ethical debate

Last September, hungry villagers stole 500 bags of maize from a WFP storeroom in Monze, Zambia. For the villagers, the loot was fast food. For the authorities, a big problem. The maize was genetically modified (GM) food aid from the United States, awaiting the Zambian government's approval. A few weeks later, Zambia became the first developing country to reject GM food aid officially.

In the midst of a severe food crisis combined with a soaring HIV/AIDS epidemic, when 2.3 million people needed food aid, President Levy Mwanawasa affirmed he would not feed "this poison" to his people. "It was immoral to bring GM maize into an independent country without our approval, and immoral to ignore a clause in our legislation that prevents GMO [genetically modified organism] introduction," fumes Bernadette Lubozhya, an agronomist.

Many humanitarian operators disagree. "This is not the right time to debate GM food when people are starving," says the UN's Andrew Timpson, in Zimbabwe. Lesotho, Mozambique, Swaziland and Zimbabwe decided to accept GM maize if it was milled before or upon arrival, so that it could not be planted. Only Malawi, lacking milling capacity and reeling from thousands of hunger-related deaths, allowed unmilled GM maize – in theory, only until the planting season.

Critics worry about the impact on biodiversity and health. Through cross-pollination, GM traits could contaminate local non-GM crops and, through the feed chain, livestock. This could jeopardize valuable agricultural exports to the EU, which bans GM food. "GMOs could pose a danger to the human organism and public health in the medium and long term," said the UN's rapporteur for the right to food, Jean Ziegler, a Swiss academic.

Some campaigners say the US, the world's largest GM producer, tried to use the food crisis to gain a foothold for its GM crops in non-GM markets. "It is ethically questionable why donors insist on sending GM grain when recipient countries have made it clear they lack the mechanisms to monitor the agricultural or health impact of these foods," says Glenn Ashton of Safeage, an environmental group in South Africa.

Much of the anxiety about GM food aid stems from a scandal involving Starlink, an insect-resistant maize genetically modified with a bacterial toxin. Starlink is approved in the US for animal feed but not for human consumption, because it might cause allergic reactions. In September 2000, however, it was found in over 300 food products. Despite a moratorium on Starlink sales and planting, it appeared again the following year in a cornsoya blend donated by USAID to hungry Bolivian children. The scandal hit the news during the Food Summit in Rome, fanning mistrust of food aid. In May 2002, WFP stated that it merely channels food approved in the donor country and respects the sovereign right of every country to accept or reject GM food aid.

Back in Africa, solutions were found. South Africa offered to mill 60,000 tonnes for free, other donors paid for additional milling and the EU gave cash to buy non-GM maize locally. Across the region, hungry people received milled GM grain, while in theory local non-GM crops were protected from contamination (except for Malawi). But the controversy will remain, long after the fleets of maize-laden trucks and ships move elsewhere. ■

who are seen as expendable," says Dan Mullins, regional HIV/AIDS coordinator for the British charity Oxfam.

Mrs. Mkaka's spirit is not broken – yet. "We survived by the grace of God," she says with a toothless grin. She proudly shows a visitor the dog-eared exercise book of her oldest grandchild, 14, the only one to attend school. "I tell him: study hard for a better life," she says.

The Mkaka family, and southern Africa's growing masses of poor people, need more than traditional short-term emergency assistance – food, seeds and tools – to bounce back. They need serious policy changes in poverty reduction, health care, agriculture, food security and women's empowerment – with poor people's lives and livelihoods at the centre. Otherwise, the vicious cycle of hunger, poverty and AIDS will not be broken.

Part 3 Zimbabwean NGOs and churches unite and speak out

In Zimbabwe, a consortium of national NGOs is – against all odds – carrying out food security monitoring and advocacy of internationally recognized ethical principles guiding humanitarian aid. Every month, a report from sentinel sites covering all of Zimbabwe's 57 districts details food needs, household stocks, maize prices, supply and availability, government, commercial and aid agency deliveries, and problems in accessing food aid. The information is compiled by community-based monitors from 24 NGOs, members of the Food Security Network (FOSENET), set up in March 2002 to share experiences, views and resources for an ethical, effective and community-based response to the food crisis.

By early 2003, 7 million people – more than half of Zimbabwe's population – needed food aid. Chaotic land seizures have destroyed commercial agriculture and a dry spell in 2002 compounded the disaster. The economy is in meltdown, with annual inflation running at 180 per cent. Cereal production has dropped by two-thirds, against a background of political repression, violence and acute impoverishment. Meanwhile, one in three adult Zimbabweans is infected with HIV/AIDS, decimating the nation's chances of recovery (see Box 3.3).

The government denied the food crisis until the flawed and violent presidential election of March 2002 was over. The election, which led to Zimbabwe's suspension from the Commonwealth, returned President Mugabe's ZANU-PF party to power. According to a 2002 report by the International Crisis Group, the ruling party, once back in power, manipulated the food supply: "ZANU-PF has politicized its

Box 3.3 Zimbabwe factfile

- Anticipated food deficit by March 2003: 239,000 tonnes
- Price of black-market maize: up 167 per cent in four months to December 2002
- By December 2002: only 38 per cent of maize-growing area replanted
- Annual inflation rate: 180 per cent
- Black-market rate for Zimbabwe dollar: 2,700 per cent more than official rate
- Decline in gross domestic product in 2002: 12 per cent
- National rates of HIV/AIDS among adults (15-49 years): 33.7 per cent (as at December 2001)
- Grant to Zimbabwe from US$ 866 million Global Fund to Fight AIDS, TB and Malaria: US$ 6.7 million to tackle malaria only (as at 31 January 2003)
- Total population: 12.5 million
- Estimated population in need: 7,182,000 (57 per cent of total population)

(Information correct as at December 2002, unless stated otherwise)
Sources: Zimbabwe National Vulnerability Assessment Committee; Global Fund to Fight AIDS, Tuberculosis and Malaria; UNAIDS.

distribution through a variety of methods, including: monopolizing imports; distributing it based on political calculations; controlling eligibility for its purchase and for the milling of grain; removing MDC [opposition] supporters from food-for-work programs; allowing party officials or commercial allies to profit from re-sale of food at exorbitant black market prices; confiscating maize at informal roadblocks; putting the party's youth militia in control of grain depots; and requiring party membership as a condition for purchasing food in some locations."

International human rights groups have documented the government's systematic starvation and torture of political opponents, and its obstruction of the relief effort. In November 2002, following a fact-finding mission to Zimbabwe, Danish Physicians for Human Rights concluded that: "ZANU-PF appears to be maintaining a situation where there is too little food in the country, by controlling all sales and imports. Too little food is serving a dual purpose: it allows political control through controlling who accesses food; it facilitates the creation of a ZANU-PF dominated black market, thus enriching the ZANU-PF hierarchy... If it is not possible to increase non-partisan food supplies into the country, it is our opinion that starvation and eventually death, will occur along party political lines in Zimbabwe."

In November 2002, UN Secretary-General Kofi Annan appealed to the Zimbabwe government "to ensure that political considerations do not affect food aid efforts". FOSENET, meanwhile, as a national, politically non-partisan NGO network, locates itself in the space between the two main actors in Zimbabwe's food crisis: the government (which tightly controls the supply of the staple food, maize) and the UN-led relief operation (which feeds several million people).

FOSENET monitors flows of food and confronts all actors with its findings. A key concern is data quality and validity, improved through training, supervision and verification crosschecks and peer review from relief operators to enable feedback and follow-up. The reports are widely circulated, published in the local press, sent to donors and presented to members of parliament of all political parties.

In December 2002, FOSENET documented the political manipulation of both food aid and governmental grain supplies in 38 per cent of districts surveyed – up from 15 per cent in August. Such manipulation included political agents denying food to opposition supporters, getting preferential access to food themselves, seeking party identity cards for food access, manipulating lists of food aid beneficiaries and simply stopping relief distributions. More generally, FOSENET has reported gross speculation by traders, corruption in the sale of government maize, massive food price increases among milling companies and, last but not least, the continued inability of the poorest and most vulnerable – orphans, the elderly and the sick – to access relief food. "Orphans find it very hard to plug into the relief network – nobody represents them," says Rene Loewenson, FOSENET's monitoring coordinator.

Paradoxically, the marginalization of national NGOs in the UN relief operation offered them a space for independent monitoring. In some emergencies, like Angola, the UN played a unifying role by pulling together all NGOs, big and small. In Zimbabwe, the UN originally kept its distance from local NGOs, which were perceived to be pro-opposition. "Careful management of toxic waste – that is how we were treated at the first meetings," says one FOSENET participant. "It got better with time." At a meeting in early 2002, FOSENET members proposed that, faced with government interference, all NGOs and the UN should act in solidarity, as if "injury to one was injury to all". The idea did not prosper with the UN agencies and its foreign NGO partners, recalls Reverend Tim Neill, director of the Zimbabwe Community Development Trust. "We missed a strategic opportunity that would have strengthened the relief operation," he says. Instead, repression and aggression were treated as localized events and each international agency dealt with its problems separately. Meanwhile Rev. Neill's organization combined with 20 other national and community-based NGOs to produce a set of "principles for ethical conduct in food and humanitarian relief", along with a set of conditions needed to implement those principles (see Box 3.4).

As regards UN agencies, the Zimbabwean government has allowed them to operate under strict control, which in practice has meant the slow vetting of NGO partners,

Box 3.4 Humanitarian principles – text signed by Zimbabwean NGOs

National NGOs, as non partisan organizations, believe that participation in relief under the highly polarised political conditions prevailing in Zimbabwe must be based on a platform of ethical principles applicable to all parties. These principles should be advocated and monitored at community, local, national and international NGO, donor and state levels in relation to Zimbabwe's food and humanitarian relief.

They derive from international humanitarian law and the humanitarian organisations' Humanitarian Charter (SPHERE).

The proposed **principles** call for inclusion into relief of:

- The right to life with dignity and the duty not to withhold or frustrate the provision of life saving assistance;
- The obligation of states and other parties to agree to the provision of humanitarian and impartial assistance when the civilian population lacks essential supplies;
- Relief not to bring unintended advantage to one or more parties nor to further any partisan position;
- The management and distribution of food and other relief based purely on criteria of need and not on partisan grounds, and without adverse distinction of any kind;
- Respect for community values of solidarity, dignity and peace and of community culture;
- Linkages between humanitarian relief and longer term strategies for reducing vulnerability and increasing economic and food security.

To achieve these principles in the current situation the following **conditions** need to be urgently addressed:

- Unimpeded access to ALL communities in need for food and relief distribution;
- Respect for and enforcement of rule of law;
- Disbanding and law enforcement against partisan groups operating outside the law, increasing displacement and vulnerability and obstructing food access (armed supporters, militias);
- The entitlement of civilians to immunity from attack and cessation of violence deliberately perpetrated against specific population groups, undermining food access;
- Active community participation and networking in relief programmes as a basis for enhancing community control and reducing dependency;
- Involvement of local capacities and national organisations operating at community level to strengthen sustained national responses to vulnerability;
- Repeal of legal provisions, including the Public Order and Security Act and Access to Information and Protection of Privacy Act that disable national organisation, information flow and community activity and networking needed for civic responses;
- Transparent, evidence based, safe, competent and accountable relief programmes.

Text signed by 21 Zimbabwean NGOs
Source: FOSENET

intimidation, assaults on UN staff, looting of food aid, stopping of aid deliveries, manipulation of beneficiary lists, distortion of quotes from senior UN officials in the government press, to name a few of the many hassles quietly borne by the international body.

"We've been too diplomatic, too wishy-washy, but there are reasons for not saying things that ought to be said," says Chris Kaye, regional emergency coordinator for the UN Office for the Coordination of Humanitarian Affairs (OCHA) in Johannesburg. Among these, he mentions that President Mugabe has the upper hand in relief matters; that the UN risks being seen as a tool of American imperialism; and that neighbouring countries, especially South Africa, do not support a stronger UN stance.

However, John Prendergast, director of the International Crisis Group, is critical: "In Zimbabwe, the UN's weak leadership has compromised the ability of aid agencies to get assistance to those in need. The aid-providing community have leverage to the extent that they remain united, and aid is best maximized if a strengthened UN is leading efforts to maintain access and fight manipulation," he says.

Iden Wetherell, editor of the weekly *Zimbabwe Independent*, argues that the UN has a humanitarian imperative to feed people, a political responsibility to point out the structural problems and government policies that led to the famine, and a moral responsibility to demand that signatories of the UN Declaration of Human Rights – which include Zimbabwe – abide by it.

Yet the big aid agencies appear the most reluctant to denounce abuses with food and violations of human rights. "We can't compromise our humanitarian space," says OCHA's Kaye. One international NGO involved in food distribution told a correspondent with a European newspaper that a story on the charity's work should dwell on HIV/AIDS and not on politics. "We cannot be party to anything that would jeopardize our position in Zimbabwe," read an e-mail sent to the reporter.

So the protest is left to Zimbabwean members of struggling NGOs, who don't have a foreign passport, cannot be relocated quickly and put their livelihoods, security and families at risk. Several workers with local NGOs, including FOSENET members, have been arrested and tortured in the course of their work. For this reason, food monitors remain anonymous.

One who will not remain silent is the Catholic Archbishop of Bulawayo, Pius Ncube. The small, frail archbishop appears exhausted from the burden of seeing so much misery. Starving, desperate people besiege his office daily. Matabeleland, his diocese, is the poorest and most neglected region of Zimbabwe, home to the minority Ndebele people, where at least 10,000 people disappeared or were killed during massacres of political opponents in the mid-1980s. "This government doesn't care if people starve to death," said Ncube in a telephone interview from Bulawayo. "It bullies aid agencies and the UN has been very poor in stopping it. The only thing we can do against this evil is to speak out."

In November 2002, Ncube made international headlines with an eloquent speech about Zimbabwe, which he delivered in Cape Town at a meeting attended, among others, by Nobel Peace Prize winner Archbishop Desmond Tutu. In return, Ncube has received death threats and is forced to sleep in safe houses.

Shortly afterwards, a group of clergy from five Christian denominations accused the government of frustrating their relief efforts. They criticized the regime's partisan supply of food and its campaign of violence, intimidation and torture. "Hijacking food supplies, hindering the work of NGOs... only increases the suffering of the poor," they wrote in a public letter. Around 30 of the signatories were arrested and beaten for carrying the protest letter and three crosses to Bulawayo's police headquarters.

Each in their own way, the churches and FOSENET's NGOs speak out so that the world can hear the voice of the poor, almost inaudible in the din of Zimbabwe's political crisis.

Part 4 Save the Children's experience in the Zambezi valley

In September and October 2002, all of Save the Children's (SCF) operations in Zimbabwe – including vital food aid to over 150,000 vulnerable people in the Zambezi valley – were temporarily suspended by the national authorities. While the organization was urged by rights activists to adopt an openly critical stance towards the government for withholding the rights of hungry people to food aid, SCF chose a more discreet path of negotiation in the belief that this would better serve the interests of the affected population. The ethical challenge facing charitable organizations – that of public commitment to humanitarian principles on the one hand, versus the practical demands of operating in complex political environments on the other – is a very real one.

In the late 1950s, with the construction of the Kariba Dam in north-western Zimbabwe, the entire Tonga population of the Zambezi river valley was forcibly evicted from the land that had sustained them for centuries. On the Zimbabwe side, the displacement forced thousands of people on to the arid, impoverished soils of the escarpment that overlooked their former homeland. Today, these 200,000 people are among the most impoverished in the country, hostage to a location that experiences chronic food insecurity, high levels of malaria and an absence of social services resulting from a history of economic and political neglect.

SCF-UK has worked in this area since 1981, embarking on a range of relief and development activities in the two districts of Binga and Nyaminyami that comprise the Tonga part of the Zambezi valley. Following a mid-season dry spell during 2001's rainy season, SCF conducted a food security and household economy assessment in September, which revealed a significant sale of assets by many families to cope with reduced food production. Half the population was shown to be vulnerable, with many children dropping out of school, growing dependency on wild foods to supplement the family diet and reduced expenditure on health care. Consequently, SCF launched a food aid programme.

On top of the drought have been soaring inflation, economic collapse and one of the worst HIV/AIDS epidemics on the continent. While a third of Zimbabwe's adult population is estimated to be infected, a majority of mothers attending antenatal clinics in Binga tested HIV-positive in a recent study. Grandparents are often left looking after families of 10 to 15 grandchildren. Prostitution among Binga's young girls, desperate to help provide for their families, has risen. Although increased malnutrition was not evident in 2001, the rationale for food aid was to help the population recover the following year, since assets such as cash, livestock and labour need to be maintained to allow for a subsequent investment in agricultural production. Meanwhile, protecting the rights of children to education, health care

Almost 3 million children under 15 are infected with HIV in sub-Saharan Africa. The disease claimed the lives of over 6,000 Africans a day in 2002. The pandemic is both a cause and an effect of disaster, challenging the traditional boundaries between relief and development.

Marko Kokic/ International Federation, Lesotho.

chapter 3

and freedom from exploitative labour also formed a core part of the organization's considerations when deciding to intervene with food aid.

Signing up to key operating principles

In the fraught political environment that has characterized Zimbabwe since the parliamentary elections of 2001, the decision by the organization to embark on a targeted food aid programme was not without its difficulties. Fifty per cent of the population of Binga was to be fed. The other 50 per cent would not be. A significant worry was the necessity to avoid the perception that the choice of beneficiary was based on political affiliation, a concern expressed within several communities during the period of registration. In order to help prevent this from happening a detailed agreement was signed between the district authorities in the Zambezi valley and SCF, which enshrined several key humanitarian principles:

- **The principle of impartiality** stipulated that need would be the sole criterion of targeting, that issues of race, ethnicity, religious or political affiliation would not be permitted to influence the selection of beneficiaries.
- **The proper attribution of aid** meant communities would be informed that food was being provided as an independent, charitable donation. While impartiality ensures that aid is not targeted at beneficiaries on the basis of an existing political position, proper attribution ensures that aid does not get used to encourage people to adopt a particular political standpoint. At a time when the two main political parties were actively trying to win votes in forthcoming elections, this measure was designed to ensure that no mileage could be made by either party from a humanitarian programme.
- **The principle of neutrality** indicated that aid would be provided with no political intent or desire by SCF to further any religious or other cause.
- **The safety of humanitarian personnel** was guaranteed in the agreement, with an obligation placed on the authorities to ensure that SCF staff were protected in the discharge of their duties.

The above agreement stipulated that an infringement of any of these principles could lead to the suspension of the programme. While it was duly signed by the local authorities and SCF's representative in Zimbabwe, little attempt was made to ensure a clear understanding of what these principles involved, either at national or local levels. Zimbabwe's disastrous drought of 1992-93 had witnessed an extremely effective partnership between government and NGOs, without spelling out humanitarian principles. So, a decade later, further discussion of principles and how they might be operationalized wasn't considered necessary.

Furthermore, in September and October 2001 when SCF's food aid began, the UN in Zimbabwe was not geared up for an emergency response. Consequently it was not in a position to broker an agreement with the government that might have offered its own agencies and NGOs the kind of protective umbrella available in other countries. In hindsight, the omission by the UN, NGOs, donors and government to fully explore the principles and practice of humanitarian aid is partly responsible for allowing a situation to develop where foreign aid agencies and their partners are viewed by authorities with considerable suspicion.

Running into difficulties

For almost a year the programme ran without any major problems. The registration lists were checked regularly to ensure compliance with the criteria of selection. The authorities were invited to attend food aid distributions in order to verify that the principles of neutrality and impartiality were being upheld. As a result of these measures, SCF was able to avoid the hostilities that developed between, for example, the Catholic Commission for Justice and Peace (CCJP) and the government authorities in Binga, which led to a suspension of CCJP's food aid on the grounds that it was being used to support a civic education programme criticizing the ruling party.

However, during the parliamentary elections of 2002 and the rural district council elections a few months later, the population of Binga registered a strong vote for the opposition. This fueled speculation among some ruling party activists in the district that SCF had 'politicized' food aid distributions in order to win votes for the opposition. At the same time, as relations between the Zimbabwe and UK governments continued to deteriorate, the neutrality of the organization was questioned. Some more strident voices indicated that as a UK-based organization their agenda could only be a subversive one.

In September 2002, all SCF's operations nationwide, including humanitarian interventions, were suspended by the national authorities with a clear instruction that programmes would not resume until the agency's situation in Zimbabwe had been regularized under a new agreement. No time scale was given for the resolution of this problem. A major concern of the organization at this time was the halt to the programme in Binga. The food security situation had noticeably worsened as the result of a disastrous harvest earlier in the year, leading to a beneficiary list that comprised almost the entire population of the district. The suspension of food aid raised considerable international attention, with several press reports claiming that the population of Binga was being penalized for how they had voted in recent elections.

Ethical dilemma – and response

The organization was presented with an ethical challenge. What should be the balance between public advocacy and private negotiation? Should it adopt a strident, vociferous position, which criticized the authorities for their decision and reminded the international community that the right of hungry people to life-saving food aid, on the basis of need alone, was being undermined? Or should it adopt a more discreet and less public position, so as to reassure the authorities about its political neutrality, that the agenda was not to 'show up' the government and increase its international isolation, but to resolve the issue as amicably and as speedily as possible?

In the end, a decision was made that while negotiations were ongoing SCF would avoid any public confrontation around what had happened and would pursue a more diplomatic strategy of discussion through the UN and senior government officials to reach a solution which would allow the organization to resume food aid. This approach attracted some criticism from civil society actors, who felt that the protection of humanitarian space in Zimbabwe required a more robust and confrontational response by implementing NGOs.

SCF's decision was guided by a mixture of pragmatism and principle. One of the core criteria for informing strategy is the assessment of what constitutes 'the best interests of the child' – a key principle of the UN Convention on the Rights of the Child. In this case, SCF believed that the best interests of children facing hunger in the Zambezi valley would be better served by efforts to negotiate a speedy resumption of food deliveries than through engaging in the kind of moral grand-standing against the authorities advocated by some.

While negotiating with the government, the organization was clear that the parameters of any formal agreement were non-negotiable, namely that any humanitarian programme should conform to the principles of impartiality, proper attribution of aid, neutrality and safety of personnel mentioned above. No pressure was placed on SCF to water down the key principle of need as the criterion of selection, or to limit the space provided to the organization to ensure that this took place in practice.

Another factor that informed SCF's approach was the question of alternatives. If SCF were prevented from feeding the Zambezi valley's increasingly hungry people, who else might do it as efficiently and as speedily? For another NGO to run such a programme, several months would be required to organize the staff, logistics, transport schedules, registration lists and community discussions necessary for a food aid project.

If the alternatives to providing such a basic need as food are so limited, then the space within which an organization signed up to humanitarian principles can impose 'conditionalities' or promote the protection of other human rights, such as protection from abuse or freedom of expression – is restricted. When individuals have a right to food, no matter what the circumstances, then the humanitarian imperative to save lives cannot be made contingent on other kinds of conditions. It is impossible to say, "SCF will only feed you if you or your government behaves in a particular way".

An organization involved in providing humanitarian relief cannot jeopardize this commitment by engaging in the kinds of public confrontation, human rights advocacy or civil society debate that might place its operations at risk. This is not to say that concern about human rights violations in a humanitarian context is not legitimate, but that these concerns may need to be expressed by actors other than those who have signed up to deliver basic life-saving assistance. Expecting humanitarian organizations to discharge this function is problematic, since it is often the perceived absence of any threat from humanitarians to the controlling authorities that enables them to deliver aid in the first place. As aid analysts Nicholas Leader and Joanna Macrae put it in a 2000 report: "The humanitarian sheep can only survive amidst the wolves of conflict by a subtle and paradoxical combination of political savvy and making a virtue of their harmlessness."

A final factor that informed SCF's response was the already public nature of what had happened. The press had picked up the story. Donors were aware of the halt in food deliveries. International and local pressure on the authorities to seek a resumption of SCF's activities was already present without SCF needing to add any more fuel to that particular fire. In other circumstances, when information does not flow, where a potential violation of basic human rights is not known about, then organizations might well be more vociferous in raising the public profile of what has happened and openly speak out against such infringements. In the circumstances that characterized the suspension of SCF operations in the Zambezi valley, however, it was felt that issuing a strong condemnation would not add anything new to an issue that was already in the public domain. Nor would this be welcomed by the authorities at a time when they had expressed concern that public criticism had replaced dialogue in their relationships with NGOs.

Conclusion – combine principles and pragmatism

After seven weeks of aid being suspended, SCF signed a new agreement with the national government that subsequently allowed a full resumption of activities in the Zambezi valley and other areas of operation. The agreement included the four core operating principles plus the mechanisms to put them into practice. So far, these principles have not been infringed.

On reflection, one shortcoming of humanitarian organizations working in Zimbabwe is the failure to form a more coherent and unified position in relation to key operating principles. In effect, organizations continue to pursue their own individual programmes and the events surrounding the Zambezi valley suspension revealed a lack of solidarity and joint representation to government that might have ameliorated the situation. While a joint forum for NGOs involved in emergency work was set up at the start of the food aid crisis, little practical work has been done to define more publicly the principles that underpin humanitarian relief. An agreed code of conduct between donors, government and the UN – which would help define the parameters of relief operations – has never been negotiated. Nor have any mechanisms been worked out for a collective response to a crisis that might affect any one organization.

The reluctance of organizations to come together is probably due to several factors. Previous relief interventions in Zimbabwe consisted of almost unqualified support to government institutions. Questions of access and politics didn't arise. So there was no history of joint action by NGOs to defend their humanitarian space. Secondly, what would a collective response look like, if any one operation were infringed? Can an NGO, for example, suspend a programme in Masvingo or Mutare if SCF's food aid in the Zambezi valley is halted? Definitely not, since withholding aid from some people in order to object to interference somewhere else would violate the key principle of impartiality.

But the fact that minimum conditions of withdrawal are so hard to identify in the humanitarian context does not mean that other more proactive measures cannot be put in place. Part of the rationale for a collective response, even where this might amount to no more than a public statement of solidarity or censure, is that the group lends its weight to the solving of specific problems in a standardized and coherent way. This helps protect individual organizations through appealing to common principles and standards. In order to push this forward in Zimbabwe, it is necessary to promote a discussion about the nature of humanitarianism itself, and what it means to sign up to the principles of neutrality, impartiality and independence. Sometimes, conformity with these principles is misinterpreted by the authorities as a political act by an individual organization rather than adherence to international standards that both NGOs and the government itself have signed up to.

Finally, if there is one lesson that can be derived from SCF's experience in the Zambezi valley, it is that while humanitarian principles can help guide the response to a problem, they cannot substitute for a sensitive and detailed assessment of the specific circumstances. Pragmatism, prior experience and an understanding of the local context are essential in helping define how humanitarian principles should be practically applied in the best interests of those we are trying to assist. To this end, a more systematic, documented analysis of the particular experiences of humanitarian organizations negotiating in situations of political complexity would be of immense use. This is not in order to provide a model for slavish replication, but to add to a body of knowledge that is seriously lacking.

Principal contributors to this chapter were Anna Jefferys, SCF-UK's emergency policy officer; Chris McIvor, programme director for SCF-UK in Zimbabwe; Mercedes Sayagues, a freelance writer; and Jonathan Walter, World Disasters Report *editor. Hisham Khogali of the International Federation contributed Box 3.1 and Mercedes Sayagues, Box 3.2.*

Sources and further information

Danish Physicians for Human Rights. *Vote ZANU-PF or starve*. Copenhagen: November 2002.

de Waal, Alex. *New Variant Famine in Southern Africa*. October 2002.

de Waal, Alex. 'What AIDS Means in a Famine', *New York Times*, 19 November 2002.

Devereux, Stephen. *State of Disaster: Causes, Consequences & Policy Lessons from Malawi*, ActionAid, June 2002.

International Crisis Group (ICG). *Zimbabwe's silent, selective starvation*. Nairobi/Brussels: ICG, August 2002.

ICG. *Zimbabwe: The Politics of National Liberation and International Division*. Harare/Brussels: ICG, October 2002.

Leader, Nicholas and Macrae, Joanna (eds.). *Terms of Engagement: Conditions and Conditionality in Humanitarian Action*. London: Overseas Development Institute, 2000.

Joint United Nations Programme on HIV/AIDS (UNAIDS). *AIDS Epidemic Update*. Geneva: UNAIDS, December 2002.

United Nations. *Mission Report: Lesotho, Malawi, Zambia, and Zimbabwe*. James T. Morris, Special Envoy of the Secretary-General for Humanitarian Needs in Southern Africa, and Stephen Lewis, Special Envoy of the Secretary-General for HIV/AIDS in Africa, Rome: UN, 10 February 2003.

Web sites

Famine Early Warning Systems Network (FEWSNET) **http://www.fews.net**

Global information and early warning system on food and agriculture (GIEWS) **http://www.fao.org/WAICENT/faoinfo/economic/giews/english/giewse.htm**

International Crisis Group **http://www.intl-crisis-group.org**

National NGO Food Security Network (FOSENET) **http://www.kubatana.net/html/sectors/fos001.asp**

Overseas Development Institute (ODI) **http://www.odi.org.uk/southern_africa/**

Save the Children-UK **http://www.savethechildren.org.uk/**

Southern African Development Community (SADC) Food Security Programme **http://www.sadc-fanr.org.zw**

The Food Economy Group **http://www.foodeconomy.com/**

World Food Programme (WFP) Africa Hunger Alert **http://www.wfp.org/index**

Zimbabwe news **http://www.zwnews.com/**

chapter 4

Section One

**Focus on
ethics
in aid**

Afghanistan – power politics or ethical principles?

Afghanistan represents the first in a new type of international intervention as part of the US-led 'war on terror'. As such it presents new ethical challenges to the international community. Desperately poor and by no means yet at peace, Afghans struggle to create a future that is better than the past. Many unresolved issues threaten to derail this process. Security – the number-one concern of most Afghans – is in many places worse now than under the Taliban, and continues to deteriorate while America hunts down its enemies across the country. Some parts of Afghanistan have become 'no-go' zones for humanitarian agencies. Provincial reconstruction teams – comprising both US military and civilian personnel – have been established in various regional centres to promote stability, local government and reconstruction. But their mixed mandate risks blurring the boundaries between aid workers and soldiers, putting the security of humanitarians at risk.

The diplomatic and aid communities also have a case to answer – 350 international non-governmental organizations (NGOs), 670 United Nations (UN) international staff and dozens of embassies took up residence in Afghanistan during 2002. Rents were driven sky-high, in some cases forcing local NGOs from their premises. The failure to pay public sector workers a living wage – while international aid agency staff enjoy extremely generous salaries – threatens much-publicized efforts to rebuild domestic capacities. Meanwhile, the UN's imperative to maintain order – along with a fear of provoking powerful regional warlords – risks creating a climate of impunity in which human rights abuses, past and present, go unpunished and unchecked. The moral issues of narcotics and abuses of women's rights – which formed such a central part of international condemnation of the Taliban – have yet to be adequately addressed. Opium production in 2002 was almost 20 times higher than in 2001. It would take a book to explore thoroughly, but this chapter highlights some of the key ethical issues faced by actors engaged in relief, reconstruction and development.

11 September changed things for Afghanistan. From being a largely forgotten country, struggling to cope with more than two decades of war and the worst drought in living memory, it suddenly became the focus of world attention. As soon as the hijacked planes hit the twin towers of the World Trade Center it was clear that the Taliban would be the target of US retaliation. The attack led to the fall of the Taliban regime, an agreement for a political transition and a chance of peace.

Photo opposite page:
After 24 years of war and the worst drought in living memory, Afghans need peace and security to rebuild their lives, their agriculture and their livelihoods.

Thorkell Thorkelsson/ International Federation, Afghanistan.

Yet there remain many problems. The Bonn Agreement signed in December 2001 was less a peace agreement than a deal brokered between victorious factions in the wake of a war won largely by an external power. These factions, born of the struggle with the Soviets and funded by a variety of external powers, usually for their own ends, had been fighting each other for more than a decade. The Taliban's rise to power in the mid-1990s was in many ways a result of the anarchy their conflict had created. The security that the Taliban brought was welcomed by many Afghans, despite the repressive aspects of their rule.

There had been other attempts at peace in the wake of the Soviet withdrawal in 1989 and to this end the UN maintained a political mission in Afghanistan throughout the 1990s. But, deprived of any serious political support from the major powers, it failed to make much headway with either Afghanistan's feuding factions or its interfering neighbours. Faced with political impasse, aid came to fill the gap left by the failure of politics. In recognition of this, the UN sought both to bring more coherence to the political and assistance wings of its mission and to develop the notion of 'principled common programming', a set of shared principles that the aid community could agree to and which would guide their negotiations with the Taliban authorities.

As the 1990s wore on and the Taliban took control of most of the country, the hardening of political attitudes towards Afghanistan was matched by greater aid conditionality and increasingly strict security regulations that severely limited the number of expatriate staff who could work in Afghanistan. Many in the aid community felt the restrictions were politically motivated and had little to do with the risks on the ground. Meanwhile, donors insisted that Afghanistan should stop being a base for terrorist organizations, that there should be progress on women's rights and that the growing of opium poppies must be stopped. Yet when the Taliban successfully eradicated poppy cultivation at the end of 2000, there was no positive response from the international community, either in terms of programming or in diplomatic recognition. On the contrary, the UN sanctions, which had been introduced in 1999, were followed by a further round of even stronger measures.

Post-11 September – the political context

While many Afghans were not unhappy to see the end of Taliban rule, the strategy the United States chose for fighting its war in Afghanistan – establishing alliances with various Afghan opposition forces – has had serious consequences for the subsequent political transition. Not only did it bring enormous quantities of new arms into the country, but the Northern Alliance troops which took Kabul after coalition forces bombed the Taliban front lines were, not surprisingly, unwilling to give up power. This inevitably placed constraints on what could be achieved in the negotiations at Bonn. The Afghanistan Interim Authority (AIA), which was established to govern for

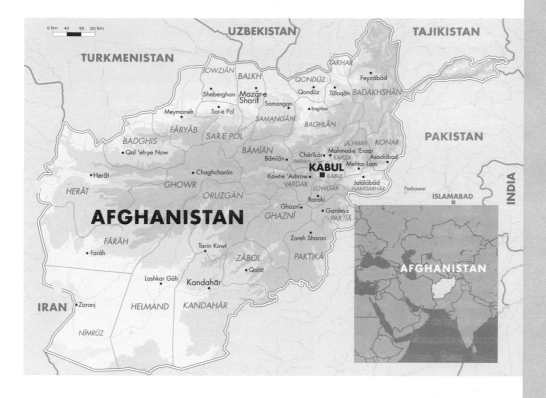

the first six months, was not only dominated by the Panjshiri faction of the Northern Alliance, but also contained a number of warlords who had been responsible for serious human rights abuses. The Pashtuns – the largest single ethnic group in Afghanistan – were under-represented and marginalized from the political process. In addition, many contentious issues, such as how the national army would be formed, were left to be resolved as part of the later transition process. Perhaps even more disabling was the failure to insist that the agreement to withdraw military units from Kabul upon deployment of the international force (Annex I to the Bonn Agreement) be upheld. This has left commanders in all parts of the country feeling they can simply ignore agreements to disarm.

A key element of the transition agreed at Bonn was the convening of an emergency *loya jirga* (grand assembly) within six months to select the Afghan Transitional Administration (ATA), which would take over from the AIA and govern until elections were held. However, the *loya jirga* process was marred by intimidation and occasionally violence. Although the new cabinet contained a few well-qualified people unrelated to factional politics, the fundamental shift in power that was required to bring about a more broad-based and representative authority did not take place. Thus, while the ATA, through its endorsement by the *loya jirga*, has a formal legitimacy as the government of Afghanistan, it has yet to achieve domestic credibility. Meanwhile, warlord power has increased and the security situation in many parts of the country has deteriorated.

chapter 4

Principles disappear from aid agenda

This lack of legitimacy presents the aid community with an ethical challenge: how should the crucial resource of aid be used? In a country struggling to emerge from conflict and with some of the worst indicators of human well-being in the world, what balance should be struck between giving aid according to the humanitarian principles of impartiality and independence, and giving support to the ATA?

More than anything, Afghans want peace and security, and this can only come through the establishment of a legitimate government. While this is primarily a job for politics, it is important that aid strategies do not undermine this process. The ATA currently has little domestic revenue. Without international aid it will not be able to provide benefits for its citizens and will lose what little credibility it has in the eyes of its people. And although it is far from perfect, if it falls apart it is more likely to be followed by a resumption of armed conflict than by a better government. But if resources are to go through the ATA, how to ensure they support the development of more legitimate government, rather than increasing factional power? For if the ATA remains controlled by factional interests and there is no transition to a more broad-based and representative entity, then violence is also likely. Those who are disenfranchised have guns, and while the presence of US forces and their formidable airpower is currently keeping the lid on the situation, this cannot be a long-term solution.

In this regard, the principles embraced by the aid community at the time of the Taliban, that international aid should be "provided on the basis of need" and that "rehabilitation and development assistance shall be provided only where it can be reasonably demonstrated that no direct political or military advantage will accrue to the warring parties in Afghanistan", are as valid as ever. Moreover, the international community needs to maintain a commitment not just to short-term stability but to the agreements made at Bonn, which included progress towards establishing a "broad-based, gender-sensitive, multi-ethnic and fully representative government" and ensuring the authorities act with respect for human rights and international humanitarian law. This does not mean working separately from the ATA, but rather engaging with the ATA in a principled manner. For a start, the international community should have an open dialogue about where the real needs lie and how they can be met, and should insist that all assistance to the ATA be channelled through the central budget, rather than, for example, through the defence ministry.

Yet the question of principles seems to have disappeared from the aid agenda. The agencies and donors that pushed so hard for women's rights under the Taliban, for example, have done little since to use their leverage to bring about change. And, as will be explored later, the commitment to investigating human rights abuses often seems wanting. Meanwhile, narcotics, an issue on which under the Taliban a principled approach was felt to be vital, has become more of a problem than ever. The area under poppy cultivation in 2002 (74,000 hectares) was over nine times higher than in 2001, and the amount of opium produced (3,400 tonnes) almost 20 times that in 2001 (185 tonnes). With the price of opium soaring to around US$ 350 per kilogram, the UN recently estimated the revenue from the sale of the 2002 harvest at US$ 1.2 billion (see Box 4.1). Worse still, in many areas poppy planting in 2003 has increased greatly even from 2002 levels.

Does Afghanistan need humanitarian aid?

The answer to this question is far from straightforward because what constitutes 'humanitarian' aid in Afghanistan is itself unclear. During the time of the Taliban, the concept of 'humanitarian' need was stretched to include everything; food shortages, health and education were all defined as 'emergencies' requiring 'humanitarian' action. This had the advantage of enabling agencies to access funding through predominantly humanitarian budget lines at a time when most donors would not invest in the 'development' of a country whose rulers they chose not to recognize. For all the limitations of its short-term nature, this at least kept programmes going in a situation of great need. But it pushed the definition of humanitarian aid far beyond the alleviation of immediate suffering. Now, when development money is again on the table, it is clear just how blurred the boundaries have become. One senior NGO worker, interviewed at the end of 2002, explained simply: "How we define our work depends on how donors define their money."

Stretching definitions in this way confuses. Humanitarian action was originally designed as a temporary response to a crisis, aimed at enabling people to survive until normality was restored and they could once again resume their lives. But in Afghanistan, 24 years of war have blurred the distinction between crisis and normality – the country's problems are critical, but they are too deep-seated to be resolved by short-term action. And Afghans are not just victims but resilient people who, often quite remarkably, find ways to survive. This does not mean they do not suffer, nor that they do not deserve aid, but it does suggest that what is normally considered as humanitarian action, with its short-term nature, free handouts and high degree of dependency on foreign staff, may not be the answer. A recent report by the Afghanistan Research and Evaluation Unit (AREU), for example, shows how in relation to refugee return the critical issue was not lack of humanitarian aid but lack of the development assistance that could help make return sustainable (see Box 4.2).

The situation is further complicated by the fact that Afghanistan is a country in which there are few statistics and even fewer reliable ones. This makes it very difficult

Box 4.1 Deadly drugs earn the poorest a living

Until 2000, hardly any aid agencies were working in Afghanistan's remote, drought-stricken Ghor province. Then, as drought raised major concerns over harvest failure, the ICRC and Oxfam mounted a relief operation. In summer 2001, after another failed harvest, ICRC increased its programme from 10,000 to 68,000 beneficiaries; 11 September stopped work, but ICRC resumed in December, flying food into an area that would otherwise have been cut off by snow.

With a much-improved harvest in 2002, ICRC downsized its relief programme and began to look at projects of long-term benefit, such as improving irrigation systems. But in 2002, wheat wasn't Ghor's only crop. Opium traders from Helmand, in southern Afghanistan, had come with poppy seeds in one pocket and cash in the other. At the time of year when people are poorest, they offered farmers 50 per cent cash upfront, the rest on harvest. It transformed the economy of the province, with the labour-intensive poppy crop providing work even for those living in areas too high to grow it themselves.

Ghor was not the only part of Afghanistan's central highlands to see this transformation. When Oxfam and the French NGO, Action Contre la Faim, started work in Uruzgan's remote Dai Kundi district in 1998, they were the first foreigners most villagers had ever seen. Dai Kundi's steep hillsides are badly eroded and landholdings are tiny. Now they too are growing poppy. As Shah Wali, the Oxfam programme manager, explains: "Every family has a small patch by their door, trying it out. The rewards have been good; last year it fetched ten times the price of wheat. In villages where people could only dream of owning a motorbike, now they have not one but several minibuses. Wait until next year, then you will see. This year people only grew small amounts. Next year it will be two, three times the amount."

Given that narcotics was one of the key issues, along with women's rights and terrorism, for the international community in the time of the Taliban, the failure to curb poppy cultivation is a matter of major concern. Yet it is hard to see what can be done to limit its spread. The writ of the government does not extend to these areas. In many remote districts no one is in control – there are just commanders with guns and their own small patch of territory. Efforts at control risk driving up prices and pushing cultivation further into the inaccessible highlands. Attempts during 2002 to pay landowners to tear up their crops backfired when farmers planted more poppy in order to get more money for subsequently pulling up what they had planted.

Crop substitution programmes on offer cannot match opium profits and much of the traditional work of NGOs (improving irrigation and reclaiming land, for example) could be used for poppy as easily as for wheat. As most Afghans do not yet use the drug themselves, the problem appears not to be theirs. But, while growing poppy provides a livelihood for many desperately poor people, it directly supports the warlords who are the cause of what Afghans name as their greatest problem: insecurity. ■

Box 4.2 Afghan refugees become political pawns

Nearly one-third of Afghanistan's entire population, some 6 million people, fled the fighting of the 1980s and 1990s and sought sanctuary in Iran, Pakistan and further afield. But since the United States bombed the Taliban out of power in late 2001, Afghan refugees have come under increasing pressure to return home. During 2002-03, Afghans applying for refugee status in Western countries were routinely refused asylum. And refugees in Pakistan's camps were threatened with eviction and camp closure to force them back over the border.

Meanwhile, the media publicity about Afghanistan's reconstruction encouraged many refugees in Iran and Pakistan to return home. President Bush spoke of a 'Marshall plan' to rebuild the country and in early 2002, donors pledged US$ 5 billion in aid. By September 2002, around 2 million refugees had returned, far more than estimated. When asked why he had returned, one returnee in the Shomali Plain replied simply: "The whole world told us they were rebuilding Afghanistan."

Yet the truth is that for most refugees who return, there are few prospects for making a living, except by growing opium poppies. After years of living in an urban refugee environment, their farming skills are rusty and they have little wish to return to their native villages. The country remains devastated by war and drought. It will take up to a decade to clear even high-priority landmined areas. The country's shattered infrastructure is still waiting to be rebuilt. Meanwhile, warlords control large swathes of territory. Insecurity for most Afghans is worse than under the Taliban.

A recent report, commissioned by AREU, argues that political pressures drove the mass repatriation. While the US and its allies, including the new Afghan government, were keen to show the benefits of their campaign to oust the Taliban, the Pakistani and Iranian authorities seized the chance to start offloading refugees from their soil. But this was in the interests neither of those returning nor of Afghanistan's long-term recovery. "Many returnees found themselves in a worse position after their return than before," says the report, while "the scale and speed of the return helped to divert yet more of the limited funds available for reconstruction into emergency assistance".

Rehm-u-din, head of a family of ten, lives in Katcha Garhi refugee camp in Pakistan. He has lived there since 1981, but was told to leave by 30 March 2003. When interviewed by UNHCR, he said: "It is not the time. When I left Afghanistan, we were five brothers and my father owned a small piece of land. Now I have two sons who are married, and five daughters. I do not have a house or job to go back to. The land is under dispute. My sons do not know anything about farming." It's not that he doesn't want to return. "My country is heaven to me. I will definitely go back," he says. "But I am waiting till I am sure that we will not die of hunger at home." ■

to measure the extent of any crisis and leaves the way open for manipulation for political ends. There have been many instances of disputed figures, but the most glaring was in the wake of 11 September, when much publicity was given to the 'humanitarian crisis' in Afghanistan. In the space of a few weeks, the numbers of people estimated at risk of severe food shortages shot up from 3.5 million (World Food Programme (WFP) report, September 2001) to 9 million. Though displacement due to bombing would clearly have had some impact, it is hard to believe that this was sufficient to triple the numbers; and with no new surveys done, there was little objective reason for WFP suddenly to decide that their earlier numbers were so drastically wrong.

The ATA is clear that more humanitarian aid is not the answer to the country's problems. They say it only treats the symptoms and that food aid distorts the agricultural economy, depressing crop prices and acting as a disincentive to farmers to plant wheat. As Afghanistan's minister for rural development told representatives of the United Kingdom's government: "Food aid will not address the causes of the poverty of our people." Yet by the end of 2002, humanitarian aid still comprised the bulk of all assistance to Afghanistan.

Most estimates are that two-thirds of the money pledged at the donor conference in Tokyo in January 2002 was for humanitarian assistance, much of it as food aid. For example, Development Initiatives (a consultancy specializing in aid policy) estimated that, out of the US's US$ 500 million pledge, US$ 200 million was for "food commodities". If Afghanistan is to switch from short-term measures to long-term strategies for solving its problems, it will mean a difficult choice between quick, top-down delivery of material aid and slower, more developmental capacity building. For all that people claim they should not have to choose between humanitarian and development assistance, the reality is that, in a country with limited human capacity, not everything can be done. Afghan capacity will remain weak for some time and aid agencies should be careful to avoid undermining it further. If Afghans are really going to be in charge, as the international community agrees they should be, it may mean going more slowly in some programmes so that this indigenous capacity can be developed.

As part of achieving this, however, the international community needs to put its own house in order. As with all high-profile crises, Afghanistan has seen an explosion of organizations, white 4x4s and spiralling rents that have made a few rich but driven many others from their homes and offices. The number of NGOs registered with the ministry of planning had soared from 250 in 1999 (of which 46 were international) to 1,005 (of which 350 were international) by November 2002. Meanwhile the number of UN international staff in Afghanistan had reached 670 by mid-2002. In addition, large numbers of embassies have returned to Kabul. The differential between the wages international organizations offer and what the government can pay is enormous, sucking what little skill and experience remains in the country away from the government (see Box 4.3). In autumn 2002, for example, an advertisement in the local Kabul paper for a driver at the US embassy

Box 4.3 Expatriate presence risks undermining recovery

At first sight, Kabul appears to be thriving. Crowds surge through the bazaars laden with goods and new restaurants and guesthouses open regularly to brisk business. Dollar salaries and the wholesale trucking-in of luxury goods, including hundreds of 4x4s, ensure a comfortable lifestyle for international aid workers, diplomats, soldiers and those who support them. The influx of over 300 international NGOs, UN agencies and diplomatic missions has created intense competition for high-quality Afghan employees and premises in Kabul. Meanwhile, many government departments lack the equipment and skilled staff needed to carry out their business.

Feelings run high on the subject of salaries. Deputy minister for reconstruction Shaheedi has contrasted his wage of US$ 50 per month with those offered by international aid agencies. Senior aid staff are paid monthly salaries ranging from US$ 1,000 with international NGOs to US$ 10,000 with UN agencies.

In a complicated twist, some government ministries are using aid money to pay expatriate Afghans UN-level wages to act as special 'advisors' – apparently justified by the need to 'get the work done' to an international standard. However, this is creating a completely unsustainable parallel structure within ministries, which does nothing to address the overall problem of below-subsistence salaries for the vast majority of civil servants. Afghanistan's transitional administration says that pledges of aid money will need to be more than doubled to meet the country's needs. Yet, ironically, the government cannot absorb more money unless its own capacity to manage the recovery process is strengthened.

Meanwhile, the aid invasion has inflated prices for accommodation. Aschiana, an Afghan NGO which provided 'drop-in' centres for street-working children in Kabul throughout the Taliban years, lost four of its centres following the arrival of international agencies. One landlord increased the monthly rent from US$ 100 to US$ 4,000. Aschiana reported that they managed to rent "a dilapidated place nearby... in order to accommodate about 900 street children who have been evicted in June 2002". This inflation may benefit a tiny proportion of wealthy landlords; but the ripple effect of rising rents makes life much harder for the majority of Kabul's 2 million residents – including those working for the government.

Ordinary Afghans are not blind to the inequalities. Baktyar Shoresh, 28, is head of a family of six, living in a Kabul suburb. He works as a flight engineer, but he struggles to afford food, clothes and schooling for his younger siblings. The road outside his house is an open sewer, with a huge pile of rotting waste at the end. "Rats and dogs and even children clamber over the rubbish. There's nothing we can do," he says. "The city council says it has no money for refuse collections or sewers."

Baktyar wants to know why so many Kabulis must live in appalling poverty in tents or run-down compounds, because they can't afford to rent houses. "Everyone is struggling, and we all share what we have with each other. That is the Afghan way, we are proud of being hospitable," he says. "But when we go into the city and see brand-new Landcruisers and all the smart houses rented by aid workers we feel angry. Surely this money sent by foreign governments was supposed to help us?" ■

offered a salary of over US$ 500 a month, while a doctor in a government clinic gets about US$ 45. Meanwhile, little of the spending has got beyond Kabul and even less beyond the regional capitals. Agencies visit, ask questions and then go away again.

Human rights – peace without justice?

Nowhere are the ethical issues more acute than over human rights. Whether it is in relation to past human rights abuses or ongoing ones, the way forward is hampered by a lack of institutions, of appropriate instruments and of political will.

Working out how to deal with past human rights abuses is always a difficult issue for countries in transition and Afghanistan is no exception. More than two decades of conflict have led to abuses by all parties, some worse than others. A number of those now in power were responsible for some of the worst excesses of the past. Not surprisingly, Afghans themselves do not agree on the way to deal with this: some argue that now is not the time for justice, others insist there can be no peace without justice. A discussion with emergency *loya jirga* delegates in Mazar-i-Sharif in September 2002 was typical of many exchanges. While some maintained, "God will punish them", others were of the opinion that action was needed now. As one woman argued: "No, God is too patient, there must be trials, there must be justice. They have committed very heinous crimes. When a mother has brought up a child and they kill him, how can she forgive these people? They must be indicted. But it must not be a personal vendetta, there must be justice and a fair trial."

Yet even if there were agreement that there should be trials, it is by no means clear how those allegedly responsible can be brought to justice in the current situation. Sima Samar, chairman of Afghanistan's human rights commission, sums up the dilemma: "We cannot have proper peace without justice. Yet we cannot start justice from today. If we do not tackle things it is like we do not remove the [land]mine, we just put another shovel of earth on it. And you know what then happens. We must start talking about justice to lay the foundation for the future. Who will do it for the past? We cannot close our eyes. Someday someone has to open this – we cannot just allow a general amnesty. At least these people should ask forgiveness, to accept the truth. At least we should have this."

The Bonn Agreement recognizes the human rights problem and in broad terms commits the UN to action. But it lays down no detail and it does not say whether the UN's mandate includes past crimes. In practice, the UN Assistance Mission in Afghanistan (UNAMA) has taken on quite a narrow interpretation of its role and took a decision not to investigate any actions occurring before 28 March 2002, the date of the formal establishment of the mission. The approach of

Lakhdar Brahimi, the special representative of the UN secretary-general, has been that currently it is impossible to have both justice and peace, and that human rights have to be seen within the overriding objective of securing a peaceful transition. Yet, as the Brussels-based International Crisis Group (ICG) argued in its reports on the emergency *loya jirga* and on judicial reform and justice, there is a danger that this sacrifices action on human rights in favour of short-term stability. Ultimately peace cannot be forged in Afghanistan without some form of reckoning with the past.

It is not only a question of the past; human rights abuses did not stop with the signing of the Bonn Agreement. In the wake of the defeat of the Taliban, Pashtuns living in the ethnically mixed north of Afghanistan bore the brunt of retributions, often for no other reason than they came from the same ethnic group as the Taliban. Yet despite the fact that this situation was predictable, the international community failed to protect them and it was not until much later that the UN managed to intervene successfully to reduce the violence targeted at local Pashtun communities. Even now, the situation is far from settled. At one level, this highlights an ongoing problem with protection work: when the situation is at its worst, international staff are almost always evacuated for security reasons (foreign staff were evacuated from Mazar-i-Sharif from September to December 2001). Yet there were sizeable coalition forces in the north and the Afghan forces accused of the violations were their military partners. Why they did not use their influence to better protect the civilian population remains one of the outstanding questions of the conflict.

Nor are the problems confined to the north. Human rights abuses have taken place in many areas and the *loya jirga* process itself was compromised by intimidation and violence, both in the delegate selection process across the country and in the final gathering in Kabul. The extent to which this happened raises serious questions about the possibility of conducting free and fair elections in 2004, a concern which is heightened by the fact that there has been no improvement in security since the *loya jirga* and there has been documented evidence of violence towards individuals involved in what could be seen as embryonic political parties.

The Bonn Agreement provided for the establishment of an independent human rights commission and this is meant to be the organization that should take the lead on human rights issues. Yet not only is it woefully under-resourced, but there is a moral problem in leaving human rights to Afghans whose safety is all too evidently at risk, unless the international community gives the enterprise adequate financial, technical and, perhaps most importantly, political backing.

Even with adequate resources, the issue of investigating human rights violations is complicated by the fact that many of those involved in Afghanistan have attempted to manipulate the human rights agenda for their own political ends. All parties to the conflict have learned that accusing one's enemies of human rights abuses is a good way to bring international wrath down upon them. For its part, the international community has often been accused of double standards – as with their condemnation of the Taliban's restrictions on women but failure to condemn abuses committed by those who took power in 1992, some of whom are now serving in the ATA. Ensuring the integrity of the human rights process therefore requires that all reports are rigorously checked and that standards are consistently applied regardless of who is in power (see Box 4.4).

Even when the truth is established, it is hard to find the way forward. Expressions of outrage by human rights agencies don't necessarily help those at risk. Afghan individuals may be clearly identified as, for example, victims of or witnesses to abuses. But if the international community is either unable or unwilling to protect them, they can be placed in more danger, as happened in the wake of the November 2002 Human Rights Watch report on Herat. Unless the international community is prepared to take a more robust line on protection, real progress on human rights issues will not be feasible. So far this has failed to happen. As one frustrated senior UN worker said at the end of 2002: "We redefine and package. There have been any number of instances when we could have confronted issues but we didn't. We fail to have a strategy for confronting issues and just pick up individual cases. We hide what is happening and justify it on the basis that we should work with this government. Where is our sense of right and wrong?"

Given that concern for human rights was made such a central plank of the international community's dealings with the Taliban, it is not surprising that many Afghans feel let down by the failure to take action now.

Civil/military operations prompt security fears

For ordinary people in Afghanistan, security continues to be the single most important issue. Whoever you speak to and wherever you go, Afghans are clear about this. As Sima Samar, chairman of the human rights commission, said in December 2002: "The main problem is the security issue. This is the problem for all of the people of Afghanistan. How long shall the guns rule this country?"

Yet security is generally worse than it was under the Taliban and continues to deteriorate. The coalition campaign has in some cases directly contributed to this deterioration though its arming of local warlords. By the beginning of 2003, disarmament had still hardly begun and progress on the formation of a professional, multi-ethnic national army and police force remained painfully slow.

Box 4.4 Can there be peace without justice?

The north of Afghanistan has seen some of the worst violence of recent years. Until the late 1990s most of the area was under the command of General Rashid Dostum and was relatively stable and prosperous, although citizens had few freedoms and scant regard was paid to human rights. This stability was shattered in March 1997, when General Malik Pahlawan, Dostum's second-in-command, mutinied, allied himself with the Taliban and ousted Dostum from Mazar-i-Sharif. The Taliban's victory was, however, short-lived. As they began disarming local forces, resistance broke out. Malik then turned against the Taliban, who found themselves trapped in the city. Hundreds of them were killed in the streets and some 2,000 taken prisoner, only to be summarily executed and their bodies dumped down wells or in the desert. This marked the beginning of a period of instability for Mazar and the first of a series of massacres. The second, of Hazara civilians in the village of Qizalabad, happened when the Taliban attacked Mazar for the second time the following September. Then, when the Taliban finally took the city in 1998, thousands of civilians were killed, along with Hazara forces trapped in the city.

Given this background of violence, it was not surprising that when the Northern Alliance (including Dostum) captured the north with the aid of Coalition Forces, further massacres occurred. Hundreds of Taliban and other combatants who surrendered after the fall of Kunduz are believed to have met their death, either by suffocation in the containers in which they were transported or by summary execution.

Bodies from all these massacres lie in mass graves across northern Afghanistan. What to do about these sites, particularly the one at Dasht-i-Leili near Shiberghan, which is believed to hold the remains of the prisoners that surrendered to the Northern Alliance forces in 2001, has been a source of contention within the international community. Although there are many who believe that a proper investigation of the graves and a dignified burial of the remains are an essential part of any accountability and reconciliation process, so far little has been done. The UN Assistance Mission in Afghanistan initiated some preliminary investigations in May 2002, but then took no further action until September, stating that the decision whether or not to investigate lay with the Afghan authorities and the human rights commission.

Concern was also expressed that it would not be possible to protect witnesses and that responsibility to the living had to take precedence over justice to the dead. International human rights groups disagreed, as did the UN special rapporteur on extra-judicial executions, who visited Afghanistan in mid-October 2002 and called for an international inquiry into past human rights violations, including the graves in the north. Finally, the UN agreed to authorize an official investigation into the sites but said that it should be limited to "finding and preserving evidence" and should have a "low profile" since systematic and full investigations "would seriously disrupt the fragile peace that the Government and international community are striving to foster and reinforce". Since then a number of witnesses to Dasht-i-Leili are reported to have disappeared or have been tortured. As one human rights worker noted: "Every time someone comes and looks, someone disappears". ■

Perhaps even more importantly, the army was still not accountable to the civil authorities, but rather to the minister of defence, who is widely seen as a faction leader.

The security problem was recognized from early on, yet despite requests from many quarters, including President Karzai and Lakhdar Brahimi, both the US and its European partners have proved reluctant to extend the remit of the International Security Assistance Force (ISAF) beyond Kabul. Instead, there have been a variety of initiatives by the coalition designed to create the 'ISAF effect'. The latest development was the creation of Provincial Reconstruction Teams (PRTs) at the end of 2002. Comprising mixed teams of US military reservists and civilian aid personnel, the PRTs are designed to operate out of eight regional centres in an initiative that, according to the US Civil Affairs Team, is designed to "remove causes of instability" through engagement with local leaders on behalf of the ATA. The proposal has caused much concern amongst aid workers who fear, among other things, that it will compromise their perceived independence.

The PRTs' remit is broad, not only playing a role in reconstruction but also in strengthening local government, negotiating between commanders, disseminating information from central government, and "assist[ing] in the establishing of national legal codes". This constitutes an extension of what has normally been part of civilian-military cooperation and takes them into the arena of the highly contested relationship between the centre and periphery. It risks sucking people into areas well outside their expertise and is full of potential pitfalls, especially as many of those involved will be on six-month tours of duty, with little knowledge of either development work or Afghanistan. It also risks politicizing the whole area of governance work, which would then undermine the role of those who ought to be strengthening the rule of law and would reduce the space in which others can have the possibility of playing an independent role.

Civil/military operations have in the past been undertaken in a number of conflict zones as part of what is formally termed 'force protection' – the idea being that undertaking tasks of benefit to the community will make foreign forces more welcome and thus safer. Where Afghanistan differs from other recent conflicts is that the coalition forces are not there as peacekeepers, or even peacemakers, but as combatants in an ongoing war. This has often left Afghans confused as to who is peace building and who is still fighting a war.

For agencies, therefore, a key challenge is to distance their work from the ongoing war and to maintain a clear distinction between military and humanitarian functions in the eyes of Afghans. There is a real danger that the blurring of lines between civilian and military will result in aid workers losing the protection that goes with being seen as independent and impartial. While civilian aid may certainly have political consequences, for example in legitimizing warring parties through entering into negotiations with them for the delivery of assistance, the intent is not political. Most aid workers (certainly from NGOs and the International Red Cross and Red Crescent Movement) see themselves as providing aid on the basis of need alone. Despite problems with putting this intended impartiality into practice, the non-political nature of such aid has been broadly accepted by all Afghan parties. This acceptance has enabled aid organizations to continue working through various regime changes, while enjoying a reasonable level of security and access to those in need. The PRTs, on the other hand, are there for another purpose – supporting the state and building stability. This threatens the perceived impartiality of all aid workers: will anyone any longer be seen as neutral?

The danger that aid workers (national or international) might be seen as part of the war effort is particularly an issue in those parts of the country where communities not only feel disenfranchised but have also borne the brunt of the US's actions against al-Qa'eda. Such actions have on more than one occasion resulted in innocent casualties, for example, the airborne attack on a wedding party in Uruzgan, near Kandahar, in

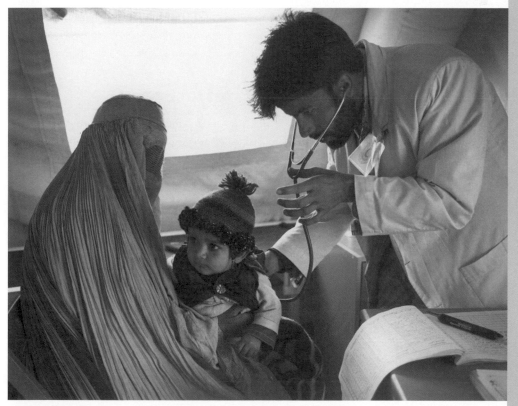

Building the capacities of Afghans to look after themselves is vital to the country's long-term future. But the influx of hundreds of international aid agencies during 2002 risks undermining this process.

Thorkell Thorkelsson/ International Federation, Afghanistan.

June 2002 that killed 54 Afghan civilians. These areas are also the main home for organized forces prepared to use violence against those seen to be part of the perceived US occupation of Afghanistan. Such security concerns became reality in March 2003, when an international aid worker was murdered while visiting a water project in Uruzgan.

There is also a fear that the PRTs' lack of military capacity on the ground will limit their ability to make any real improvement in security at the local level, and that they will just divert attention away from the real security issue, especially if US forces are occupied with action elsewhere. At the same time, their remit for self-defence, including the calling in of air support, could all too easily lead to civilian casualties and an escalation of the problems.

What is clear, however, is that such civil/military initiatives are here to stay and the aid community needs to decide how it relates to them. While the Red Cross Red Crescent Movement and many NGOs have expressed strong reservations about the deployment of PRTs, UNAMA sees a role for itself as a bridge between the PRTs and the NGO community and believes that their involvement will make a real difference to how the teams work. Yet it is not at all clear what the terms of engagement should be. Keeping the PRTs out of the dialogue might lead to many problems, but it is far from obvious how to include them and still maintain the separation between the PRTs and civilian aid workers that many believe necessary for security.

Principles must guide reconstruction

When coalition forces started bombing Afghanistan, world leaders made a promise to the Afghans that this time they would not walk away but would help them rebuild their country. In the words of US President George W. Bush, speaking in April 2002: "We will work to help Afghanistan develop an economy that can feed its people. We are working in the best traditions of George Marshall. Marshall knew that our military victory in World War II had to be followed by a moral victory that resulted in better lives for individual human beings." The Afghans are still waiting.

At the heart of the problem lies the fact that there is not yet peace in the country and warlord power continues largely unchecked. Until this is resolved, it is hard to see how real progress can be made towards either a fully representative government or substantial reconstruction. These are not problems that can be solved by aid – rather they require a sustained political engagement with the country. Those involved in the formulation and delivery of relief and development programmes, however, need to take these factors into account. Yet despite the fact that many of the root causes of injustice, inequity and impunity persist, the notion of principled programming, once so important to international agencies and key donors, seems to have been discarded. Meanwhile, poppy production is soaring, human rights abuses remain and the boundaries between aid and military intervention are becoming ever more blurred. In this context, Afghanistan needs long-term assistance to:

- address chronic humanitarian and developmental problems;
- help develop a responsible government; and
- build local capacity.

Yet what it has got is short-term humanitarian aid, often in the form of free food, and an invasion of international staff. The result is a failure to address the country's deep-seated problems and an undermining of local capacity and of the transitional authority. It would be easy to talk of the need to learn lessons, but most of the problems experienced in Afghanistan were predictable, and predicted, from the experiences of Bosnia, East Timor, Kosovo and other high-profile situations. From the spiralling rents and inflated salaries to the distorted priorities and the failures to protect, none of it is new.

Why then has the international community failed to employ this experience in making their 're-engagement' with Afghans more effective, despite their repeated public commitments to do so? The question would be important for any poor country struggling to emerge from more than 20 years of conflict – it is even more so because this latest conflict was not an Afghan war but the coalition's 'war on terror', fought on Afghan soil. Afghanistan has been the subject of other people's wars for more than two decades. The international community now owes its people the chance to live in peace and decide their own future. Some key challenges remain for the international community as a whole. For the UN and its member states, there is an urgent need to:

- make progress on security, including the formation of a national army under civilian control and the demobilization of private militias, the curtailing of the war economy and an end to the climate of impunity, and
- take a more robust stand on human rights issues, recognizing that ultimately peace will only come if some account is made for the past and protection is given for the future.

For the aid community, a major challenge is to find a way of working that strikes a balance between respect for the Afghan Transitional Administration and the need to provide aid on a principled basis. For a start, all aid agencies could agree to develop a set of principles that will guide aid in the transition period, recognizing that Afghanistan is not yet at peace and that, while the level of need is akin to a humanitarian crisis, the deep-seated nature of the problems demands a long-term response. Key principles would need to ensure that:

- priority is given to meeting basic human needs (male and female) for livelihoods, health and education;
- long-term commitments are made to funding aid programmes;
- Afghan capacity is built at all levels of the system;
- aid does not go to warring parties; and
- separation between military and civilian activities is strictly maintained.

Chris Johnson, the principal contributor to this chapter and Boxes 4.1 and 4.4, has worked in Afghanistan since 1996, first for Oxfam and then as director of the Strategic Monitoring Unit (now AREU). She currently works as a consultant. Robbie Thomson of the International Federation contributed Box 4.2. Barbara Jones, who contributed Box 4.3, is a freelance war correspondent.

Sources and further information

CARE International. *Rebuilding Afghanistan: A Little Less Talk, A Lot More Action*, Policy Brief. CARE International (Afghanistan), 2002.

Duffield, M., Gossman, P. and Leader, N. *Review of the Strategic Framework for Afghanistan*. Kabul: Strategic Monitoring Unit, 2001.

Human Rights Watch. *All our hopes are crushed: Violence and repression in Western Afghanistan*. November 2002.

Human Rights Watch. *Paying for the Taliban's Crimes: Abuses against Ethnic Pashtuns in Northern Afghanistan*, vol. 14, no. 2 (C). April 2002.

International Crisis Group. *Afghanistan: Judicial Reform and Transitional Justice*. Asia Report No 45. Kabul/Brussels: International Crisis Group, 2003.

International Crisis Group. *The Afghan Transitional Administration: Prospects and Perils*. Washington DC: International Crisis Group, 2002.

Johnson, C., Maley, W., Their, A. and Wardak, A. *Afghanistan's political and constitutional development*. London: Overseas Development Institute, 2003.

Maley, W. *The Afghanistan Wars*. London: Palgrave Macmillan, 2002.

Olcott, M.B. *Drugs, Terrorism, and Regional Security: The Risks from Afghanistan*. Testimony before the US Senate Judiciary Committee, March 2002.

Rubin, B.R. *The Fragmentation of Afghanistan: State Formation and Collapse in the International System*. New Haven: Yale University Press, 2002.

Stapleton, B. *A British Agencies Afghanistan Group Briefing Paper on the Development of Joint Regional teams in Afghanistan*. London: British Agencies Afghanistan Group, 2003.

Stockton, N. *Strategic Coordination in Afghanistan*. Afghanistan Research and Evaluation Unit (AREU), 2002.

Turton, D. and Marsden, P. *Taking Refugees for a Ride? The Politics of Refugee Return to Afghanistan.* AREU Issue Paper, December 2002.

United Kingdom, Government of. *Afghanistan: the Transition from Humanitarian Relief to Reconstruction and Development Assistance*, First Report of Session 2002-3, HC 84, House of Commons, International Development Committee, London.

Web sites

Afghanistan Information Management Service (AIMS) **http://www.aims.org.pk/**

Afghanistan Research and Evaluation Unit (AREU) **http://www.areu.org.pk/**

Agreement on Provisional Arrangements in Afghanistan pending the re-establishment of permanent government institutions **http://www.uno.de/frieden/afghanistan/talks/agreement.htm**

Strategic Framework for Afghanistan: Towards A Principled Approach to Peace and Reconstruction **http://www.pcpafg.org/programme/strategic_framework/**

chapter 5

Section One

**Focus on
ethics
in aid**

Forced migration – forgotten disaster?

For all of human history, people have moved to find new opportunities. Yet far more people today have chosen – or been forced – to migrate than ever before and they have gone to far more places. Over 175 million people now live outside their countries of birth, according to the United Nations (UN). While migration may offer an increased quality of life for some, those who are forced to migrate may face long and terrifying journeys, debts to smugglers of thousands of dollars, discriminatory immigration barriers and years of illegal labour in squalid and dangerous conditions where their needs and rights are ignored. International legal provisions to protect and assist those forced to flee from conflict or natural disaster are inadequate or non-existent. Meanwhile, the ongoing 'war on terrorism' has led to security measures that risk encouraging human trafficking and prejudicing the rights of 'genuine' refugees. Since migrants move from country to country, often via illegal channels, they risk slipping into a legal no-man's-land, where their rights and welfare become no one's problem. What ethical challenges does migration pose to governments and organizations committed to the fundamental principle of humanity, which seeks "to prevent and alleviate human suffering wherever it may be found"?

The context in which international migration takes place has changed radically in the past few decades. Technological and communications changes have helped people migrate while enabling them to stay in touch with their home communities. Would-be migrants have unparalleled access to information about other countries. Globalization means freer movement of services and labour, as well as goods and capital. Yet globalization has produced winners and losers, too often leading to greater poverty and instability in the world's poorest countries. With few opportunities at home, international migration is an attractive alternative. Meanwhile, the end of the cold war, while reducing ideological barriers to international migration, released latent nationalistic tensions which have led to ethnic cleansing and other forced movements.

Migration is often discussed in extreme terms. Throughout Europe, for example, far right-wing political parties have proposed policies to prevent all migration into countries with sizeable foreign-born populations. They argue that all asylum seekers file abusive claims aimed at gaining access to generous welfare benefits rather than safety. Conversely, many who support generous asylum systems can be equally vehement in portraying all asylum seekers as bona fide refugees fleeing persecution.

Photo opposite page:
A young Cambodian boy looks out through the barbed wire at a transit centre in Thailand. Detention of children seeking asylum is never justified, although the US, the UK, Australia and Canada all detain migrant children who fail the asylum test. Detaining children arbitrarily or denying them prompt access to legal assistance are forbidden by the UN Convention on the Rights of the Child.

© M. Kobayashi/ EXILE IMAGES, Thailand

These absolutist positions belie the complexity of the issues surrounding international migration, reducing difficult ethical choices to simplistic arguments. Seldom does international migration raise clear issues of 'right or wrong'. More often it pits competing interests that require delicate balancing of 'good' versus 'good'. Meanwhile, for the victims of conflict and extreme poverty, the choice is often a dilemma between two evils: whether to stay at home or try to find refuge outside – risking harm or even death either way.

Governments face difficult moral choices, too. A generous asylum policy may protect refugees from persecution, but attract those not in danger to risk dangerous journeys in the hope of gaining admission. Meanwhile, the legitimate interest of governments in preventing the entry of potential terrorists may unintentionally result in strengthening human trafficking networks, which prey upon migrants desperate for a better life. Growth in trafficking undermines the very security that governments seek, while increasing the vulnerability of migrants to forced labour, sexual exploitation, unsafe living conditions and even 'slavery'.

Resolving ethical challenges raised by migration requires a far more nuanced understanding of population movements than that contained in many public debates. This chapter examines the scale, causes and effects of international migration – including its benefits in stimulating development. It then focuses more specifically on those forced to flee emergencies, and addresses five areas of concern:
- Millions of forced migrants remain unprotected by aid or by law.
- Human trafficking claims up to 4 million victims per year.
- Security post-11 September risks increasing discrimination and trafficking.
- Rights of international migrants are inadequately protected.
- Lack of multilateral cooperation in managing international migration.

International migrants top 175 million

International migrants are defined as people who take up residence in a foreign country. The number of long-term international migrants has grown steadily in recent decades, from 75 million in 1965, to 84 million by 1975, 105 million by 1985, 120 million by 1990 and – by the end of the millennium – 175 million. However, the proportion of the world's population who are migrants has remained at roughly 3 per cent for the past century. The more developed countries of the North experienced significant growth in their immigrant populations during the 1990s, particularly from less-developed countries in the East and South (see Figure 5.1). According to the UN Population Division, 104 million of the 175 million migrants are in more developed countries – although much of this migration is still *within* regions, rather than trans-continental. For international migration to occur, there must be 'pull' factors, 'push' factors and networks to connect people with where they want to go (see Box 5.1).

International migrants either move voluntarily or they are forced. Voluntary migrants include people who move abroad for employment, study, family reunification or other personal factors. Forced migrants leave home to escape situations that threaten their lives and well-being. However, distinguishing between the two groups can be very difficult. People may be forced to flee from a life-threatening crisis but voluntarily choose to migrate somewhere with family ties or greater economic opportunities. Depending on why they flee from home and how they arrive in their new destination, migrants will find themselves in distinctly different legal situations:

Refugees are a subset of forced migrants with special status under the 1951 UN Convention and 1967 Protocol relating to the Status of Refugees. The UN High Commissioner for Refugees (UNHCR), which is mandated to protect and assist them, estimated that there were about 12 million refugees under its mandate at the beginning of 2002. Another 4 million Palestinian refugees are under the mandate of the UN Relief and Works Administration. Under the 1951 convention, a refugee is a person who has crossed an internationally recognized border and has a "well-founded fear of being persecuted for reasons of race, religion, nationality, membership of a particular social group or political opinion" if he or she were to return home.

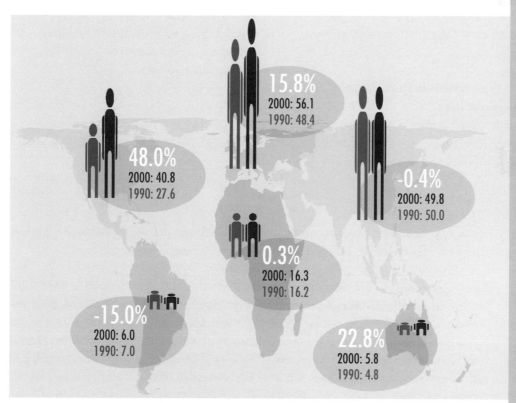

Figure 5.1
Size and growth of numbers of migrants by continent, 1990 and 2000. (Figures are in millions.)

Source: United Nations Population Division.

Box 5.1 Some factors driving international migration

"Push factors" driving migrants from their homes

- Conflict
- Crime
- Human rights abuse – including sexual abuse
- Economic mismanagement by states
- Climate change/drought/flood/natural disaster – may initiate rural-urban migration
- Increasing inability to sustain a rural/subsistence lifestyle – partly due to collapsing commodity prices
- Unfair international trade rules preventing access of developing economies to richer markets
- Poverty – although the very poorest cannot afford to migrate
- Persecution – the only qualification for refugee status

"Pull factors" attracting migrants to other countries

- Demographic change, principally ageing and reducing workforces in developed market economies
- Reluctance by workforces in developed economies to do 'three D' jobs (dirty, dangerous, difficult) – offering job opportunities to migrant workers
- Modern communications – many of the world's poor can now see living standards in developed economies on television or the Internet
- Cheap and easy access to travel
- Political freedom and respect for human rights
- Physical security of individuals

"Facilitation" – networks enabling people to migrate

- Labour recruiters
- Relatives and friends in destination countries
- Trafficking by criminal elements including organized crime
- Smuggling operations

However, those who flee war, natural disaster, violence, crime or destitution are not usually considered refugees – except by some developing countries.

Many who would be considered refugees if they fled across an international border are instead **internally displaced persons (IDPs)**, often because they cannot find refuge beyond their own borders. The Norwegian Refugee Council's Global IDP Project recently estimated there are about 25 million people displaced by conflicts within their own countries. While there is no international convention for IDPs, the UN has promoted Guiding Principles on Internal Displacement, drawn from existing human rights and humanitarian law, to provide a more comprehensive framework for protecting and assisting IDPs. Their safety and well-being remain a major concern, since simply reaching them is often very difficult, particularly if they are caught in conflict zones or if government or rebel forces deny access to international aid.

Environmental migrants, who flee natural disasters or environmental degradation, do not generally need protection from persecution or violence. But, like refugees and IDPs, they may be unable to return to now uninhabitable communities. Most move within their countries – either moving temporarily until they can rebuild their homes or seeking permanent new homes. Other environmental migrants, however, cross national boundaries. Although there are no official data, some scholars estimate there are 25 million environmental migrants – a number which may grow as global warming, desertification and other environmental problems render more areas uninhabitable.

Development policies and projects may cause large-scale migration of **'development-induced migrants'**. Involuntary relocations occur, for example, as a result of building new dams, highway construction and urban renewal. According to the World Commission on Dams, large dams could have displaced 26 to 58 million people between 1950 and 1990 in India and China alone. Some governments have tried to redistribute residents from over- to under-populated regions, even compelling relocation through force. Those targeted for relocation based on their nationality, race, religion or political opinion share similarities with refugees and IDPs. In Myanmar during the 1990s, for example, the government embarked on a massive programme of road and railway construction, clearing areas of those who might support the Mon and Karen ethnic armies. In this case, the location for a project resulting in mass displacement was chosen to lessen political opposition and to repress an ethnic or religious minority. Global statistics are elusive, partly because no international organization has responsibility for this issue – although the World Bank has established guidelines to reduce involuntary resettlement from its projects.

Human trafficking – the most insidious form of forced migration – involves exploiting migrant labour in sex trades, domestic service, sweatshops, agricultural production, restaurants and other similar activities. Victims may be held against their will for long periods in slavery-like conditions (see Box 5.2). The United States State Department estimates that between 700,000 to 4 million women, men and children are trafficked worldwide each year. Migrants may willingly arrange to be smuggled into other countries, but then find themselves in debt bondage, forced for months or years to work off the smuggling fees they incurred – around US$ 50,000 to get from China to the US. The 2000 Protocol to Prevent, Suppress and Punish Trafficking in Persons, Especially Women and Children (supplementing the UN Convention against Transnational Organized Crime) aims to tackle the issue. But while one of the protocol's key aims is to protect and assist victims, authorities too often punish those trafficked rather than the traffickers behind the crime.

Box 5.2 Trafficked survivor tells her story

Name: Ms. Vi

Country of Origin: Vietnam

Country of Destination: American Samoa

Testimony provided by U.S. House of Representatives, Committee on International Relations Hearing on the Implementation of the Trafficking Victims Protection Act November 28, 2001

I arrived in American Samoa on July 22, 1999. Two other groups of Vietnamese workers had been brought to this island before us. When I signed the contract, Tour Company 12 (TC12) told me that I would go to the U.S. and its deputy director promised that I would be paid US$408 a month. I had to borrow 4 thousand dollars to pay TC12 and another 2 thousand to pay the company official in charge of recruitment.

We were taken to American Samoa, not the U.S. As soon as we landed, our passports were confiscated. At Daewoosa I had to work from 7 a.m. often to 2 a.m. and sometimes to 7 a.m. the following day and also on Saturdays and Sundays, without pay. We had no money to buy soap, amenities, or food.

We had to pay about $200 per month for meals, which Daewoosa should have provided according to the contract. Meals at Daewoosa consisted of a few cabbage leaves and potatoes cooked with a lot of water. Those who were at the head of the line could get some cabbage and potato; latecomers got only water. Hungry, we planted some vegetables to supplement our meager diet but Mr. Lee, President of Daewoosa, destroyed our garden. Undernourished, I lost 35 lbs and weighed only 78 lbs.

Working and living conditions at Daewoosa were very suffocating. There was no ventilation. Workers sat next to each other. It was very hot. We were not allowed to step out for fresh air. The supervisor even kept count of how many times we went to the toilet.

We lived 36 people per room. Another worker and I shared one tiny bed. We could only sleep on our side. If we lay on our back, we would pile up on each other. Most of us were women. At night Mr. Lee often came to our room and lay next to whomever he liked. Once he forced me to give him a massage right in our bedroom.

He called pretty ones into his office and forced them to have sex with him. Three women have publicly denounced him for that. Once, several of his customers arrived in American Samoa; Mr. Lee pressed several female workers to sleep with them. They resisted. At the workplace, he regularly groped and kissed female workers in front of every one.

There were three pregnant women among us. Mr. Lee demanded that they undergo abortions. He fired them when they refused. Evicted from Daewoosa, they had to seek refuge at a local church.

Movement at Daewoosa was very restricted. Everyone leaving the compound was searched by American Samoan guards. Female workers were groped all over their body. Those who protested were strip-searched. Those coming back to the compound after 9 p.m. were beaten up. Once I was slapped.

Mr. Lee used big American Samoan guards to terrorize us. Once several workers staged a strike because they were not paid. He threatened that he would send these guards to short-circuit the electric cables and cause a fire to kill all of us. Everyone was fearful because two female workers, Nga and Dung, involved in a lawsuit against Mr. Lee, had just disappeared.

On November 28 of last year, there was a dispute between the supervisor and a female worker. Mr. Lee ordered the supervisor: "If you beat her to death, I will take the blame." The supervisor dragged the female worker out. Other workers came to her rescue. The American Samoan guards, already holding sticks and scissors, jumped in and beat us. Everyone was so frightened. We ran for our life.

The guards paid special attention to the 5 or 6 workers known to have supported the lawsuit against Mr. Lee. They beat them the hardest. Ms. Quyen, the key witness in this lawsuit, was held by her arms on two sides by two guards; a third guard thrusted a pointed stick into her eye. She has now lost that eye. A guard beat a male worker with a stick, breaking his front teeth and bleeding his mouth.

Another male worker was pinned to the floor and repeatedly beaten at the temple, his blood spilling all over the floor. The next day, FBI agents took picture of the bloodstains. During the assault, Daewoosa's lawyer and the police were there but did nothing. Only when the lawyer representing the workers showed up, did the guards stop the beating.

From 1999 to the above incident, TC12 and International Manpower Supply – another Vietnamese company hiring workers for Daewoosa – forced us to continue working without pay and threatened to send us back to Vietnam if we disobeyed. Everyone was deeply in debt; if sent back to Vietnam, how could we pay our debt?

Since my arrival to the US I have sent every dollar earned back to Vietnam to pay my debt. However this has barely made a dent because the interest rate is so high, 50% per year. My parents in Vietnam are very worried; their hair has turned all gray. They told me that it is fortunate that I have come to the US; otherwise we would be in a hopeless situation.

If sent back, it would be hard for me to find employment. My previous workplace will not take me back. Because of my involvement in the prosecution of Mr. Lee I am afraid of running into trouble with the government if repatriated to Vietnam.

I am getting used to life in the U.S. Here I am free to choose where to work. If dissatisfied with one workplace, I can always go to another one. I have been thoroughly helped in my first steps towards a normal life. I find everyone to be kind.

I now live with a Vietnamese family without having to pay rent. That family offers me employment. They take care of my food, transportation and other things. They also give me a phone card to call my family in Vietnam once a week.

I have received the certification letter from the Department of Health and Human Services for public benefits. I have a temporary visa, which will expire on October 30, 2002, and a work permit. I work at a nail salon in DC to pay my debt. If allowed to remain in the U.S., I would like to go back to school because in Vietnam I had to stop schooling at 7th grade. I also wish to be reunited with my child left behind in Vietnam.

I am thankful to everyone who has helped get me out of American Samoa and everyone who has assisted me in my new life in the U.S.∎

A final group are **economic migrants,** some fleeing poverty and severe deprivation. Historically, the world's poorest lacked the resources, networks or information necessary to move across borders. International economic migrants tended to be better-off – under-employed or under-paid rather than unemployed or destitute. But in recent decades, cheaper transport and communications, combined with the growth of smuggling networks that 'advance' travelling costs, have increased the pool of potential economic migrants dramatically. Unlike refugees who fear persecution if returned home, economic migrants are assumed to be able and willing to accept the protection of their own countries. However, as long as developing countries cannot compete with subsidized industries in developed countries (and are further penalized by restrictive import terms), those who can afford it will keep searching for better economic opportunities abroad.

Remittances worth more than world aid

While international migrants may suffer from a bad press in developed countries, they are an important resource for the development of their home countries – a resource not sufficiently tapped. Migrants remit about US$ 80 billion per year to developing countries – considerably more than the US$ 50-55 billion of official development assistance (ODA) that flows from rich to poor countries every year. Furthermore, whereas ODA may be 'tied' to the purchase of goods and services originating in donor countries, migrants' remittances are mostly spent on helping their own families with food, shelter, health care, education and other inputs to economic development. So the money goes directly where it is most needed. When used to purchase locally produced items, these remittances have a multiplier effect in stimulating local economic activity.

Remittances may be the difference between life and death during disasters and other emergencies. After El Salvador's twin earthquakes in 2001, their president successfully argued that the US should grant legal work permits to Salvadoreans, having estimated that legal status could increase remittances by US$ 250 million per year – a far greater sum than was likely to be given in foreign aid. Migrants have provided similar assistance to help Armenia, Honduras, India, Mozambique, Turkey and other countries cope with the effects of earthquakes, hurricanes and floods.

Governments from Mexico to Mali have encouraged migrants living abroad to invest in local infrastructure. Mexican hometown associations in the US and Malian associations in France have responded by contributing to the construction of health clinics, schools, sanitation systems, roads, small factories and other infrastructure. Sometimes home governments match migrants' contributions to increase the value of remittances (see Box 5.3).

Box 5.3 Migrants promote hometown reconstruction and recovery

Forced migrants are not just victims of horrific situations. They can also help communities in their home countries recover from the devastation of conflict, natural disaster and extreme poverty. The United Community of Chinameca, an association of Salvadorean migrants in the Washington DC (USA) area, was formed a decade ago to help their hometown, 120 kilometres from San Salvador. Able to return when peace came to El Salvador, they were struck by the devastation that the war had brought. They wanted to help their families and friends to rebuild. Since then, they have contributed a new Red Cross clinic, an ambulance, a public laundry, a septic tank, and helped rebuild the school. They throw parties and sell home-baked delicacies to raise money, as well as soliciting donations from businesses. Members estimate they have raised more than US$ 300,000 for their hometown.

Thousands of kilometres away, migrants from Marena village in Mali are contributing to the development of their home community. The migrants, who live in France, also have an association that supports community projects back home. They have funded a local school and pay the teacher's salary, and built a health clinic. In an interesting twist, the migrants pay health insurance to cover the cost of medical care for their relatives in Marena. The premiums they pay each month guarantee the continued operation of the health clinic. This also benefits residents without family members abroad, who pay a small fee for health services they receive.

Recognizing the important role of Malian migrants, France and Mali have signed a Franco-Malian co-development framework. A fund of 2.6 million euros will supplement financing by the Malian diaspora of local projects. The countries also plan to develop a registry of skilled Malians in France who could help build the Malian economy. As a further element of co-development, a contract will be signed with a Malian bank to guarantee loans to small businesses started by returning migrants who require additional funding for expansion of their activities.

Several Mexican states are facilitating the efforts of migrants abroad to help develop their home communities. Under a '3-1' programme, Mexican federal and state governments provide three dollars for each dollar contributed by clubs of Mexicans living in the United States. According to *Migration News*, the Southern California Zacatecas Federation, which includes 55 clubs linked to an equal number of towns in Mexico's Zacatecas state, remitted US$ 2.5 million in 2001, which was matched by US$ 7.5 million in government funds. Projects supported by the 3-1 programme include a US$ 1.2 million potable water and drainage system, for the farming village of Las Animas with the help of US$ 300,000 in club contributions. The 20 associations that make up the Illinois Federation of Zacatecanos also raise money for their hometowns. According to one association board member, Elena Duran, the overseas Mexicans are involved in the projects from start to finish. "Our funding through 3-1 helps make the government more accountable. If we raise money through raffles and dances for a road," she says, "we make sure the road gets built." ■

Migrants who return home ('returnees') are a valuable resource for development, but their countries' capacities to reintegrate migrants vary. In some cases, returnees are expected and governments help migrants invest resources earned abroad. But other countries are ill equipped to support reintegration of returnees – especially in post-conflict situations where massive reconstruction of the economy, housing, legal and political systems is needed. Moreover, until peace and reconciliation are secured, the security of those returning may be threatened. It would be unethical to encourage refugees to return under such circumstances. A recent report on Afghan repatriation in 2002 concluded: "Many returnees found themselves in a worse position after their return than before."

Programmes to help returnees reintegrate take many forms, ranging from immediate assistance in travelling home and finding temporary accommodation, to longer-term support for self-sufficient livelihoods. The communities to which migrants return need help too, in demobilizing combatants, demining, human rights monitoring and the restoration of basic education, health, water, sanitation, infrastructure and judicial systems. If these basic conditions for a safe and secure life are not met, then people may be forced to migrate once again.

Millions of forced migrants remain vulnerable

Addressing humanitarian crises involving migration has strong ethical, security and developmental implications. However, the legal and institutional system created after the Second World War to address refugee movements is proving inadequate to assist and protect the full range of forced migrants needing attention today.

The 1951 UN convention's definition of refugees as persons fleeing across borders to escape persecution is narrow, encompassing only some of those in life-threatening situations. It does not include people fleeing conflict, generalized violence, natural disaster or environmental crisis. Nor does it include the increasingly large numbers of IDPs trapped within their home countries. While convention refugees clearly deserve international protection, far larger numbers of forced migrants remain vulnerable and under-protected (see Box 5.4).

Some advances have been made. The Guiding Principles on Internal Displacement provide a framework for the international response to IDPs, emphasizing the need to: prevent forcible displacement; gain access to those displaced; provide basic assistance and protection; ensure their safety and that of those providing humanitarian assistance; and secure their resettlement or return home. National governments are primarily responsible for protecting their own nationals, including IDPs. But if they are unwilling or unable, the international community has a humanitarian responsibility to help provide IDPs with aid and protection. In Bosnia, East Timor, northern Iraq,

Box 5.4 Burundi's displaced women face disease and destitution

Conflict in Burundi has lasted more than 30 years, the most recent crisis developing in 1993. During this period, more than 200,000 Burundians have lost their lives, over 600,000 have fled abroad and another 500,000 are internally displaced. In August 2000, a peace agreement was signed by most, but not all, of the parties to the conflict. No ceasefire was agreed upon so the peace remains fragile. The UN Office for the Coordination of Humanitarian Affairs estimates that a recent outbreak of new conflict may be generating as many as 100,000 new displacements each month.

Of all the civilians affected by conflict in Burundi, none are more victimized than the women and children forced to flee their homes. They are divided into three categories: the 'displaced' who live in formally recognized IDP (internally displaced people) camps; the 'regrouped' who are forced into camps established when the army removes local populations to facilitate military operations; and the 'dispersed' who live in the forests and marshes or have sought refuge with relatives and friends. Some refugees who have returned from neighbouring countries in the hope of peace have subsequently become internally displaced as fighting reached their villages. Urban street children and other homeless populations have grown in size because of the conflict, although they tend not to be considered IDPs.

The case of 'GM' is typical. When fighting started, her home was destroyed and she and her family were forced to move to a regroupment camp. "My husband died when I was four months pregnant with my baby daughter.

We were both sick, but we had no medicine when we were living in the regroupment camp," she says. "I was so sick I didn't even realize my husband had died." In addition to her own seven children, she also cares for an unaccompanied girl whose brothers and sisters had died of dysentery and malnutrition. The girl had wandered the camp begging for clothes and food until she found GM. "If I can find food for my seven children, surely I can find food for eight," says GM. When the regroupment camp closed, GM was fortunate. Her old house had been destroyed in the conflict, but she found new quarters in a commune near the camp. She received food, blankets and a kitchen set from the World Food Programme.

Others are less fortunate. Many women and children have been living in forests, moving nightly to escape the violence around them. Most of them have no sources of income, except for occasional humanitarian aid. Even aid operations have been targets of attack in Burundi, making it particularly difficult for agencies to reach vulnerable populations. Many women are so desperate for money they resort to prostitution, despite the enormous risks in a country where around 20 per cent of the urban population is thought to be HIV-positive. Spès Manirakiza, director of the Women's Center for Peace, describes the case of one woman who, she says, "would prefer to feed her baby and die herself of AIDS". Unprotected by refugee law, too poor to migrate in search of a better life, and beyond the effective reach of aid agencies or human rights conventions, her situation is truly desperate. ∎

Kosovo and Somalia, armed interventions attempted, among other objectives, to ensure that IDPs received aid and protection. But this is rare, as it may be seen as an issue of sovereignty, so millions of IDPs remain beyond the reach of international help.

Complicating the situation is a gap within the global system for protecting internally displaced people. No UN agency has this mandate, although the UN secretary-general has appointed a special advisor on IDPs. In the field, UNHCR assumes responsibility on a case-by-case basis if, for example, refugees and IDPs are returning to the same home communities after a conflict ends. At present, about 5 million of the estimated 25 million IDPs are under UNHCR's mandate. The International Committee of the Red Cross (ICRC) cares for those internally displaced by armed conflict, but its mandate does not extend to people displaced for other reasons. Solutions to address this gap range from the assignment of a lead agency (according to the context) to the creation of a new organization – for example, a UN High Commissioner for Forced Migration. However, the political will for such an agency is currently very weak.

Reform is also needed in responding to *international* movements of forced migrants. The vast majority of refugees seek protection and assistance in the developing world. More than 80 per cent of the 16 million refugees worldwide live in less developed regions. While only a limited number of refugees reach Europe, North America or Australia, asylum policies and practices in the developed world seriously compromise the security of the large numbers of refugees who remain within their home regions.

When developed nations deny entry to their territories, the message is clear: find protection elsewhere. Australia adopted a new policy to address boat arrivals of asylum seekers in late August 2001, not long before national elections were to be held. Under the new policy, Australia refuses to allow such arrivals into Australian territory and sends them to other countries in the Pacific, where their refugee claims are assessed. UNHCR has expressed serious concern that Australia's actions could send a negative message to impoverished nations closer to conflict zones, which often take in hundreds of thousands of refugees. Iran, for example, has played host to around 2 million Afghan refugees since the 1980s, at a cost of an estimated US$ 1-2 million per day. If a relatively wealthy country like Australia restricts the intake of refugees to a few thousand per year, less wealthy 'front-line' states may be tempted to do the same.

Roadblocks to asylum have become widespread in developed countries during the last two decades. Asylum seekers struggle even to reach the territory of developed countries, deterred by strict visa requirements and sanctions against air and road carriers transporting people without adequate documentation. Receiving countries may bar asylum applicants from what are considered 'safe' countries of origin or transit, regardless of the merits of individual cases. The slow processing of asylum claims, tight deadlines for filing applications and detention of asylum seekers during the application process also discourage or bar asylum seekers from receiving protection in developed countries. Officials justify these measures by pointing to the large number of failed asylum applications as evidence that the system is being abused. Yet migrants fleeing conflict and extreme political insecurity may view themselves as 'refugees', even if they do not meet the persecution test of the UN convention.

In recognition of the limits of the convention, governments increasingly grant at least limited protection to forced migrants on other grounds. The US, for example, provides Temporary Protected Status to people fleeing conflict and natural disaster, which enables them to remain legally in the country until conditions in their home countries improve. However, the government has great discretion in granting this status and those temporarily protected do not have the right – which individuals granted asylum have – to become permanent residents. The issue of complementary protection was raised during UNHCR's global consultations, and governments acknowledged the need for greater harmonization of policies to improve protection of vulnerable groups.

'Genuine refugees' face tremendous risks due to the failures to reform asylum systems, to ensure security for all migrants requiring it and to provide economic migrants with entry routes other than asylum. The policies to deter asylum seekers from reaching developed countries end up channelling refugees, along with other migrants, into the hands of smugglers. This makes the forced migrants' quest to escape and seek protection far more risky. One solution to reduce the pressure on Northern asylum systems could be to issue economic migrants with work visas (so-called WTO visas) to enable them to access countries that need their labour. Given the rapid ageing of the population in many developed countries, such labour migration could help offset the looming financial crisis which will occur when there are too few workers to support the generous pension systems for those who have retired. By definition, most labour migrants migrate to work, not to claim social security. Moreover, many keep a foot in each camp – at home and in their country of work. Increasing their options for legal immigration would reduce the role of smugglers and shorten the queue for those genuinely in fear for their lives.

Meanwhile, inefficient asylum procedures are expensive to refugees and governments alike. The systems for deciding on the eligibility of asylum seekers and caring for them cost developed countries billions of dollars. By contrast, funding for the far larger number of refugees and IDPs in developing countries has declined to dangerously low levels, leaving millions with inadequate food, shelter, health care or durable solutions. According to the US Committee for Refugees, the anticipated shortfall in UNHCR funding of almost US$ 200 million in 2002 had the following impacts: 35,000 Congolese refugees in Zambia faced a 50 per cent cut in food rations, resulting in higher malnutrition rates; up to 80,000 Sudanese refugees in Kenya faced a 25 per cent cut in food rations; 40,000 refugees from Chad and Nigeria received little or no assistance because budget constraints forced UNHCR to close its office in Cameroon; 40 projects to help Senegalese refugees support themselves in Guinea-Bissau were cancelled; and nearly half of the 2 million Afghan refugees returning home would receive no non-food reintegration supplies from UNHCR. In addition to declining funds for refugees and IDPs, funding to address the root causes of the instability that drives migration – underdevelopment, overpopulation, environmental degradation, disease – is woefully inadequate.

The danger is that the most vulnerable are the least protected. A recent study of displacement by conflict in Sri Lanka and Somalia indicates that those migrating to developed countries are more affluent, while the poorest cannot afford to find international protection. There may be a gender bias, too. About 80 per cent of refugees in developing countries are women and children, whereas a high proportion of asylum applicants in developed countries are men. While refugees who make it to the North and refugees or displaced people in the South are equally deserving of protection, the imbalance of resources available to help them may well be the real 'asylum crisis' facing the world today. In short, too much money is spent keeping asylum seekers out of the North and not enough is spent helping them in the South.

Up to 4 million people trafficked each year

Human trafficking has become one of the most explosive branches of organized crime. Long-distance, intercontinental trafficking of people to exploit their labour is increasingly organized by well-known crime syndicates (e.g., mafia, triads), which form global alliances linked to local networks of employers and enforcers. Attracted by the prospect of apparently better job opportunities and living conditions in rich countries, between 700,000 and 4 million men, women and children fall victim every year.

Three principal approaches can combat human trafficking: law enforcement; educational programmes; and efforts to protect the rights of those trafficked. Law enforcement can deter criminals by increasing legal penalties, improving intelligence, breaking up trafficking and smuggling rings, increasing arrests and prosecutions of smugglers, disrupting traditional routes and safe houses, and improving cooperation between local and foreign law enforcement officials. Legal attention has also been focused on the employers of trafficked aliens, enforcing labour laws, and regulating marriage, modelling and escort services to ensure they are not involved in trafficking for forced prostitution. Too often, however, prosecution is misplaced, with heavier penalties for the victims than for traffickers themselves or the businesses that benefit from forced labour.

Education strategies have been targeted at two groups: would-be users of trafficking and smuggling operations, and the officials who may come across such operations. Campaigns to combat trafficking in women have received particular support from governments. If accurate, timely information about trafficking is disseminated to potential migrants, they can make an informed choice and avoid being misled by those seeking to exploit them. For example, a Polish women's organization, La Strada, uses leaflets, lectures, video presentations and school visits to educate potential victims. It runs telephone hotlines to offer advice and reliable information to women considering migration to western Europe. Campaigns of this type are under way throughout the world but remain inadequate, given the continued growth in trafficking. Moreover, few programmes can address the main reason why so many are vulnerable to trafficking – the absence of other economic opportunities at home.

Meanwhile, governments grapple with defining the standards to govern the treatment of migrants entering their country. First, migrants attempting illegal entry have the right to be protected from physical abuse by smugglers, other predators and immigration officials. Secondly, the successful prosecution of traffickers often requires the testimony of their victims, who may rightly fear retribution. They generally need witness protection and other support – however, rather than being a right, this is at the discretion of the authorities. Third, trafficked people need help to return home safely, since they often lack the necessary resources. Abused migrants may need special help.

The need for education and protection programmes far outstrips what is available. Governments and civil society must cooperate to ensure that the rights of trafficked migrants are protected. Survivors often ask for help from non-governmental organizations (NGOs) – more trusted than government agencies. NGOs and Red Cross and Red Crescent societies can play an important role in helping survivors to settle in their new country or to return home safely. Humanitarian organizations with networks in countries of origin and destination could prove particularly useful in assessing which option is in the best interests of the trafficked survivor.

On a broader level, the control of trafficking requires a more effective international migration management regime which can curb unauthorized flows of migrants and set realistic policies for the return of migrants no longer permitted to remain. When unauthorized migrants violate immigration policies with impunity, the credibility of legal admission systems suffers. A public that perceives immigration to be out of control may react negatively to all forms of migration, not necessarily distinguishing between legal and unauthorized immigration, or voluntary and forced migration.

Controlling unauthorized movements presents many ethical challenges, particularly for democratic governments that seek to protect human rights. Strategies must reduce the incentives and possibilities for migrating through illegal channels, while simultaneously ensuring that individual migrants are not physically harmed or their rights trampled. The indefinite detention of unauthorized migrants poses particular ethical problems, particularly when used to deter would-be refugees from seeking asylum. Detention of children seeking asylum is never justified – although the US government, for example, argues that when it detains unaccompanied minors it is for the children's own safety. Australia, Canada and the United Kingdom also detain migrant children who fail the asylum test. Detaining children arbitrarily or denying them prompt access to legal assistance is in contravention of Article 37 of the widely ratified Convention on the Rights of the Child. Moreover, the detaining authorities become the children's legal guardians, raising more ethical concerns – including the paradox that the authority responsible for a child's rights is the same authority that locked that child up. Finally, when they release unaccompanied children, governments need to take special measures to protect them from exploitation. The person who claims to be a close relative may actually be the trafficker who plans to put the child into a brothel or sweatshop.

New security measures risk discrimination

Since the events of 11 September 2001, governments and the public have become increasingly concerned that terrorists and others who pose security threats are able to move freely around the world, with few controls over their movements. The 19 airline hijackers entered the US legally with visas and had spent considerable time in other democratic countries prior to accomplishing their suicide missions.

Governments' responses to terrorism have raised questions about the balance between security and civil liberties. Recognizing that immigration officials lacked access to the intelligence needed to screen migrants for terrorist connections, the US, EU and other countries have tightened visa information systems – including, for example, fingerprint checks. Currently in the US, foreign nationals from 25 designated countries (mainly Islamic) are required to register with immigration authorities, raising concerns of discrimination based on religion and nationality. The deadlines for registration have already caused a flight of migrants across the Canadian border.

Long-term detention of suspected terrorists is also on the increase. Often, authorities cannot establish a criminal case against these individuals but can hold them for violating immigration policies. If there are good reasons to believe the person intends to commit terrorist acts, then neither releasing them into the community nor removal to another country is an attractive alternative. Consequently, governments may find themselves 'between a rock and a hard place'. Added to which, if the suspected terrorist were returned to a country known to use torture, this would contravene not only the binding obligations for signatories to the UN Convention Against Torture but also the principles of customary law which are binding on all states.

Maintaining generous refugee policies in light of terrorist threats is a challenge for all countries. Not surprisingly, many refugees come from states known to harbour terrorists – including Afghanistan, Somalia and Sudan. The repression and instability that makes them safe havens for terrorists also produces refugees who are fleeing those same conditions. Immediately after 11 September, the United States suspended its programme of resettling refugees in the US in order to undertake a security review. Even after its resumption, the movement of refugees into the US has been very slow. In the meantime, refugees remain in unsettled, sometimes dangerous situations awaiting approval of their cases.

Women and children account for 80 per cent of refugees in developing countries. This Senegalese woman sought asylum in neighbouring Gambia, after fighting broke out in and around her village.

Marko Kokic/ International Federation, Gambia.

Chapter 5 **Forced migration – forgotten disaster?**

Rights of international migrants poorly protected

Just as important as the rules governing entry and exit is what happens to migrants once they reach destination countries or return home. Receiving countries differ significantly in the rights they grant migrants, such as citizenship, participation in elections, obtaining gainful employment and qualifying for public benefits. The availability of language training and cultural orientation – which helps both newcomers and the communities in which they settle – also varies.

Migrants' rights are spelled out in a number of global agreements. The International Labour Organization (ILO) has initiated international labour standards for the benefit of migrants. The 1951 Refugee Convention spells out the rights of refugees. In 1990, the UN General Assembly adopted the International Convention on the Protection of the Rights of All Migrant Workers and Members of Their Families. The convention recognizes that migrants – especially those smuggled or trafficked – are often in a vulnerable position. It aims to guarantee minimum protection for migrant workers and their families, whether they are working legally or illegally. Unfortunately, support for the convention has only come from the source countries of migration. In March, Guatemala became the 20th state to ratify, paving the way for the convention to enter into force on 1 July 2003. But no destination countries have ratified it, nor have they indicated their intention to do so. This is despite the convention being identified as one of the most fundamental of the seven human rights treaties.

Given the weakness of the international regime, migrants will generally have to rely on national governments and civil society to protect their rights. Under customary law, governments are obliged to protect the rights of all people on their territory – whether they are there illegally or not. Unfortunately migrants continue to be discriminated against (see Box 5.5). Many countries need to implement active programmes to combat racism, xenophobia and discrimination. Strategies to better protect migrants' rights include: identifying varieties of discrimination that exist in society; establishing laws and mechanisms to guarantee equal opportunity; and developing ways to measure discrimination, so that policies can be adjusted accordingly.

New international migration regime needed

In an increasingly interconnected world, multilateral cooperation is essential in addressing global migration. Cooperation must involve national governments that regulate migration, plus the international organizations, NGOs, corporations, labour unions and migrants that have a stake in the outcomes of migration policies. While every country has a sovereign responsibility to protect its own borders, unilateral actions are no longer adequate. Few countries can erect sufficient barriers

Box 5.5 Asylum rules risk repeating apartheid

In October 2002, Lord Joffe, formerly legal advisor to Nelson Mandela, during a debate in the British House of Lords on the National Asylum and Immigration Bill, was moved to comment: "I could not help but be struck by certain parallels between this Bill and legislation in apartheid South Africa. That legislation initially deprived selected groups of some of their human rights and, subsequently of most of those rights. In the Bill before the Committee, a group of people, asylum seekers, have been singled out and are to have many of the rights enjoyed by everyone else stripped out or diminished."

A national who commits a crime in many modern democracies can only be imprisoned for a few days before their case has to be heard by a competent and impartial judicial authority. Yet an asylum seeker whose identity or origin is in question can be locked up indefinitely pending a refugee determination process. This can take several years. If the migrants fail the refugee test and if their country of origin does not want them back, they can remain in detention for an unspecified period of time, with no idea as to a release date.

In the UK, the Secretary of State may detain non-nationals indefinitely without charge or trial, based entirely on evidence that the detainees may never get to see. In his report on one British detention centre, former chief inspector of prisons Sir David Ramsbotham stressed – as an important point of principle – that the decision to deprive anyone of their liberty should be overseen by the judicial process. He noted: "In accordance with the International Covenant on Civil and Political Rights – Article 9(4) – detention must always be authorised and reviewed through a court process." Unfortunately, people who have committed no crime continue to be detained indefinitely without judicial scrutiny.

Women and children are detained under the same circumstances, often in the same facilities as convicted criminals. In the case of an unaccompanied minor, the detaining authority becomes the child's legal guardian. Paradoxically, this means the authority that is responsible for detained children's rights is simultaneously denying some of their rights under international law. Law aside, detaining children indefinitely may have severe psychological effects. As John Mone, Scottish Bishop of Paisley, has remarked: "It is a disgrace that young children from perhaps the age of 5 to 14 are held in a prison environment."

Even the right to life may be denied to asylum seekers. In 1997 a Chinese woman, Zhu Qingping, who sought protection for her unborn baby against China's 'one-child policy' lost her battle for asylum in Australia and was forcibly deported back to China. Once in China, the eight-and-a-half-month pregnant woman was forced to undergo an abortion at the hands of the state, since her pregnancy would otherwise have delivered her second child. Australia's immigration minister Philip Ruddock stated, "She was denied refugee status because a fertile woman is not a member of a social class", and hence did not qualify for asylum under the strict rules of the 1951 Refugee Convention. Security concerns aroused by the 'war on terrorism' have led governments in the developed world to impose ever-more stringent immigration policies. The rights of migrants are under threat as legislation seeks to classify them as second-class citizens. In the face of this discrimination, humanitarian agencies – which have signed up to protect 'life with dignity' regardless of race, creed or nationality – must ensure that this most forgotten of vulnerable groups is accorded its basic rights. ■

to stop unauthorized migration, particularly if the nation wishes to benefit from, for example, competitive labour, tourism or business travel. Meanwhile, commitments to human rights, including international refugee law, rightly limit a country's options.

With the exception of refugees, there is no international regime to set rules regarding movements of people. Nor is there a common understanding as to the costs and benefits of freer or more restrictive immigration policies. No body of international law or policy governs responses to labour migration or to the full range of forced migrants seen today. The obligations of states to protect and assist internally displaced persons, conflict refugees, environmental and development-induced migrants have not been spelled out. Nor is there agreement on even the basic outlines of the multilateral cooperation needed to address these situations. If such cooperation is to emerge, there must be a greater consensus that harmonizing policies will make migration more orderly, safe and manageable while still protecting the rights of migrants. New, comprehensive legal frameworks and global institutions with migration-related mandates are badly needed.

Conclusion: protect *all* those forced to flee

With over 175 million people living outside their countries of birth, international migration has more than doubled in the past 25 years. Meanwhile the welfare and security of tens of millions of migrants forced from their homes by political, economic and ecological insecurity is of enormous concern. Countries need to cooperate in finding legal and humanitarian solutions for forced migrants. While the ideal solution would be 'stay at home' development, for the foreseeable future the world will be faced with millions seeking safe and dignified lives outside their home communities. Moreover, while labour migrants can time their departure and choose their destination, forced migrants have little choice but to migrate to save themselves and their families.

Since 1951, the international community has agreed that the protection of people fleeing persecution outweighs the sovereign right of countries to protect their borders from unauthorized entries. However, today's refugee system does not meet the needs of modern society, where reasons for migration are highly complex and hard to measure.

Receiving countries should offer protection and assistance to the full range of forced migrants seeking safety from life-threatening situations at home, not only to refugees as defined by the 1951 convention. Often, forced migrants may need only temporary protection before returning home when conditions there permit. But if repatriation threatens migrants' safety, then more long-term solutions are necessary.

Protection of forced migrants is hampered by the lack of agreement on the range of people deserving international attention. Improving data on forced migration would help identify those in need, as well as providing better information on the reasons for flight and the potential for solutions. Meanwhile, the piecemeal legal and institutional arrangements for refugees and IDPs make international responses ad hoc and, too often, ineffectual. Serious consideration should be given to establishing a UN High Commissioner for Forced Migrants, which would assume responsibility for refugees as well as IDPs and others forced to flee. Locating responsibility in one agency would help ensure equitable treatment for all types of forced migrants. It is essential, however, that increased protection for internally displaced persons should not be used as an excuse to prevent people from seeking asylum in other countries.

In addition, the international community must do more to help provide safe conditions for the majority of refugees who remain in developing countries. This means restoring adequate levels of funding to UNHCR and its implementing partners, and working with countries of asylum to ensure the safety of refugees fleeing into their territory. International organizations, governments and NGOs should seek to ensure that refugees receive adequate assistance and, where possible, access to employment to reduce their vulnerability to exploitation and abuse. Developed countries can play an important role in improving protection by offering resettlement opportunities to refugees whose situations are insecure in their countries of first asylum and who have few prospects for repatriation. Finally, for those who return home, there need to be adequate measures to ensure that repatriation is voluntary and safe.

Meeting these challenges is complicated by the twin threats of terrorism and trafficking. Immigration systems have proved vulnerable to manipulation by people who pose a security threat as well as those who exploit the labour of others. Combating these twin threats is in everyone's best interests – whether governments, civil society or migrants themselves. Security must not, however, be used as an excuse to prevent forced migrants from reaching safety. With governments leaning towards more restrictive policies, it is up to civil society to advocate for more humane and effective policies to protect forced migrants throughout the world.

The main contributor to this chapter was Susan F. Martin of the Institute for the Study of International Migration, Georgetown University, Washington DC, USA. She also wrote Boxes 5.3 and 5.4. Box 5.4 is based on her participation in the Women's Commission for Refugee Women and Children in October 2000. Some of this material has been published in the commission's report, Out of Sight, Out of Mind: Conflict and Displacement in Burundi. *Robbie Thomson of the International Federation wrote Boxes 5.1 and 5.5, and Box 5.2 is reprinted with permission of the Protection Project of the Johns Hopkins University School of Advanced International Studies, USA.*

Sources and further information

Adams, Richard H. Jr. *The Effects of International Remittances on Poverty, Inequality, and Development in Rural Egypt.* International Food Policy Reseach Institute, 1991.

Binational Study of Mexico-US Migration. *Migration between Mexico and the United States.* Washington, DC: US Commission on Immigration Reform, 1997.

Castles, Stephen and Miller, Mark. *The Age of Migration: International Population Movements In The Modern World.* New York: Guilford Press (2nd ed.), 1998.

Cohen, Roberta and Deng, Francis M. *Masses In Flight: The Global Crisis Of Internal Displacement.* Washington, DC: Brookings Institution Press, 1998.

Cornelius, Wayne A. and Martin, Philip L. *The Uncertain Connection: Free Trade and Mexico-US Migration.* San Diego: Center for U.S.-Mexican Studies, University of California, San Diego, 1993.

Global IDP Project. *Internally Displaced People: A Global Survey.* London: Earthscan Publications, 2002.

International Organization for Migration (IOM). *World Migration Report 2000.* New York: United Nations Publications, 2000.

Martin, Philip L. *Trade and Migration: NAFTA and Agriculture.* Washington, DC: Institute for International Economics, 1993.

Martin, Susan. '*Complex Forced Migration and the Humanitarian Regime*', presented at the International Association for the Study of Forced Migration, Chiang Mai, Thailand, January 2003.

Martin, Susan. *Environmental Migration.* Geneva: IOM and the Refugee Policy Group, 1991.

McNeill, William H. and Adams, Ruth S. (eds.). *Human Migration: Patterns And Policies.* Bloomington: Indiana University Press, 1978.

Myers, Norman. 'Environmental refugees: a growing phenomenon of the 21st century', in *Philosophical Transactions: Biological Sciences*, Vol. 357, No. 1420, pp. 609-613, April 2002.

Sassen, Saskia. *Globalization and its Discontents*, New York: New Press, 1998.

Smith, James P. and Edmonston, Barry (eds.). *The new Americans: economic, demographic, and fiscal effects of immigration.* Washington, DC: National Academy Press, 1997.

Teitelbaum, Michael S. and Stanton Russell, Sharon. *International Migration and International Trade.* Washington, DC: World Bank, 1992.

Teitelbaum, Michael S. and Winter, Jay. *A Question of Numbers: High Migration, Low Fertility, and the Politics Of National Identity.* New York: Hill & Wang, 1998.

Turton, David and Marsden, Peter. *Taking Refugees for a Ride? The Politics of Refugee Return to Afghanistan.* Afghanistan Research and Evaluation (AREU) Issue Paper, December 2002.

UN High Commissioner for Refugees (UNHCR). *2001 Statistical Yearbook*, Geneva: UNHCR, 2002.

UN Population Division. *International Migration Report.* New York: United Nations, 2002.

UN Statistical Division and European Community Statistical Office. *Final Report of the Expert Group Meeting on International Migration Statistics.* New York, 10-14 July 1995 (ESA/STAT/AC/50/9).

US Commission for the Study of International Migration and Cooperative Economic Development. *Unauthorized Migration: An Economic Development Response.* Washington, DC: Government Printing Office, 1990.

US Committee for Refugees (USCR). *World Refugee Survey 2002.* Washington, DC: USCR, 2002.

US State Department. *Victims of Trafficking and Violence Protection Act of 2000: Trafficking in Persons Report.* 5 June 2002.

Van Hear, Nicholas, *"I went as far as my money would take me": conflict, forced migration and caste',* presented at the International Association for the Study of Forced Migration, Chiang Mai, Thailand, 2003.

Web sites

Protection Project, Johns Hopkins University, Washington, DC, USA
http://www.protectionproject.org/main1.htm

International Convention on the Protection of the Rights of All Migrant Workers and Members of Their Families
http://www.unhchr.ch/html/menu3/b/m_mwctoc.htm and
http://www.december18net/UNconvention.htm

chapter 6

Section Two

**Tracking
the system**

Measuring the impact of humanitarian aid

Measuring both the positive and negative impacts of humanitarian aid would appear, self-evidently, to be a good idea. Knowing and being transparent about the effects of one's actions is part of being an accountable organization. Yet, surprisingly, the process of developing the right tools to carry out this job is still in its infancy. Progress is being made to improve the quality of project evaluations. Yet the measurements of success in the humanitarian world too often focus on 'outputs' only – how many tonnes of food aid or blankets delivered, how many cubic metres of clean water provided, how much cash spent per capita. These crude measures fail to analyse the actual results of such aid – whether lives have been saved, health and nutrition have improved, money was well spent – and whether these results were because of the aid effort or for other reasons. Many challenges – both technical and ethical – face those aiming to assess humanitarian aid's results. Which impacts do you measure – immediate outcomes or longer-term changes? How can you be sure that a specific impact is the result of a specific aid intervention? Who makes these critical judgements – foreign agencies or indigenous groups? Does an obsession with measurement encourage agencies to intervene only where impacts are easily measured? Can impacts be assessed quickly enough to affect real-time decisions, or will lessons remain unlearnt on a dusty shelf? This chapter aims to address some of these issues and chart a way forward in this increasingly important field.

During the 1990s, a growing critique of the effectiveness of humanitarian aid (especially during emergencies in Bosnia, Rwanda and Somalia) led to a broader questioning of the role, legitimacy and capacities of non-governmental organizations (NGOs). Humanitarian agencies have responded to this critique by developing clearer ethical principles and minimum technical standards through the Code of Conduct for the International Red Cross and Red Crescent Movement and NGOs in Disaster Relief (the Code of Conduct) and the Sphere project. More recently, the Humanitarian Accountability Project was established to improve the accountability of agencies to the people they seek to benefit. And much effort has been invested in greater inter-agency exchange and learning through, for example, the Active Learning Network for Accountability and Performance in Humanitarian Action (ALNAP), the Groupe Urgence Réhabilitation et Développement (Groupe URD) and the Global Study on Consultation and Participation by Affected Populations in Humanitarian Action. Meanwhile, the second half of the 1990s saw several publications devoted to impact assessment in both the development and the humanitarian arenas.

Photo opposite page: Measuring the success of humanitarian aid means more than simply quantifying the amount of food or water donated. Impacts – such as lower mortality and improved health – must also be tracked.

Marko Kokic/ International Federation, Guatemala.

At the same time, a number of other significant changes have been occurring. Among donor governments, there has been a further emphasis on 'results' and 'results-based management'. The increasing militarization of humanitarianism has culminated in what some have called the first 'humanitarian wars' in Kosovo and Afghanistan. NGOs have become more involved in humanitarian advocacy and policy work, which itself has recently come under increased scrutiny. And there is – according to last year's *World Disasters Report* – a growing recognition that for humanitarian agencies, "the challenge now is to turn still rather exceptional examples of accountability into regular, institutionalized practice".

These developments raise a number of key questions. To what extent are the efforts being made to improve impact assessment, accountability and learning bearing fruit? How far have these initiatives got to grips with assessing both direct, short-term outcomes and direct *and* indirect longer-term impacts of humanitarian work? What methodological developments and innovations have occurred in the last few years? How far does an ethical approach to these issues assist? What do organizations need to do to institutionalize these processes further?

Assessing impacts during disasters

For the purposes of this chapter, impact is defined as 'a significant or lasting change in people's lives brought about, at least in part, by a given intervention'. These changes may be positive or negative, expected or unexpected. Change may result directly from a given intervention, for example saving lives by providing food or water; or indirectly, for example through lobbying a third party to protect a group of people. This definition suggests that impact – or significant change – can be a short-term phenomenon. A life-preserving action, even if temporary, may well be viewed as significant, not least to the person whose life has been saved. If impact is defined in this way, the key questions then become: what has changed, is it significant or lasting, and to what degree can it be attributed to a given set of actions? Equally important: who decides?

In addition to these challenges, impact assessments during emergencies face a range of distinct issues which need to be factored into any methodology. Direct threats to the lives, health and livelihoods of civilians (including agency staff) can distort findings or simply render the process irrelevant. Any assessment will be complicated by the often high levels of confusion, contradictory information and lack of agreement about what is happening and why. Meanwhile, the swiftly changing environment of many emergencies may mean that objectives shift significantly. Tracking why objectives have changed over time becomes an important part of any impact assessment. Furthermore, high-profile emergencies play host to a plethora of organizations, increasingly including military forces, which may make the attribution of impacts to single agencies more difficult.

Different groups on the ground may have different interests in curtailing or sustaining conflict. Equally, some groups may differ in their ability to command support from others, including aid agencies, or to meet humanitarian needs. These differences need to be properly taken into account in any impact assessment. The best longer-term development processes try to assess such differential needs and interests, and then build the capacity of local organizations accordingly. But in emergency situations, the priority of meeting immediate needs is usually more pressing. This can lead to local organizations being ignored or undermined by international agencies – even though they may make more impact on humanitarian needs – as happened in the response to the Gujarat earthquakes in 2001. Impact assessments during emergencies should avoid these dangers by exploring the relationships between local and external organizations. This is important not only in terms of assessing immediate impacts on people's lives, but also in gauging the degree to which local capacity has been supported to respond to shocks and disasters in the future.

Measuring expected outcomes or significant changes?

Although there are many different approaches to impact assessment, one of the key debates concerns the degree to which impact assessments focus on 'expected results', secondary/indirect impact, or broader contextual change. This has given rise to three different ways of approaching impact assessment:

The 'project-out' approach, which involves defining project impacts or outcomes in advance and then assessing whether they have been achieved. A 'logic model' will be constructed, which indicates the links between activities/outputs and impacts/outcomes, and establishes a small number of 'objectively verifiable' indicators for each. Just how these indicators can be verified will usually be determined in the project design phase. The assessment then seeks to test whether the outcomes have been achieved, usually by determining if the indicators have been reached. The narrow use of Sphere's minimum standards would fall into this category of evaluation.

Assessing broader impacts. This approach still takes a given intervention as its starting point, but assesses broader, unexpected changes that may have resulted. This often involves collecting and analysing different stakeholders' opinions of changes brought about by a given project and how they happened. The approach can use frameworks or checklists, such as an aide-memoire or set of organizing principles, for assessing impact. The use of the Code of Conduct in the evaluation of the 2001 Gujarat earthquake by the UK-based Disasters Emergencies Committee (DEC), falls into this category (see Box 6.1).

Box 6.1 Comparing Gujarat responses using the Code of Conduct

In an attempt to assess responses to 2001's Gujarat earthquake against not only short-term goals but also 'connectedness' to longer-term issues, the evaluation of the Disasters Emergencies Committee (an umbrella organization of leading UK NGOs) used the principles of the Code of Conduct for the International Red Cross and Red Crescent Movement and NGOs in Disaster Relief. Apart from interviews with key 'stakeholders' and agency staff, the evaluation also involved a major public opinion poll of 2,372 rural and urban dwellers who survived the earthquake.

A subsequent study of the response of the Self Employed Women's Association (SEWA) – a local union of nearly 300,000 members in Gujarat – also used the Code and a smaller poll of survivors' opinions. This enabled the responses of international NGOs and this local membership organization to be compared. The table below indicates the scores out of ten for each of the principles as determined by the evaluators.

The study concluded that not only was SEWA's response better linked to longer-term development concerns, but was also faster, more efficient and better targeted. This was in particular because of SEWA's membership structure and, it is argued, because it worked primarily with and through women. Where SEWA performed worse than international NGOs was in its accountability to donors. While the study indicated that SEWA could improve this aspect of their response, it also suggested that the fact that SEWA remained accountable to its members was a key element in its success. It concluded that SEWA "occupies the moral high ground on this issue".

This use of the Code of Conduct illustrates some of the strengths of using a common set of criteria, notably: it sets norms and standards for the sector as a whole; it allows for local interpretation of these standards depending on context; and it enables a comparative performance of different agencies to be undertaken. Of course, some of these strengths can become weaknesses: the breadth of the principles could lead to such different interpretations as to be meaningless, and it could foment further competition and rivalry between agencies. But the study has contributed enormously to key debates about the role of local agencies, especially women's organizations, in disaster response, and how agencies should handle multiple accountabilities. ∎

Source: Vaux 2002.

Code of Conduct principle	DEC agencies	SEWA
1 Humanitarian imperative comes first	5	9
2 Non-discrimination of aid	8	8
3 No furtherance of religion and political agendas	9	9
4 Independence from foreign policy	n.a.	n.a.
5 Respects local culture and custom	6	9
6 Builds on local capacities	5	10
7 Involves beneficiaries	4	10
8 Reduces future vulnerabilities	3	9
9 Accountable to beneficiaries	6	10
Accountable to donors	8	4
10 Dignity in images	5	8
Total	**59**	**86**

The 'context-in approach', which starts by assessing significant changes in people's lives and environment, and then seeks to explore the sources of those changes. This approach attempts to locate changes attributable to a particular action or agency within a broader context. In so doing, it allows for a comparative analysis of changes brought about by different actors and processes, as well as an assessment of how different actions combine to promote change. Importantly this can help assess the degree of relevance that a specific project might have in a rapidly changing environment. For example, when this approach was tested in northern Ghana after a severe bout of ethnic conflict in 1994-95, it revealed not only how different actors (local groups, government, international NGOs) responded to the conflict, but also the different value that local people put on those responses.

A combination of the third approach with one of the first two is preferable but may not always be feasible. The tendency for impact assessments – like evaluations in general – to focus too much on 'project-out' approaches can lead to rather 'egocentric' results which exaggerate the importance of interventions and diminish the role of other actors, not least survivors' own ingenuity and actions.

Which indicators best measure change?

Some dimensions of change have been commonly cited as important in assessing humanitarian work. For example, the Organisation for Economic Co-operation and Development (OECD), in its 1999 report *Guidance For Evaluating Humanitarian Assistance in Complex Emergencies*, includes the following:

- **Mortality and morbidity rates** – a significant indication of public health. These data are not only important in designing appropriate responses but also in adapting them over time. It may often be appropriate for several agencies to pool resources to assess changes in these rates.
- **Coverage and differential impact** – the proportion of men, women and children who have been covered by a particular intervention.
- **Protection and security** – the degree to which the human rights of individuals or groups have been protected over and above their material needs.
- **'Connectedness'** – how far short-term emergency responses 'connect' to, or support, longer-term recovery and sustainability.
- **Coherence and coordination** – the degree to which different agencies' policy agenda are consistent and the degree to which organizations coordinate their actions.

There is currently some debate as to the relevance and utility of these indicators – especially whether NGOs can or should 'connect' to longer-term issues or advocate for broader policy change and coherence while also undertaking life-saving humanitarian relief. For example, Tony Vaux, Oxfam's former global emergencies coordinator, recently described how poorly-conceived attempts to leverage a change in the Taliban's policy towards women may have led to an increase in humanitarian suffering (see Chapter 2). On the other hand, it is also clear that agencies have been manipulated by warring parties since the Biafra war at least, and that they can and should make better judgements about the secondary or unintended consequences of their actions.

Some have criticized not the idea of indicators themselves but the ways in which they are used. For example, the fluidity and unpredictability of emergencies require flexible responses adapted to the changing context. In such situations, indicators of change can be useful to help organize information but not for predetermining activities, as these may no longer be relevant. This has led to a greater emphasis on monitoring and impact 'tracking' – an ongoing assessment of impact. Recent attempts at real-time evaluation in Afghanistan and elsewhere by the Office of the United Nations High Commissioner for Refugees (UNHCR), the World Food Programme (WFP) and the Humanitarian Accountability Project are examples of this (see Box 6.2). This could mean a continual process of assessing change against indicators determined at the outset of a project, and adapting and changing these indicators over time. However, it also requires being attentive to unexpected changes which, by definition, will not have been anticipated at the outset.

Broader frameworks for measuring impact

In addition to indicators or dimensions of change, there are a number of broader frameworks which emphasize particular elements of performance. These include Sphere's minimum standards and the Code of Conduct. In the central Mindanao region of the Philippines, experience of using Sphere's standards complemented by other approaches suggests that the use of minimum standards alone may not provide sufficient evidence for effective decision-making (see Box 6.3).

For some critics like Groupe URD, the development of universal standards, such as those embraced by Sphere, is highly controversial. They emphasize the need for diversity rather than universality. They stress the importance of participation and an understanding of context in order to assess impact. This, they argue, is not consistent with 'pre-set formulae' and universal standards.

The Code of Conduct is probably the most widely accepted set of humanitarian principles among the global NGO community – 227 organizations had signed up to this voluntary code by March 2003. The use of the Code's ten principles in evaluating the response to the Gujarat earthquake illustrates how such frameworks can enable comparative assessments between different agencies, while exploring the difficult trade-offs that may have to be made between different dimensions of performance.

Box 6.2 Impact and accountability in Afghanistan – a moving target

In 2002, the Humanitarian Accountability Project (HAP) piloted a project to promote accountability in western Afghanistan. The experience showed that accountability requires an ongoing effort to monitor the impact of programming on the lives and perspectives of beneficiaries. Priorities and problems change rapidly as needs shift from the management of overcrowded IDP camps to rebuilding livelihoods in scattered, isolated and devastated villages. Needless to say, following the moving target of accountability was found to be neither cheap nor easy. Rigorous assessment of accountability requires a major investment in training and mobilizing field teams to interview beneficiaries. HAP's limited successes in Afghanistan came primarily from joining with agencies that were already themselves making efforts to reflect on the quality of their programmes. Through encouragement and exchanging information between agencies, HAP helped to provide deeper and more rigorous analysis of issues that had already been identified by agencies on the ground, and also provided an extra 'push' for ongoing efforts to address concerns raised by beneficiaries.

A particular challenge was how to maintain a focus on humanitarian (as opposed to developmental) accountability. Currently in Afghanistan, developmental actors are at the forefront of recreating accountability within new governance structures and in selecting reconstruction and reintegration priorities. It is in developmental circles that an increasing proportion of the decisions will be made regarding which services a returning IDP or refugee might hope to access back in his or her village.

The debate around accountability means finding a balance between rights-based approaches and the day-to-day efforts of humanitarian agencies to ensure that target groups obtain what they need to survive. Agencies must prioritize from an overwhelming array of pressing failures to defend the rights of disaster-affected people. It is not self-evident which 'rights' should come first. Even greater uncertainty arises when, as is the case in much of rural Afghanistan, there is no agency prepared to declare itself responsible for more than a narrow set of beneficiaries and a narrow set of rights. Finally, the difference between humanitarian entitlements and the need to apply developmental solutions to deal with chronic vulnerability is hazy. A difficult question for agencies that claim to have an ethical commitment to a rights-based approach is how to avoid merely creating frustration by drawing attention to a collection of rights that is difficult to prioritize.

HAP dealt with these difficult questions by providing practical advice and data collection (structured surveys) related to accountability issues in the IDP camps near the city of Herat. They were acutely aware, however, that the IDP camps were not the most strategic focus within the broader spectrum of accountability issues facing Afghanistan's western region. HAP chose its camp focus because it lacked the capacity to reach and solicit the perspectives of war- and drought-affected people once they left the camps. If those promoting accountability are to find their feet in the countryside of places like Afghanistan, major investments are needed in getting an empirical perspective on what is happening out in the villages to which people are returning. So far, this has not happened on a wide scale. Tools such as Sphere are useful, but there is also a need for far more money, staff, vehicles and time to get out and see whether programmes are yielding the impact that was expected. ■

Box 6.3 Central Mindanao – mix of data helps fine-tune response

An upsurge in conflict in the Mindanao region of the Philippines in 2000 displaced over 800,000 people. Evacuation centres set up to host displaced families became overcrowded, and inadequate shelter, water and sanitation facilities posed a severe threat to public health. Several local and international organizations, including Oxfam GB, Acción contra el Hambre and the ICRC, intervened to help improve public health and nutritional status. However, continuing unrest meant families remained in the centres into 2001.

Oxfam worked throughout 2001 to protect displaced families from preventable health risks. Progress was monitored – and interventions adapted – by tracking both outputs and impacts using a mix of data gained from measurement, observation and discussion.

The increasing attainment of Sphere standards was used as one of the proxy indicators of the impact of the programme. In January 2001, the average number of people using each waterpoint was 252; by November, it had fallen to 153. These figures were achieved despite the arrival of another 1,200 families in 2001. Not all Sphere standards were achieved. Following a mid-term review, Oxfam made greater efforts to attain the 3.5-$4.5m^2$ shelter indicator in one evacuation centre. Anecdotal evidence from householders suggested it had significant impact on their lives beyond the shelter it provided.

Nevertheless, project staff recognized they had to monitor other data to complement the Sphere standards, which by their nature measured outputs only. These complementary data included morbidity and mortality statistics, which indicated a sizeable reduction in diar-rhoea-related deaths since 2000. The data were collected by, among others, Médecins sans Frontières-Belgium, the ICRC and the government's Regional Epidemiological Surveillance Unit. The resulting information provided an overall picture of the situation, which allowed Oxfam to highlight where morbidity increases were occurring and enabled a speedy response to health problems. Close cooperation between public health and medical agencies enabled all actors to amend their activities to meet any changes.

As Oxfam's annual report for this project notes: "While Sphere was useful as a planning tool, actual needs for facilities were monitored through observation of usage patterns (e.g., no queuing at waterpoints or latrines), the practice of the beneficiaries (e.g., no open defecation), and morbidity and mortality data. If the number of facilities provided did not match Sphere standards, but observations and focus group discussions showed that facilities were still sufficient to meet the needs of the population; extra facilities were not provided."

Tracking a mix of mortality and morbidity data, Sphere standards and people's behaviour and opinions allowed staff to confirm that no negative impact was observed even when all Sphere standards, or outputs, were not achieved. Likewise, tracking changes in outputs and changes in people's lives enabled staff to make connections between project activities and impact, and to adjust activities accordingly. Fine-tuning the project in response to real-time data ensured that resources were more efficiently used and the lives of disaster-affected people were enhanced. ■

One criticism of the Code is that the generalist nature of its principles allows them to be interpreted so broadly that they become meaningless. For others, however, this is the Code's great strength, as it allows for local interpretation and adaptation to different contexts. Tony Vaux, who was part of the evaluation team, recently said that he was "struck by how precise the Red Cross Code actually is. It is important to make the assessment not against each simple principle but also against the paragraph that goes with it and interprets it".

A wide variety of other tools and methods can also be used to assess impact in humanitarian situations – ALNAP's online training modules provide a useful summary of work in this field. New approaches are constantly being invented, for example the Groupe URD's Quality Project (see Box 6.4) and the Humanitarian Accountability Project. The choice ranges from surveys and interviews through to a variety of participatory tools, observation and research methods. The key skill is selecting a judicious mix – and sequence – of tools and methods, appropriate to the circumstances. This in turn usually depends on the purpose and focus of the assessment, the context, the organizations involved and the resources available. The ability to develop appropriately rigorous methods and to adapt these as the study progresses, is at least as important as the knowledge and skill required for individual methods. However, two particularly problematic areas of methodology – participation and attribution – remain the subject of much debate.

Participation – double-edged process?

Much of the evaluation literature presumes an important, if not primary, role for international agencies in delivering relief and developing policy. As a result, there have been consistent calls for greater involvement of affected populations and local actors in assessing impact. Put simply, the argument goes that the key people in assessing how significant change is should be those who are ultimately supposed to benefit.

While at one level this is clearly true, ensuring greater participation of affected people in all stages of project design, implementation and evaluation is not without its problems during emergencies. Despite the limited examples of good practice that seem to exist – and the apparent gap between what humanitarian agencies say and do – a number of lessons are emerging, based on experience and research.

There are several challenges to participatory research in general, which are equally relevant during emergencies. Much research at best ignores existing inequalities in power and social relations (including those between researcher and population in question) and at worst further strengthens or legitimizes these inequalities.

Box 6.4 Tracking three years of impacts in El Salvador

At the turn of the millennium, El Salvador was hit hard by three natural disasters: Hurricane Mitch in 1998, then two major earthquakes in 2001. Initial assessments of the humanitarian response to Mitch in 1998-99 were followed by a series of evaluations and workshops in 2001, forming part of Groupe URD's Quality Project. The process included an assessment of responses to the 2001 earthquakes and an evaluation looking back over the two to three years since Mitch.

This approach mixed a 'real-time' methodology (in the sense that agencies were still working in the area) with an extended approach to develop a more considered assessment of impact over a longer time frame. Thus it built upon the 1999 assessment of the original responses to Hurricane Mitch, and explored the degree to which these original interventions enhanced local capacities to cope with the 2001 earthquakes. The findings suggest some important lessons:

■ Short donor lead-times (pressure to spend money quickly) can lead to poor long-term impact, particularly if it precludes effective local assessment.
■ When effective alliances between exter-nal agencies and local organizations are built, there is a marked gain in quality.
■ Housing reconstruction is more than simply an emergency response – it is a key part of reconstructing livelihoods.

The El Salvador study confirmed one of its central assumptions: that the time at which an evaluation is undertaken will determine how an action is assessed. This is an important lesson for impact assessment. In particular, it appears that some negative consequences tend to become more visible after a period of time, while some of the more positive consequences tend to fade. So there is a danger in assessing impact only at the end, or soon after the end, of a short-term operation. To establish a balanced assessment of both positive and negative effects, subsequent reviews will be necessary. The study also highlighted the importance of 'bilateral' rather than 'multilateral' discussions with agencies, so that any advice offered is likely to be acted upon. And important questions were raised regarding the willingness of donors to accept changing programmes as a result of 'real-time input'. ■

Researchers often fail to respect local time constraints and priorities, or ignore the views of the most marginalized. Participatory processes can lead to the views of certain groups becoming so dominant that researchers fail to cross-check their findings with other methods or sources.

During a participatory impact assessment of Oxfam's Ikafe refugee programme in Uganda, certain groups 'used' the process to lobby for their own purposes, which led to an exaggeration of impact attributable to the project. For example, the host population raised several complaints related to the influx of refugees in general – such as greater insecurity and a decline in moral standards – in addition to issues directly related to the project. On the other hand, their involvement revealed important, but unexpected, secondary effects such as the violation of cultural sites due to some of the resettlement activities that the project was promoting. So, while staff on the project welcomed this new information, they also felt frustrated that the participatory process led to refugees and the host population often criticizing those problems over which the project and its staff had little control.

This suggests that if more participatory methods are to be introduced into humanitarian impact assessments then clear criteria must be developed to define what effective participation means and what it looks like in disaster situations. This will involve distinguishing between different levels and purposes of participation, from consultation in a predetermined aid response through to deeper and fuller local involvement in determining not just responses but the performance of agencies more broadly.

Furthermore, if the findings of participatory research are actually going to be acted upon, then key changes in organizational culture, incentives and behaviour will be needed. These include: rewarding good local analysis and understanding; investing in listening to local people and coping with divergent and dissonant information; and being more able to modify approaches and plans in the light of feedback.

Despite these challenges, there are examples which indicate that participation – applied sensitively – can go a long way to improving programme quality. But firstly, evaluators must recognize that the space and time available for participatory research will vary according to context. This means adapting the range of existing tools and methods to the specificities of emergency situations. Secondly, greater attention must be paid to ensure the views of vulnerable groups are heard while dealing with the political risks of this process – for example, by ensuring the confidentiality of interviewees for security reasons. This in turn has implications for the degree to which evaluation methods can be exposed in the public domain.

Encouraging the participation of local people in assessing the impact of humanitarian aid will ensure that those who judge the value and causes of those impacts are not solely external evaluators. In the DEC's Gujarat evaluation, for example, a formal, independent public opinion survey of over 2,300 people was undertaken in 50 rural and urban areas. This not only helped to reduce potential bias towards the views of agency staff or evaluators, but also revealed important areas of success and major issues of concern, based on a large sample of the population affected. The vast majority of respondents felt satisfied with the quality, accessibility and reliability of food and nutrition services provided, as well as the quality and affordability of drinking water. However, satisfaction with support for rebuilding livelihoods was much lower.

Some of the most negative findings of the survey related to agencies' efforts at consultation and participation. For example, people tended to distrust agencies that were only involved in relief. Many people criticized the way 'participation' and 'consultation' were handled – they felt that many agencies arrived with pre-determined projects and sought only minor modifications or simply free labour from local people. They also felt strongly that agencies' tendency to disregard cultural norms, such as who should eat with whom, was inappropriate – those surveyed wanted to make such choices for themselves. The usefulness of this approach and its findings led the evaluators to recommend that this sort of public opinion survey be a necessary part of future DEC evaluations.

Pressure to prove results creates dangerous disincentives

The challenge of how to attribute impact to individual interventions or agencies remains one of the key issues for impact assessment. This is particularly the case when assessing ultimate impacts, since other influences multiply as one moves further along the 'impact chain'. Because of this – along with demands to improve accountability – there is a tendency, particularly among major donors, to assess only those outcomes for which individual agencies can be held accountable. Two potentially contradictory trends have emerged: a growing emphasis on results-based management and impact assessment; and a growing demand for predefining intermediate outputs and objectives, along with activity and output reporting. This risks creating at least three perverse incentives:

- **Agencies will take fewer risks,** sticking only to those interventions that they can report on most easily – and that, increasingly, they have been contracted to deliver. This will happen even if agencies believe that undertaking other less easily reportable, or different, actions would ultimately make a greater difference to people's lives.
- **Tendency to undermine the role of professional judgement.** Performance indicators within results-based management systems are often selected for ease of measurement, comparison and control, rather than because they accurately reflect the quality of what is achieved. This may not only reduce the discretion of staff in making qualitative judgements about performance, but also restrict their initiative to improve things in the light of changing circumstances and learning. There is a growing fear that aid staff under such regimes are being constrained to serve their paymasters rather than their publics.
- **The pressure to show attributable results will limit cooperation** with other agencies, where it might be more difficult to distinguish between the contributions of different actors – even if cooperation would have a greater longer-term impact.

These disincentives reflect a broader paradox noted by some commentators, that in an era of ever-more standards, quality assurance processes, audits and accountability mechanisms, the trust in public institutions has never been lower. Worse still, if past or future 'results' become the main criteria for the disbursement of funds, then these disincentives will become even greater. This will further compound what many see as the failure of the global aid regime to distribute resources according to need alone.

The problem of attribution can sometimes be addressed by expensive and detailed evaluations which use control groups and comparisons of 'before' and 'after' data. But often the data will not be available and more 'real-time' assessments of performance may be required in order to feed back into decision-making. New approaches are required. One avenue worth exploring is 'contribution analysis' developed in 1999 by John Mayne of the Canadian Auditor General's Office. Mayne recognizes that even if it is difficult to *prove* attribution to outcomes and impacts, agencies can do a lot more to increase understanding and knowledge of their contribution to ultimate results – thereby reducing uncertainty. Contribution analysis looks for 'plausible association' and suggests a number of actions to achieve this:

- recognize and discuss the problem;
- define the logic of the programme and identify links where causality will be hard to show;
- ensure that significant – especially qualitative – changes are adequately documented and recorded;

Evaluations of the impact of aid responses to the 2001 Gujarat earthquake found that a major local women's NGO responded more quickly and efficiently to people's needs than the collective intervention of British NGOs.

Patrick Fuller/ International Federation, India.

- use a limited number of sensitive indicators (this takes thought and effort);
- assess patterns of change over time and space. For example, have changes happened where and when they might be expected, or failed to happen in other locations?
- discuss and test alternative explanations. Put findings into the public domain and invite others to provide more plausible explanations of contribution. Cross-check findings; and
- if necessary, undertake a more in-depth evaluation.

This sort of approach might help in dealing with some attribution problems. However, addressing the disincentives noted earlier will require more radical changes to the ways in which results-based management has been implemented to date. Greater emphasis is needed on partnership and collaboration, and assessing the degree to which different agencies and actors *combine* to promote significant change. This in turn will require some fundamental shifts in how donor governments and their audit and treasury offices relate to aid administrations. There are also implications for the accountability of governments and aid agencies to tax-payers and the public, in whose name the push for narrow attributions of impact and the promotion of donor visibility are often made.

Ethical aspects of impact assessment

There are several ethical dimensions to impact assessment. The first relates to its practice: are the methods and approaches ethical? The second relates to the assessment of how ethical an intervention is, or will be. The third relates to the organizational context within which impact assessments are undertaken.

Impact assessments and evaluations are now seen as key tools across the public sector to assess the effectiveness of policy choices. Many national evaluation societies have recognized the growing responsibility of evaluators by developing codes of conduct and ethical checklists (e.g., those produced by the Canadian and American evaluation societies). These guidelines address, among other things, the competence and ability of the evaluators, their integrity in relation to their stakeholders and their accountability – normally to their clients.

In the development and humanitarian arenas, a number of more specific recommendations have been made regarding the ethics of assessment methods, including:
- avoid raising expectations that can't be met;
- promote evaluation exercises that are meaningful for local people rather than aiming purely to extract information;
- respect informants' personal and time constraints in conducting interviews and research;

- recognize that evaluation processes (particularly in conflict situations) can increase tension, put informants and evaluators at risk and increase trauma for affected populations and staff;
- ensure that, in situations where wide power inequities exist, the voices and experiences of the least powerful and most marginalized are privileged;
- strive to put evaluation reports into the public domain, to enhance transparency and accountability; and
- make the lessons available to others, thereby contributing to improved practice.

While this guidance is useful, a couple of challenges remain which demand good judgement from agencies commissioning evaluations and promoting more ethical practice. The first relates to the appropriate balance between learning and accountability. For example, it may be difficult to ensure openness and honesty among field staff in an evaluative process, if it is known that the results of the evaluation, in its entirety, may be publicly available.

Secondly, any agency has a moral responsibility not just to the population it supports in a particular project, but also to other populations it currently supports, as well as to groups it might support in the future. So evaluations may impose certain 'costs' on individuals, whether staff or affected people, who do not accrue the benefits. In other words, there may be important lessons which need to be drawn from a particular experience for application in future work elsewhere – lessons which may not benefit those involved in that evaluation. These challenges require frameworks for decision-making which enable difficult choices to be made.

Assessing the ethics of decision-making and interventions

In his 1997 article, *Doing the right thing: relief agencies, moral dilemmas and responsibility in political emergencies and war,* Hugo Slim proposed a framework for ethical analysis which asks a number of questions about organizational practice and decision-making. These include assessing the degree to which an agency:

- has a duty-bound (life-saving) or consequentalist (life-enhancing) ethic;
- acts on the basis of sound motives or other considerations;
- gathers enough information to inform its decision-making properly;
- actually has the capacity to do anything differently;
- is adequately committed to debating the consequences of difficult decisions and minimizing the likelihood of negative impacts; and
- promotes the ethical skills and knowledge of its staff.

As a tool for impact assessment, these questions can be useful both for prospective impact assessment (i.e., a forward-looking assessment of the degree to which decisions and programme design will make a difference to people's lives) and for retrospective analysis. Slim's paper includes examples of how this framework can be used to assess the choices made by agencies in Africa's Great Lakes region and Somalia.

There are few recent examples of either prospective or retrospective impact assessments which use Slim's ethical framework to its fullest extent. However, during early 2003, several agencies used elements of this framework in their deliberations over the situation in Iraq. One of the key issues for many international NGOs was whether they should take money from 'belligerent' governments for relief operations associated with any ensuing war.

Within international NGOs, the Iraq crisis led to intense discussions about the likely humanitarian impact of any war, the possible impacts of different types of humanitarian intervention – at operational and advocacy levels – and the potential consequences of accepting or refusing funding from a range of sources for these interventions. Those agencies that have a 'consequentialist' ethic believe that they should be held accountable, at least in part, for the wider, longer-term consequences of their actions. This involves making prospective assessments of anticipated wider outcomes and impacts, which in turn should be based, to a lesser or greater degree, on past assessments and experiences of impact. Thus if, in making decisions about taking certain types of funding, an agency believes that this will ultimately have negative impacts on people's lives, then there is an ethical case for not taking the money. Of course, the difficulty lies in who makes those judgements – aid agencies or local people? And on what basis, given all the problems with attribution and prediction, as well as the difficulties inherent in assessing the counterfactual, i.e., what would have happened if that money had been accepted.

For some agencies these debates were greatly assisted by the kinds of questions that Slim poses. In the end, Oxfam International refused to accept funding from 'belligerent' governments in all but the most exceptional circumstances. For Oxfam this meant only taking such money if there were a situation where they alone could provide humanitarian relief and the only source of funds were from 'belligerent' governments. Others, such as Save the Children, agreed to accept funding from the US and UK governments.

These are not easy questions, but the Iraq example illustrates how a clear framework can prove useful as a means of ethical assessment and in particular for prospective impact assessment purposes. This kind of exploration of organizational values and ethics provides insight into not just how decisions are, or might be, taken, but also the way in which the impacts that the agency achieves are valued and judged. This in turn can start to affect deeper organizational practices, including recruitment and retention of staff. If an agency's values are not clear, then they can be open to distortion, particularly in relationships with powerful donors, which are increasingly moving towards subcontractual rather than partnership arrangements.

Some of the key dimensions of Slim's ethical framework refer to the degree to which organizations gather and use knowledge to make ethical decisions. This relates to issues of organizational learning and the context in which impact assessments occur. Evaluations and assessments may in themselves have little effect on organizational practices and policies if agencies are unwilling, or unable, to learn, follow up and change. Some commentators suggest that agencies should commit to real-time monitoring of their work by independent bodies according to agreed standards. However, significant changes to organizational cultures, incentives and resources are also required if learning and practice within agencies and the sector as a whole are going to improve (see Box 6.5).

Conclusion: make impact central to all programmes

The momentum to improve the ways impact is assessed is liable to continue. It will be driven by accountability requirements as well as the need to learn how to improve practice. A variety of tools, methods and approaches are emerging which, in various combinations, offer practical ways to assess both short- and long-term change. These include frameworks to assess the ethical dimensions of impact, inform decision-making and improve good practice. However, there are potential disincentives to enhancing quality and impact, emerging from the practical experience of implementing results-based management. For progress to be made, it will be important to test different approaches in real situations and understand which approaches are more cost-effective and useful.

Meanwhile, if the organizations undertaking impact assessments do not improve their capacities to learn from them, then no matter how good the methodologies, little real change will occur. Avoiding this entails developing methods that provide useful and timely feedback to decision-making, such as those found in 'real-time' evaluations or 'impact tracking'. It also requires more profound changes in organizational cultures and behaviour so that agencies are better able to cope with discordant and unpalatable findings. Similarly, across the humanitarian sector, improvements in collaborative learning, evaluation and research are required to gather a greater body of evidence and put it in the public domain. The initial efforts

Box 6.5 ALNAP: improving performance through improved learning

The 2002 ALNAP review focused on learning in the humanitarian sector. Information was sought from a number of players within the sector, including bilateral donors, UN agencies, the Red Cross Red Crescent movement and NGOs. In addition, a literature review was undertaken on organizational learning and knowledge management, and learning mechanisms in other sectors were explored. Some of the key findings include:

- **Defensive behaviour,** commonly employed by individuals to protect themselves and their organizations from critical examination, blocks the ability to learn from experience. Overcoming such behaviour requires environments and organizational cultures where the admission of mistakes is encouraged and the allocation of blame discouraged.

- **Examples of good practice** include 'after action reviews', the creative use of information technology (shared drives and intranets), communities of practice, and common networks and sources of learning such as ALNAP, ReliefWeb and the Humanitarian Practice Network.

- **Learning versus accountability.** The humanitarian sector does not adequately distinguish between learning and accountability approaches to evaluation. The increasing use of self-evaluation and internal evaluation approaches may well reflect that externally-driven, accountability-oriented, independent evaluations are not conducive to genuine learning.

- **Low priority for learning.** The development of mechanisms in the humanitarian sector does not compare favourably

with other sectors considered. Analysis of the UK's army, health sector and construction industry reveals stronger political and managerial support and resourcing for learning and training.

- **Unclear objectives, high staff turnover,** weak links between training and action, inappropriate approaches which do not address the preferred learning style of many people, and weak mechanisms for cross-organizational learning are all constraints to improved learning in the sector.

- **The structure and funding** of the sector as a whole contribute to many of the weaknesses identified. These include short-term funding, pressures to maintain low overheads, and the competitive behaviour of agencies in an environment where subcontracting is becoming more common.

The report concludes that there are a number of actions that individual organizations and the sector as a whole could take to improve the current situation. At an organizational level these could involve: assessment of current learning practice and preferred styles; development of organizational programmes to support learning; and clearer signals from the leadership that this is a priority. For the sector as a whole this could include: concerted action to reduce staff turnover; improved resource provision for learning; support to communities of practice; development of mechanisms of cross-organizational learning; setting up of annual sector awards for learning; development of an electronic library; and the establishment of a university for the sector and/or better collaboration with research bodies and universities. ■

of ALNAP and Groupe URD in this regard are encouraging and offer strong platforms on which to build.

Humanitarian agencies aiming to improve their ability to assess whether their work makes a significant or lasting change in people's lives need to look at addressing the following:

Make the question of impact central to *all* programme design, monitoring, reporting and evaluation processes. Starting or stopping programmes on the basis of input and output information alone can put lives at risk. Monitoring and evaluation systems need to provide information in time for good decisions to be made.

Ensure the right stakeholders are involved in judging impact – those who are best placed to assess the degree to which significant change in people's lives has occurred, including the disaster-affected themselves. Make sure their views are cross-checked and validated.

Examine agency culture, behaviour and incentives. Are learning and innovation rewarded tacitly or formally? Are errors and mistakes buried or used as a means to improve? How does the agency react to criticism and negative feedback? What unintended disincentives to improving genuine impact and learning exist?

Explore how to work with others, in specific situations, in order to pool information and learning, and to make more effective and timely decisions. Creating a shared understanding of impacts could act as a barometer of change, which in turn would inform decision-making processes with the realities facing those at risk. This will require all agencies to cede some sovereignty to others and to be more concerned about how change is fashioned together, rather than how single agencies fail or succeed.

Develop ethical frameworks to help navigate through the dilemmas of an era when geo-politics is increasingly played out under the guise of 'humanitarian wars'. Furthermore, a commitment to communicating the knowledge agencies gain from past experiences and impacts will increase the likelihood of sound and ethical decisions being made by themselves and others in the future.

Principal contributor to this chapter and all boxes except Box 6.2 was Chris Roche, who works with Oxfam Community Aid Abroad and is the author of Impact Assessment for Development Agencies: Learning How to Value Change. *Box 6.2 was written by Ian Christoplos, a consultant in humanitarian and rural development issues.*

Sources and further information

Active Learning Network for Accountability and Performance in Humanitarian Action (ALNAP). *Humanitarian Action: Improving performance through improved learning, ALNAP Annual Review 2002.* London: ALNAP, 2002.

Christoplos, I. *Evaluation; The Humanitarian Accountability Project Field Trial in Afghanistan May 2002-July 2002.* Geneva: HAP, 2002. (available at http://www.hapgeneva.org)

Collinson, S. et al. *Politically informed humanitarian programming: using a political economy approach.* Humanitarian Practice Network Paper 41. London: Overseas Development Institute (ODI), 2002.

de Geoffroy, V., Levron, E. and Carid, J. *Iterative Evaluations with Mini-Seminars, Three Years Post Mitch, El Salvador After the 2001 Earthquakes.* Mission No. 1 Summary Report. Plaisans, France: Groupe URD, 2001. (available at http://www.projetqualite.org)

Duffield, M. 'The Symphony of the Damned', in *Disasters,* Vol. 20, No. 3, 1996.

Groupe Urgence Réhabilitation Développement (Groupe URD). *Global Study on the Participation of Affected Populations in Humanitarian Action.* Interim Report, June 2002-September 2002. Plaisans, France: Groupe URD, 2002. (available at http://www.globalstudyparticipation.org/)

Grunewald, F. *Iterative Evaluations with Mini-Seminars, Three Years Post Mitch, El Salvador After the 2001 Earthquakes.* Mission No. 2 Summary Report. Plaisans, France: Groupe URD, 2001. (available at http://www.projetqualite.org/ancient/it_eva.htm)

Macrae, J. et al. *Uncertain power: the changing role of official donors in humanitarian action.* Humanitarian Policy Group Report 12. London: ODI, 2002.

Mayne, J. *Addressing Attribution Through Contribution Analysis: Using Performance Measures Sensibly.* Discussion Paper of the Office of the Auditor General of Canada, 1999. (available at http://www.oag-bvg.gc.ca/domino/other.nsf/html/99dp1_e.html)

Minear, L. *The Humanitarian Enterprise: Dilemmas and Discoveries.* Bloomfield, US: Kumarian Press, 2002.

Neefjes, K. *Participatory Review in Chronic Instability: the Experience of the Ikafe Refugee Settlement Programme in Uganda.* Humanitarian Network Paper 29. London: ODI, 1999.

O'Neill, O. *A Question of Trust.* BBC Reith Lectures 2002. Cambridge: Cambridge University Press, 2002. (available at http://www.bbc.co.uk/radio4/reith2002/)

Organisation for Economic Co-operation and Development (OECD). *Guidance For Evaluating Humanitarian Assistance in Complex Emergencies.* Paris: OECD, 1999.

Porter, T. 'An Embarrassment of Riches', in *Humanitarian Exchange,* 21 July 2002.

Rieff, D. *A Bed for the Night: Humanitarianism in Crisis.* New York: Simon & Schuster, 2002.

Roche, C. *Impact Assessment for Development Agencies: Learning How to Value Change.* Oxford: Oxfam, 1999.

Slim, H. 'Doing the right thing: relief agencies, moral dilemmas and responsibility in political emergencies and war', in *Disasters*, Vol. 21, No. 3, 1997.

Sphere Project. *Humanitarian Charter and Minimum Standards in Disaster Response.* Geneva: Sphere Project, 1998.

Terry, F. *Condemned to Repeat? The Paradox of Humanitarian Action.* New York: Cornell, 2002.

Vaux, T. *Disaster and Vulnerability: SEWA's Response to the Earthquake in Gujarat.* Ahmedabad: Disaster Mitigation Institute with SEWA (Self Employed Women's Association), 2002.

Vaux, T. *The Selfish Altruist: Relief Work in Famine and War.* London: Earthscan, 2001.

Wood, A., Apthorpe, R. and Borton, J. *Evaluating International Humanitarian Action: Reflections from Practitioners.* London: ZED Books/ALNAP, 2001.

Web sites

Active Learning Network for Accountability and Performance in Humanitarian Action (ALNAP) **http://www.alnap.org**

ALNAP's Online Training Modules: Evaluation of Humanitarian Action **http://www.alnap.org/modules/training.html**

American Evaluation Association, Guiding Principles for Evaluators **http://www.eval.org/EvaluationDocuments/aeaprin6.html**

Canadian Evaluation Society, CES Guidelines for Ethical Conduct **http://www.evaluationcanada.ca**

Code of Conduct for the International Red Cross and Red Crescent Movement and NGOs in Disaster Relief **http://www.ifrc.org/publicat/conduct/code**

Global Study on Consultation and Participation by Affected Populations in Humanitarian Action **http://www.globalstudyparticipation.org**

Groupe Urgence Réhabilitation et Développement (Groupe URD) **http://www.urd.org**

Humanitarian Accountability Project **http://www.hapgeneva.org**

Sphere Project **http://www.sphere.org**

chapter 7

Section Two

**Tracking
the system**

Measuring disasters: challenges, opportunities and ethics

chapter 7

How many people are killed or affected by disasters globally every year? Where and when do disasters occur? What causes the casualties? Which countries and communities need help now to save lives? Where should more money be invested to reduce the risk of future disaster?

These questions appear simple, yet the answers are vitally important for informed decision-making. The right kinds of information can prove life-saving. While sudden earthquakes and flash floods make good media stories, other more deadly disasters lurk in the shadows. Humanitarian aid tends to follow in the wake of high-profile conflicts, such as in Afghanistan, the Balkans, East Timor and Iraq. Less reported or less strategically significant crises risk attracting less aid. High-quality data on all kinds of disasters – especially slow-onset famines and war-related disease and mortality – is currently lacking.

Lack of good data has urgent ethical implications. Without it, thousands of disaster victims die before humanitarian organizations even register their need. Poor-quality or inaccurate data in the field can result in flawed decision-making that may cost lives or squander valuable resources. And without accurate information on global needs, no one can accurately judge whether or not humanitarian spending is really impartial.

This chapter examines different kinds of disaster databases – their users, sources and ways of operating. While the idea of a database sounds dry and technical, someone, somewhere has to get hold of the raw information first-hand. Problems in gathering high-quality data in the field are analysed in the context of disasters from Malawi and Congo to Bangladesh and Afghanistan. Simply gaining access to disaster zones in order to gather the right information, or deciding whether people are affected by conflict or famine or disease, can prove enormously difficult.

The chapter examines some of the ethical dilemmas which confront the collation and interpretation of disaster data. During acute emergencies, for example, is it right to divert potentially life-saving resources towards gathering information? Should agencies conduct assessments when they lack the resources to act on that information? Will searching for certain kinds of data put locally-based staff at risk?

Photo opposite page:
Accurate and timely data can save lives. But too often, particularly in the aftermath of disaster or conflict and in famine zones, reliable data are lacking.

Yoshi Shimizu/ International Federation, Sierra Leone.

We conclude by arguing that donors have neglected the significance of data collection for too long. High-quality information gathering is the nervous system of the humanitarian enterprise. Without it, any form of principled action – whether now or in the future – is paralysed.

Global disaster databases and users

Developing a global database measuring the effects of disasters seems a straightforward and useful idea. A global database can provide essential information on the occurrence, recurrence and location of disasters and disaster trends over time. It can also give an idea of the magnitude of their impact on countries and affected populations.

The emergencies database (EM-DAT) operated by the Centre for Research on the Epidemiology of Disasters (CRED), based at Louvain Catholic University in Belgium, has attempted to collect, analyse and provide disaster data since 1988 – with considerable success, but also not without great difficulty. Other databases exist, operated by insurance companies (such as Swiss Re/Sigma and Munich Re/Natcat), national or regional groups (e.g., DesInventar in Latin America) or specialist centres in academic institutions. They all have their strengths but arguably their greatest collective weakness is that these databases are not inter-connected and comparisons between them are difficult.

Global databases like EM-DAT serve a global market and are widely used by a diverse group of clients with an interest in disaster preparedness and response. These users and their needs include:

- Multilateral organizations: such as the World Bank or United Nations (UN), to mobilize funding for disaster preparedness or mitigation activities.
- Bilateral donors: for example Organisation for Economic Co-operation and Development (OECD) countries, to determine priorities for the global allocation of funds (including changing priorities).
- Host governments: e.g., Philippines, to justify national allocations to disaster preparedness or mitigation activities.
- The International Red Cross and Red Crescent Movement and non-governmental organizations (NGOs): to help determine priority countries for interventions; to monitor trends over time and assess the need for further action.
- Academics, researchers and students: to place localized or national events in a global context; to provide baseline data for research purposes and teaching.
- Insurance industry: to help validate and/or complement their own databases.
- Military: purpose not clear, but probably to monitor global security (as some disasters can have a destabilizing effect); to develop simulation exercises for their staff.

■ Interested individuals and humanitarian activists: who use information to lobby their own governments for additional funds or more political support.

The needs of these 'global' users are clearly very different from those of a disaster manager at field level who needs reliable first-hand information to make difficult decisions about the allocation of scarce resources. Several attempts have been made to link global databases like EM-DAT with local and national disaster information systems. However, since such systems are designed for national rather than global purposes, they collect somewhat different data and use it in varying ways.

Disaster – a relative term

Different definitions of disaster are often used. Some local, national and regional databases do not appear to have a distinct definition for disaster at all. They may include any event, however small, that results in loss of life or damage – for example, someone being eaten by a crocodile or three houses collapsing after a minor earth tremor. While this is a tragedy for the individuals and their families, it does not constitute a disaster according to EM-DAT or UN criteria.

EM-DAT classifies an event as a disaster if at least "10 people are killed and/or 100 or more are affected and/or an appeal for international assistance is made or a state of emergency declared". This definition is easy to apply in practice and will include most disaster types – more in fact than if the UN definition were used. The UN's definition of disaster is, according to a 1992 disaster training programme: "A serious disruption of the functioning of a society, causing widespread human, material or environmental losses which exceed the capacity of the affected society to cope using only its own resources".

EM-DAT aims to catch significant events as defined by the UN, but needs to avoid information overload. It therefore excludes those that do not meet either the UN or EM-DAT definition. EM-DAT will capture some events that the UN definition misses, for example, serious transport and technological accidents. While each single accident may be fairly localized, cumulatively they account for a significant mortality and morbidity. Having captured the disaster event, however, the definition of what constitutes an 'affected' person remains highly debatable.

Other global databases, operated by major reinsurance companies such as Munich Re or Swiss Re, are not always accessible to the public and tend to concentrate on insurable events and damage which can be measured in monetary terms. Therefore they are biased towards natural disasters (earthquakes, floods, subsidence) rather than complex (often uninsurable) emergencies involving war, famine or disease. They also focus on countries with business potential – middle income and richer countries which potentially have more to lose, in economic terms, than poorer countries. Estimates of financial losses may bear little relation to levels of humanitarian need. The coping capacity of poorer countries is often so undermined by endemic poverty that even a relatively small disaster can trigger enormous human needs – yet financial losses remain small when compared to richer countries. Not surprisingly, insurance companies appear to value risk to property more highly than human costs and their data should be interpreted in this light (see Box 7.1).

Importantly, most databases, including EM-DAT, miss significant human suffering in complex emergencies involving conflict, political violence, famine and disease. This is mainly because databases rely on secondary data provided by others – and reporting from complex emergencies, as we shall see later, is notoriously difficult.

So different data sets are collected for diverse purposes and consequently use different criteria for inclusion or exclusion. In some cases, databases have no transparent criteria at all. Comparisons between the different types of database are therefore difficult or misleading.

Box 7.1 Munich Re – values exposed

In March 2003, the reinsurance giant Munich Re, which tracks natural disaster trends across the globe, announced its latest publication, *Topics: Natural Catastrophes 2002*, saying: "Munich Re's experts have developed an index for the world's 50 largest metropolitan areas which quantifies their risk potentials for all natural hazards, including the vulnerabilities and concentrations of values. As might be expected, metropolitan areas like Tokyo-Yokohama, San Francisco, and Los Angeles are particularly high up the scale, whilst others, like Rio de Janeiro, Delhi, or Lagos are much lower down the scale because the exposed values and the hazards there are smaller. The index makes it possible for the first time to make a realistic comparison of the risk of various megacities."

Not surprisingly, Munich Re rates rich-world cities in Japan and the United States as at greater risk from natural hazards than poor-world cities such as Rio, Delhi or Lagos. Munich Re's analysis clearly focuses on cities with a high insurance density located in areas of high earthquake, and therefore mega-disaster, risk. The less 'catastrophic' disasters afflicting developing world cities, such as poor water and sanitation, low air quality, dangerous slum dwellings and contagious diseases, are more insidious, silent urban disasters whose effects barely figure on the economic bottom line. Yet these urban hazards probably exact a much higher toll on human life and health than the once-in-a-century mega-disasters. The 'exposed values' of the insurance markets are clearly a world away from 'humanitarian values'. ■

Method in the madness?

Just as disaster databases differ in their methodologies, so too do assessments from the disaster front line. Assessments can measure a whole range of different things – physical damage, economic losses, humanitarian needs, impacts (of disaster or of aid), local capacities, risks, vulnerabilities, food security, household economy. They may be initial, rapid, epidemiological, qualitative, quantitative or cluster-based assessments. But they are mostly carried out with a similar purpose in mind – to estimate the scale and severity of the disaster, to identify those affected and to determine the level and type of needs.

Although tools and methods exist for collecting disaster data, many were created originally for use in development situations and have been adapted for emergency situations. The methods themselves are often not objectively tested or validated under acute emergency conditions. There is little standardization between agencies. Each has its own preferred approach or variation. Common methodological problems include a lack of consensus over agreed criteria (how does one define who is 'affected' or 'in need'?) and sampling sizes (how many households need to be assessed to gain a reliable overview of the scale and severity of the disaster?).

Often, similar methods are used by different organizations, but in a variety of different ways. This failure to standardize methods, definitions and criteria means that direct comparisons of results cannot be made due to methodological differences. In addition, data collection methods used by different agencies are often not clearly explained or evaluated, so it is hard to judge the quality of the data and 'guesstimates' that are generated. Errors or misunderstandings in collecting and recording data (including observer errors) are not uncommon.

Problems occur in the interpretation of data too. Many disasters are complex and politically fraught. Well-developed analytical skills are needed to make sense of the data in chaotic and highly politicized contexts, especially when pre-disaster baseline data is lacking. Relief workers often lack the necessary skills and training for rigorous analysis under challenging field conditions.

A number of unanswered questions remain. We know that many deaths in some types of emergency go unreported, but it is not clear which deaths. Is the death of a single woman or unaccompanied child less likely to be reported? Or is failure to report deaths more a feature of geography (there is no one nearby or locally responsible to report to)? Perhaps deaths from specific causes are less likely to be reported (e.g., war wounds, HIV/AIDS or death in childbirth). Or maybe there are no surviving family members left to make the report. We simply do not know. Yet a better understanding of these problems is essential in trying to estimate deaths, especially in war and famine zones.

In short, there is a high risk of inaccuracy and partiality in data collection, due to problems with physical access, limited resources, differing methodologies and the agenda or bias of data sources (see Box 7.2).

Prioritizing data sources

Databases like EM-DAT use data from various sources. In the aftermath of a disaster, needs assessments are usually conducted by district-level government teams, UN agencies, Red Cross Red Crescent teams or NGOs. These primary reports detail specific geographic areas or localized problems and provide essential insights into disaster-affected areas. However, disasters do not respect borders and many such reports lack an overview of the situation, especially when several districts, countries or regions are affected. Moreover, certain agencies have specific mandates – to care for children, refugees or the disabled – so their assessments may be angled towards these groups.

Disaster assessment data is often widely shared and repackaged in the form of consolidated reports or secondary data. Consolidated reports – for example, UN or Red Cross Red Crescent country or regional reports, or national-level government analyses – often provide a better overview of the problem. As well as incorporating primary data, consolidated reports make use of early warning system data where it exists. EM-DAT prioritizes secondary data – mainly from UN and Red Cross Red Crescent sources – as it provides an independent overview. This data is often supported by other secondary data from insurance companies, research centres, bilateral donors or host governments.

Sometimes tertiary data is used in the absence of anything judged to be more reliable – such as summary reports using data synthesized from primary and secondary sources. Media reports may be used (e.g., Agence France Presse, BBC or Reuters) when best estimates of deaths or damage are given – particularly for transport accidents or disasters where the key disaster relief organizations are not involved. In media reports, the sources of the original data are usually not clear or not cited, making it hard to judge the credibility of the data. However in some cases, media reports are the first and only source of information and to ignore them would risk missing some disasters.

Not surprisingly, serious discrepancies in figures may emerge when comparing data from different sources. Often after scrutiny, either UN data or information provided by the government will be used. Sometimes differences are irreconcilable. In those cases, both sets of figures are given in the accompanying comments on the data, so that users can decide for themselves which are the most relevant for their purposes.

Many data problems occur at, or shortly after, the point of collection. While this may prove inconvenient for database operators, discrepancies in data collection can mean the difference between life and death for some of the world's most vulnerable people.

Box 7.2 Obstacles to better data collection

Physical access

- Often agencies simply cannot visit areas devastated by war or disaster in order to gather the right information, because it's too difficult, too dangerous or too remote. Disasters leave bridges broken and roads impassable. Conflict not only hampers immediate access, landmines may prevent access for years to follow.
- There is a sheer logistical challenge of how to mobilize professional, well-trained assessment teams rapidly in a challenging or dangerous environment.
- Gathering data uses valuable resources (people, time, money, equipment such as helicopters, vehicles) which may be needed to save lives in acute emergencies.
- A vicious spiral can develop where no access leads to no information, no appeals, no resources, no aid agencies and no one on the ground to gather the information needed to break the cycle.

Methodology

- There are no standard definitions of what a disaster is or what constitutes a disaster-affected person. Is HIV/AIDS a disaster?
- Agencies differ over how, where and when they gather disaster data. They use a variety of often unspecified and unevaluated data collection methods and tools, over differing time frames. They may apply findings from one survey area across a much wider area. Comparisons of results are therefore very difficult.
- Different definitions and interpretations are used that often relate to the variety of purposes for which data is collected and used.
- Lack of accurate pre-crisis baseline data (on population numbers, mortality and morbidity rates) makes it hard to judge the effects of particular disasters. Information management systems are often shattered or non-existent during disasters and conflicts.
- Deaths are routinely under-reported in certain types of disaster such as conflict, famine and epidemics.
- Problems in data interpretation and analysis: some disasters are complex and multi-causal. Did the person die as a result of the drought/flood or because of concurrent famine, economic crisis, epidemic or conflict?

Bias

- Data is never entirely neutral. Different data sources will have different agendas.
- Governments may have political reasons for over- or under-reporting the effects of disaster. They may overstate the effects of disaster to gain additional aid or understate it to minimize problems in the face of public criticism. Governments may try to prevent data collectors from gathering sensitive data or discredit their findings.
- Aid organizations may only focus on the numbers of people they feel capable of helping: the 'beneficiaries'. This figure will depend on an agency's resources, mandate and access. The total of beneficiaries is usually lower than the total of those affected or in need.
- Disaster-affected people may have incentives not to report deaths to authorities: they may lose out on aid rations, they may not wish to attract the attention of hostile authorities. There may simply be no benefit to reporting deaths in the family, or no one nearby to report to. ■

As the following example from Bangladesh shows, the key to good data gathering – and therefore to saving lives – lies in gaining access to those in need.

Active surveillance saves lives

In conflict zones, physical factors often inhibit access to disaster victims. Agencies simply can't visit areas devastated by war or disaster in order to gather the right information, because it's too difficult, too dangerous or too remote.

As violence, disaster or famine increase, so do population movements. These are often unplanned and unpredicted, making it extremely difficult to get accurate population or death data. Most victims die away from relief centres, hospitals or registration points and therefore go unreported. Even in clearly defined refugee or relief camps (which offer more opportunity for collecting reliable data), many deaths are not recorded. Previously unpublished data from refugee camps in south-eastern Bangladesh in the 1990s clearly illustrates this problem (see Figure 7.1).

Deaths in the camps were recorded using two different methods: 'passive' surveillance (deaths reported at health centres or the camp administrator's office) and 'active' surveillance (counting graves, interviews with religious leaders and relatives of the

Figure 7.1
Active and passive mortality surveillance compared: data from 12 refugee camps in south-eastern Bangladesh, 1992-1993.

Source: P. Diskett, 1997.

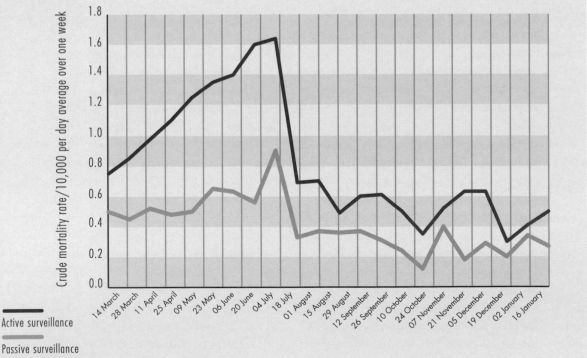

Active surveillance

Passive surveillance

dead). When comparing deaths from both systems, it is clear that many deaths were not officially recorded, especially during the early, acute phase of the crisis.

When compared to international standards (where more than two deaths per 10,000 people per day indicates an emergency out of control), the discrepancy in death rates obtained from the two methods represented the difference between a situation under control and a looming disaster. Most strikingly, from mid-May to mid-June – just before the height of the crisis – passive surveillance data suggested that mortality was decreasing, while active surveillance showed it was actually increasing. At one point, the active method measured nearly three times more deaths than the passive method.

If decisions had been based only on passive surveillance data, the severity of the deteriorating situation (between March and July) would have been catastrophically underestimated. Active surveillance revealed the need for urgent action whereas passive surveillance did not. This provides a valuable example of how accurate and timely data can be used to save lives.

There seemed to be three clear reasons for the under-reporting of the passive surveillance system:

- The name of the deceased would be removed from the family's food ration card. Refugees rapidly calculated that the value of the free burial shroud (given as an incentive for reporting mortality) was considerably less than the value of a continuing food ration.
- Those living furthest from health centres and government offices were less likely to report deaths, especially as there was no apparent benefit. Likewise, the further away families lived, the fewer were the deaths detected by clinic staff.
- The government at the time was promoting repatriation. Many refugees were afraid to return home to a situation that arguably had not changed. They did not want to do anything that would attract the attention of government officials, as they feared they would then be targeted for repatriation.

Calculating mortality in complex emergencies

Refugee camps are fairly clearly defined, making active surveillance possible. However, in war and famine zones, people may be scattered in remote, inaccessible or insecure areas. Active surveillance for all locations is clearly impossible. In complex emergencies, attempts have been made to estimate death rates based on random retrospective mortality surveys, or on active surveillance in selected locations. These localized rates are then multiplied up to estimate deaths across a wider area (see Box 7.3). One series of mortality studies estimated that 3.3 million people had died due to war in the Democratic Republic of the Congo (DRC), from 1998-2002. Of these deaths, 86 per cent were caused by communicable diseases and malnutrition.

Box 7.3 Counting the cost of conflict, famine and disease

The famine in southern Sudan during 1998-99 resulted in high levels of malnutrition and mortality among both adults and children. Estimates of deaths occurring as a direct result of the famine varied from 60,000 to 300,000. Famine-afflicted people often gathered around airstrips and distribution points in crowded, unsanitary conditions with only limited access to health care. The combination of destitution, malnutrition and increased risk of infection led to very high death rates in these sites. However, mortality rates in the countryside were unknown. They may have been higher, due to the effects of conflict or lack of health care and food. Or they may have been lower, since the risks of infection are less among more widely dispersed populations, and those living on the land may have had access to some food and shelter. We simply do not know. So attempts to apply death rates from around airstrips to the whole of the countryside are clearly problematic.

During 2000-01, attempts were made to assess war-related mortality in the Democratic Republic of the Congo (DRC). On behalf of the New York-based NGO, International Rescue Committee (IRC), an epidemiologist and relief workers carried out a series of random cluster surveys to assess mortality. Using pre-war population data as their starting point, they made some assumptions about population growth and variations in mortality rates. Rigorous statistical methods were then used to calculate mortality across the region. They estimated that a staggering 2.5 million people had died as a result of the war, over a 32-month period from August 1998 to April 2001, deaths which were in addition to what would be expected normally. They found that the overwhelming majority of deaths were due to common communicable diseases and malnutrition. Just 14 per cent of deaths (350,000) resulted directly from violence over the same period.

In order to check their results, the team then recalculated their figures changing some basic underlying assumptions (e.g., 'normal baseline' mortality rates in the areas, variations in mortality rates across the surveyed areas and variations in the impact of the war). The results that they came up with were still shockingly high (over 2 million deaths) regardless of which basic assumptions were modified.

In summary, they found that "in four of the seven areas visited, about 8 per cent of the population are dying annually and deaths outnumber births in those areas by about two or three to one". There was an absence of younger children as a result of fewer births and extraordinarily high death rates in this vulnerable group. They concluded that "approximately 2.5 million deaths have occurred in DRC, making this perhaps the most deadly African conflict in recent decades". A subsequent nationwide mortality survey, conducted by IRC in late 2002, revised the death toll upwards to 3.3 million.

One big message emerges: regardless of debates about which figures are nearest the mark, the scale of death and suffering is enormous and should trigger a major humanitarian response. At the very least, doubt about the statistics should lead to greater efforts to establish better data on which to base a proportionate response. ■

Such excess mortality calculations are often controversial, as they are based on a range of assumptions whose accuracy is difficult to prove – for example, that similar mortality conditions to the survey site apply across wider areas, or that pre-disaster population and mortality statistics are available. Conflicts, however, lead to the collapse of public services – and information systems are among the first to be affected. Often, we don't have accurate baseline data. For example, how many people lived in the area before the disaster? What were the normal (pre-disaster) death and malnutrition rates? Did they vary at different times of year?

Accurate population figures are required to estimate the scale of a major disaster, calculate death rates and plan interventions. Yet such data may not be easy to obtain. For example, in Goma in 1994, approximately 850,000 people arrived from Rwanda within a five-day period, while others fled to Tanzania, northern Burundi and different locations in Zaire (now DRC). According to the subsequent evaluation of responses to the genocide, in the ensuing chaos, the number displaced from Rwanda was inflated by as much as 40 per cent and a census was delayed (for logistical and political reasons). In northern Iraq in 1991, *The Lancet* reported that a random survey estimated the displaced population to be 70,000, while a figure of 128,000 was provided by the authorities.

Population figures may be inflated by refugees, agencies or governments for political reasons, to attract more aid or simply because the speed, scale and complexity of population movements makes registration difficult. Numbers may also be underestimated. A 1990 study from Pakistan, published in the *Journal of Biosocial Sciences*, concluded that the Afghan refugee population was underestimated by at least 10 per cent – which meant around 250,000 Afghans were not included in official planning figures.

Disasters are dynamic, rapidly evolving phenomena and not single, static events – so not surprisingly, numbers of those affected change over time. It is not always clear if these changes are 'real' or simply reflect changing criteria for data collection, different definitions, poor reporting, inaccurate counting or political massaging. Further work is urgently needed to develop and test appropriate methods for estimating deaths in conflict zones.

If the figures from DRC and other war or famine zones are correct, it would appear that mortality and suffering from conflict and food insecurity globally far exceed the total of those killed or affected by 'natural' disasters. Criticisms have been levied at the DRC study from a methodological viewpoint – in particular, the underlying assumptions and population figures have been challenged. However, it is currently the best estimate we have using rigorous statistical methods and confirms the problems of accessing and analysing data from war zones.

Furthermore, it is unethical simply to ignore data from complex emergencies and focus only on data from safer, more accessible areas. Equally, it is wrong to discount or discredit data just because it brings unwelcome news. Those in greatest need are often the least visible and have no political voice. There is a moral imperative for humanitarian agencies to investigate proactively precisely those areas where data sets are incomplete yet may point to a major, but hidden, catastrophe. When findings are disputed or contested, further verification becomes even more important, to confirm or refute reports and to identify opportunities to prevent further suffering.

Are malnutrition and disease disasters?

The mortality surveys in DRC suggested that disease and malnutrition accounted for the vast majority of war-related deaths from 1998-2002. Infectious diseases cause significant morbidity and mortality in non-war situations as well. According to the World Health Organization (WHO), communicable diseases (mainly acute respiratory infections, HIV/AIDS, diarrhoea, tuberculosis, malaria and measles) claimed 13.3 million lives worldwide in 1998. Many of these diseases are endemic (always present) but have the potential to become an epidemic (WHO definition: "an unusually large or unexpected increase in the number of cases of the disease for a given place, period or time"). We need to know what is normal (where and when) in order to determine what is abnormal. As seen in the DRC example, this baseline is often not available for war zones, rendering calculations of excess mortality very difficult.

Because communicable diseases are so common in poor countries and health infrastructure is often weak, many deaths go unreported. A long-term burden of disease and underlying malnutrition, with the additional threat of epidemics, can have a severe impact on the economy of a country and the life of its people – even in the absence of war. A review of how these problems are analysed and reported on is urgently needed.

In addition, we should ask the question: is the current HIV/AIDS epidemic a disaster? In many countries and regions, the answer would be a strong yes. But disaster statistics and databases rarely include HIV/AIDS deaths. In Kenya, for example, deaths from HIV/AIDS have been estimated to be equivalent to two 747 jets crashing every day in the country. If indeed the latter happened every day, there would be an international outcry. But because deaths caused by HIV/AIDS happen slowly, often secretly and hidden from view, somehow the statistics have less impact.

The HIV/AIDS pandemic has reached such devastating proportions – particularly in sub-Saharan Africa – that all data on HIV/AIDS and other disease epidemics should now be routinely included in global disaster databases, to place the severity of the situation (and of other disasters) in context. In order to promote a global humanitarian system which responds in a genuinely impartial way to all suffering according to need alone, reliable data on all types of disaster is an essential first step.

Currently, the effects of both epidemics and malnutrition are under-reported in global disaster databases. A new categorization of disasters is needed, which reports on both the primary impacts of disaster (earthquake, flood, war) and the secondary impacts (malnutrition and disease). The question of how to distinguish between deaths from primary or secondary causes presents major methodological challenges and further research is needed. In the meantime, as a pragmatic compromise, databases could develop a new category of disaster – *complex emergency*, which would include mortality from both primary and secondary impacts (e.g., war, violence, hunger and disease).

Inextricable causes – the case of Malawi

When comparing information from a variety of sources – especially regarding complex emergencies – there is often a lack of agreement over the numbers killed or affected by a disaster and the extent, severity or cost of the damage. These differences reflect several common, underlying problems – such as how to define who is

Simply gaining access to some disaster zones and highly vulnerable groups (e.g. women), in order to gather the right information, can prove very difficult.

Thorkell Thorkelsson/ International Federation, Afghanistan.

Chapter 7 **Measuring disasters**

'affected' and by what. Malawi, which has become caught in a cycle of floods, drought, food insecurity and epidemics, clearly illustrates these problems (see Box 7.4). The current food crisis results from droughts that disrupted normal agricultural patterns (1994-95, late 1990s-2002) and floods that damaged or washed away crops (1997, 2000-01, 2003).

Like many other countries in southern Africa, Malawi is also in the grip of the HIV/AIDS epidemic, which has seriously undermined its mainly rural economy, as people are too ill or weak to work. More than one in seven Malawians of productive age (15-49) is infected with HIV. The situation is further complicated by an ongoing cholera epidemic, which by the end of 2002 had, according to WHO, led to around 33,000 cases and almost 1,000 deaths. Meanwhile, the Malawi Economic Justice Network, a collection of 45 local NGOs and church groups, claims that – on the basis of medical reports, death certificates, affidavits and media reports – 398 people died from starvation between December 2001 and March 2002 (see Chapter 2, Box 2.1). And according to Ben Wisner, a US-based disaster expert, reports from NGOs working in rural areas suggested that up to 10,000 Malawians – including some with AIDS – may have died by May 2002. When extracting information from reports like these for entry into a database, serious questions arise:

- Is this ongoing food crisis a single event spread over a number of years or is it a series of separate but linked events? How should it be recorded?
- Do we record the continuing food crisis or the floods or drought to which the food crisis is secondary?
- Should deaths be attributed to hunger, disease, floods or drought?

If we record only the primary events (flood and drought), we risk underestimating the total impact. While very few died as a result of the floods, we simply don't know how many have suffered or died as a result of the secondary impact (hunger, malnutrition and epidemics). These 'casualties' are either not accurately reported or completely missed.

It is often easier to extract data on single, clear-cut events like earthquakes. In contrast, food crises are spread over a prolonged time period, cover a large geographic area and usually occur in areas where poverty is endemic (and where infrastructure and reporting systems are weak). Food crises and famine are less clearly defined, as they have multiple (but linked) causes. With drought, flood, hunger, disease and poverty so inextricably intertwined – and with different data sources focusing on different aspects of the crisis – attributing numbers of killed or affected to particular causes becomes virtually impossible.

The data problems identified in Malawi are not unique – similar issues are evident in reports from Ethiopia and the Democratic People's Republic of Korea (DPRK). The

Box 7.4 Defining who is disaster-affected in Malawi, 1997-2003

An examination of over 20 reports on Malawi's food crisis, used by EM-DAT, graphically illustrates many of the problems faced when quantifying the scale and severity of ongoing disasters.

For a start, humanitarian organizations use a plethora of different terms in their reports, such as 'displaced', 'most vulnerable', 'affected populations', 'homeless', 'victims', 'most vulnerable affected', 'in need', 'beneficiaries', 'injured' or 'sick'. Do these terms refer to the same people, to different categories of 'affected' people or to degrees of need? It is far from clear. There is, in short, no widely used definition for someone 'affected' by disaster. Variations in numbers across the different reports almost certainly reflect the different criteria and terminology in use rather than objective differences.

Numbers may be expressed in different ways; for example, 'families', 'households', 'individuals/people', 'vulnerable groups' or 'communities'. It is often not clear, even in the same report, if the people, households or communities referred to are the same or different, or if the vulnerable groups mentioned are an additional group or are already included in the overall total. As a result, reports about the impact of floods in Malawi in January 2003 range from 15,000 *people* affected to over 50,000 *households* affected. Flooding restricted access to the most severely affected areas and, as a result, numbers were often 'best guesses' rather than 'real' figures. Agencies used different data collection tools and assessment methods (usually unspecified), which may also account for some differences.

When analysing the subsequent food crisis, the number 'affected' and the final number of 'beneficiaries' rarely agree even in the same report. This is often because agencies' management or logistical problems mean that not all those in need can be reached, so numbers are revised downwards. Thus in June 2002, the World Food Programme (WFP) reported that 3.2 million Malawians were in need, yet by August only 541,300 beneficiaries had been reached. WFP then increased this figure to 2.3 million by December. The numbers 'affected' also vary between reports from different agencies, often because they refer to a different time frame or only cover part of the country.

Even in the more accessible drought-prone areas, deaths were under-reported as most deaths occur away from relief centres or clinics and the health information system in Malawi is, as in many poor countries, weak. Deaths are also under-reported because many are perceived to have died from infectious diseases (exacerbated by underlying malnutrition), rather than from pure starvation. The real scale and severity of the food crisis in Malawi, in terms of numbers killed, affected or malnourished, is therefore not known with any reliability. While it is possible to draw rough conclusions about the range of numbers affected, there is little credible information on mortality due to the crisis. ∎

Malawi example confirms that the quality of information in any database is only as good as the expertise of data collectors and the appropriateness and reliability of the data collection tools and methods used.

Dangers and dilemmas of disaster data

Reliable information is needed to support decision-making at every level. However, it is also clear that reliable information is no guarantee of good programme decisions, management or quality. Like any tool, data have to be used responsibly and ethically to be effective. Collecting data at the height of a disaster – when there are pressing and obvious humanitarian needs – can pose particular ethical dilemmas. With resources scarce and hard-pressed, should time, money and effort be spent on gathering data or on saving lives as quickly as possible? This dilemma became acute in northern Afghanistan in the wake of the devastating earthquakes in 1998, high in the snow-bound Hindu Kush mountains. The only way to access shattered villages quickly enough was by helicopter. But very few aircraft were available in the early stages of the disaster, and the poor mountain weather meant they could only fly at certain times. Should they be used to ferry doctors into disaster-struck villages and bring injured Afghans back to field hospitals? Or should they simply fly from one disaster site to another, assessing overall needs as quickly as possible? Should precious space be given to journalists, who could publicize the tragedy across the world and thereby help raise life-saving funds?

There are no easy answers. Some would argue that it is unethical to delay relief responses until accurate, reliable data have been gathered, as delays in assistance can prolong suffering and lead to avoidable deaths. Others would argue that relief programmes should be based on objective assessments of disaster impact and community needs. In Afghanistan, how would you know whether there was another village over another mountain ridge which was even harder-hit than the villages that you had already reached – unless you did a full assessment? There is clearly a trade-off between the time spent collecting data and the time needed to get relief programmes up and running quickly enough to save lives. It becomes a matter of humanitarian judgement.

For some far-flung disasters, there simply isn't enough political will or media interest to raise the money for humanitarian assessments or relief. Africa is littered with examples of disasters too dangerous or remote to raise sufficient international interest: eastern DRC from 1998 to the present; vast tracts of Angola, prior to the fall of UNITA in 2002 (see Chapter 1, Box 1.2); and Liberian refugees in Guinea in 1991. Very little aid means that few relief workers are active in the region. That in turn means data are patchy or non-existent. Without reliable data on the scale of the problem, appeals cannot be launched, awareness cannot be raised and aid does not arrive. This creates a vicious spiral of suffering which may go unnoticed by aid agencies and governments alike. Is it ethical to ignore areas where there is little international interest? The answer is obviously no, but the question of how to get reliable data under such circumstances remains.

Data sets are sometimes challenged by those who cannot or will not (often for political reasons) accept the results. One of the more notorious examples is that of the food crisis in DPRK from 1995-98. Many close observers put deaths from a series of floods and malnutrition at between 800,000 and 1.5 million. Some estimates were as high as 3 million lives lost. Figures given by a government official in 1999, however, suggested nearer 222,000 had died. The Pyongyang government has consistently rejected any higher figures. The truth will probably never be known. Equally, the scale of the disaster described in the DRC mortality study is frightening because of the immensity of suffering and the wide-ranging implications for governments and international agencies. The report could be interpreted to reflect badly on the international community for failing to mitigate the situation, unwilling perhaps to respond to large-scale human suffering in areas of little geo-strategic interest.

Meanwhile, is it ethical to collect data on disaster impacts and humanitarian needs, if there is no intention of responding to those needs? The world's high-profile crises are replete with stories of 'assessment fatigue' – disaster-affected people exhausted by answering the same questions posed over and over by a stream of different aid agencies, many of whom they may never see again. Such practice is arguably unethical, but with one notable caveat: even without an immediate response, research data from the field can be used to lobby for change and useful lessons can be learned to benefit similarly affected populations in the future. But if this is the purpose, then data collection must be part of a wider information dissemination and advocacy policy.

Humanitarian advocacy itself leads to a range of new dilemmas, explored more fully in Chapter 1. The data used in advocacy can be open to manipulation for political purposes. Those in power may not like the message being delivered and may therefore try to discredit the evidence or discourage data collection in the future. A number of examples exist where data collectors have been arrested, jailed and even beaten because they have uncovered unwanted news – perhaps about atrocities or high death rates in certain areas. Agencies have been banned from collecting data and their staff threatened with expulsion from the country. Specific cases of such intimidation from Uganda in the 1980s and Bangladesh in the 1990s are too sensitive to describe in detail, since individuals remain at risk to this day.

These problems are more common in insecure areas where serious human rights abuses are committed by controlling authorities – for example, aid manipulation, political violence, torture, rape or genocide. Aid agencies have to make difficult judgements about whether to use their data to speak out and risk expulsion, or remain silent and be accused of colluding with the perpetrators. Expulsion means agencies can no longer protect and assist potential victims, nor can they gather the data needed to lobby for change. Many agencies find a compromise by keeping quiet in public, discreetly releasing information in a way that is non-attributable and simultaneously continuing their life-saving work. Often, different NGOs take different approaches according to their mandate and the context, as has happened in the southern Africa food crisis (see Chapter 3).

The benefits of sharing and using reliable information are self evident. However there are also risks. In conflict zones, aid agencies may be working alongside local military factions or international contingents. There is a risk that aid agencies may be fed false information, for political or military purposes. They may feel unable to share information with the military because it could be manipulated and used as military intelligence, perhaps leading to further suffering. Relief agencies are rightly concerned about issues of impartiality and neutrality. Any suspicion that information, provided by them, was being used for military purposes would jeopardize their security and credibility. Guidelines drawn up in 2002 by the Geneva-based Steering Committee for Humanitarian Response recommend that data shared between humanitarian agencies and the military should be confined to information on security conditions, conditions in shared logistical space (airfields, aid movements, transport), and general estimates about the scope of the emergency.

Challenges and recommendations

It is urgently necessary to improve the quality of data on all kinds of disaster, but especially for war and famine zones. Data quality needs to be improved from the point of collection right through the whole process to entry in global databases. Improvements in the quality of data collected at source would have a highly beneficial impact on the utility of global databases such as EM-DAT. Good-quality information is needed to inform decision-making at all levels. Recommendations to improve data quality – at both national and international levels – are summarized in Boxes 7.5 and 7.6. Key recommendations include:

- **Standardize disaster definitions** and data collection systems, to enable direct comparisons.
- **Improve proactive data collection** in 'forgotten disasters' – especially chronic conflict and famine zones.
- **Create new data categories** (e.g., 'complex emergency') to capture the full, combined effects of war, malnutrition and disease.

These recommendations need to be sufficiently financed to become reality. There is a consensus in the humanitarian community that information projects are not yet adequately supported by donors. It is important to raise awareness in the donor community about the need for, and benefits of, better quality and more timely disaster data. The difficulties associated with gathering data from war and famine zones mean that mortality and suffering during such disasters is underestimated in the

Box 7.5 Recommendations for action at national level

- *Develop or review national disaster data collection systems.* Monitor existing systems and address issues such as developing a reliable national (pre-disaster) baseline, coordination and standardization of data from different sources (to include data from humanitarian relief agencies) and quality control.
- *Revisit and standardize definitions.* Develop standardized criteria to allow links to other databases and facilitate comparisons with regional and international databases.
- *Develop linkages between disaster data and vulnerability data.* Different types of data need to be compared to minimize the risk of drawing misleading conclusions and to improve the quality of analysis.
- *Review linkages between data collection and response.* Despite data indicating rising levels of need, disaster responses are often insufficient. More effort is needed to link reliable data with appropriate and timely response at all levels.
- *Disseminate information.* Make relevant information available to a wide variety of users, including relevant database operators. ■

global context. Urgent action is needed to develop appropriate tools and methods to confirm the scale and extent of conflict- and famine-related impacts. However, information alone is not enough. It must be used to direct international attention towards addressing the humanitarian consequences of disaster.

One of the biggest challenges is how to depoliticize data, to avoid it being covertly manipulated for political, military or commercial purposes. As disasters become more complex and politically fraught, we need to consider the feasibility of developing an international code of ethical data collection and use, along the lines of the existing voluntary Code of Conduct for the International Red Cross and Red Crescent Movement and NGOs in Disaster Relief. Such a code would need to consider the collection and use of data not only for disaster preparedness and response, but also for research purposes – to benefit future populations in danger. The code could be a starting point that leads to the development of detailed standards, guidelines, tools and methodologies for data collection and use, leading to improved practices and better-informed decision-making. The code and accompanying guidelines could be developed through consultations similar to those which created Sphere's minimum standards in humanitarian response. A culture of information sharing must be developed that is built not only on trust but on objective, high-quality assessments of disaster impacts and needs. Information about the impact of disasters is a powerful tool for decision-making and learning. If used wisely, it can greatly improve our preparedness and effectiveness to save more lives in future.

Box 7.6 Recommendations for action at international level

- *Revisit and standardize definitions of disaster and disaster-affected.* Develop standardized criteria to allow links to other databases and facilitate comparisons with national and regional databases. The current work in developing GLIDE (global identifier numbers for disasters) and SHARE (structured humanitarian reporting) criteria are one step in that direction but further work needs to be done, especially to agree on a definition of 'affected' and how to assess this.

- *Reclassify some disaster types.* Introduce new categories of food crisis (where there is no conflict but there is increased malnutrition and mortality from communicable disease) and complex emergency (war or insecurity, food crisis, human rights violations and excess mortality from disease) to replace existing categories such as drought or conflict.

- *Reappraise and standardize assessment tools and methods.* Work with humanitarian organizations to review their data collection tools, methods and guidelines to try to standardize criteria, methods and procedures.

- *Proactively seek out mortality data in areas where reliable data are lacking.* Conduct proactive studies and active surveillance in neglected disaster zones (e.g., DRC and southern Sudan) wherever possible and where security permits.

- *Develop tools and methods* designed specifically for assessing mortality in war and famine zones where the population may not be easily accessible.

- *Conduct field-based studies* (in war and famine zones) and test out methods of statistical or mathematical modelling.

- *Conduct more rigorous evaluation of data sets* that are currently collected and disseminated, by better training of staff and through developing links with centres of excellence and academic institutions, to allow better data verification and data use for research purposes.

- *Carry out retrospective analyses of earlier disasters* to check if earlier analyses or assessments of deaths and of those affected are reliable and trustworthy (e.g., Rwanda crisis).

- *Meta-analyses.* Often, many conclusions can be drawn by bringing data sets from many disasters together and carrying out meta-analyses to gain an overview of mortality and morbidity. There is a potential for new lessons to be learned through meta-analysis.

- *Develop a code of conduct for ethical data collection and use* in order to ensure data or data collection are not misused for political, military or commercial purposes. ∎

Patricia Diskett, director of the Centre for Public Health in Humanitarian Assistance, Uppsala University, Sweden, contributed this chapter and all boxes except Box 7.1, which was contributed by Jonathan Walter, editor of the World Disasters Report.

Sources and further information

Danida/Overseas Development Institute. *The International Response to Conflict and Genocide: Lessons from the Rwanda Experience.* Steering Committee of the Joint Evaluation of Emergency Assistance to Rwanda. Copenhagen/London: Danida/ODI, 1996.

Diskett, P. *Evidence-based decision-making and managerial chaos in population displacement emergencies (PDEs): A case study of Rohingya refugees in Bangladesh 1992-1993.* Ph.D. Thesis, Liverpool School of Tropical Medicine, University of Liverpool, UK, 1997.

Hirnschall, G. *International Trip Report; Guinea (1990).* Atlanta: Centers for Disease Control, 1991.

Pecoul, B. and Malfait, P. 'Caring for Kurdish refugees' in *The Lancet,* vol. 338, p. 190, 1991.

Roberts, L. et al. *Mortality in the Democratic Republic of Congo: Results from a Nationwide Survey.* New York: International Rescue Committee, April 2003.

United Nations. *An overview of disaster management: disaster training programme. Geneva:* UNDP/UNDRO/DHA, 1992.

Van der Veen, A., Diskett, P., O'Keefe, P., Wekesa, F., Nyaba, P., Zangabeyo, M., Mowbray, R. and Huss, R. *Evaluation of the impact of WFP emergency food aid interventions in Operation Lifeline Sudan (Northern and Southern Sectors), 1999.* ETC UK report for Dutch Government and DFID, Khartoum/Nairobi, 1999.

World Health Organization. *Communicable diseases 2000.* Geneva: WHO, 2000.

Yusuf, F. 'Size and socio-demographic characteristics of the Afghan refugee population in Pakistan' in *Journal of Biosocial Sciences,* vol. 23 (3), pp. 269-279, 1990.

Web sites

Centre for the Epidemiology of Disasters **http://www.cred.be/emdat/**
Project Ploughshares **http://www.ploughshares.ca**
ReliefWeb **http://www.reliefweb.int**
Smithsonian Institute, Glocal Volcanism Program **http://www.volcano.si.edu/gvp/**
UN Environment Programme, Awareness and Preparedness for Disasters at Local Level **http://www.uneptie.org/pc/apell/disasters/lists/disastercat.html**
USAID **http://www.usaid.gov/hum_response/ofda**
World Food Programme **http://www.wfp.org/index**
World Health Organization **http://www.who.int**

chapter 8

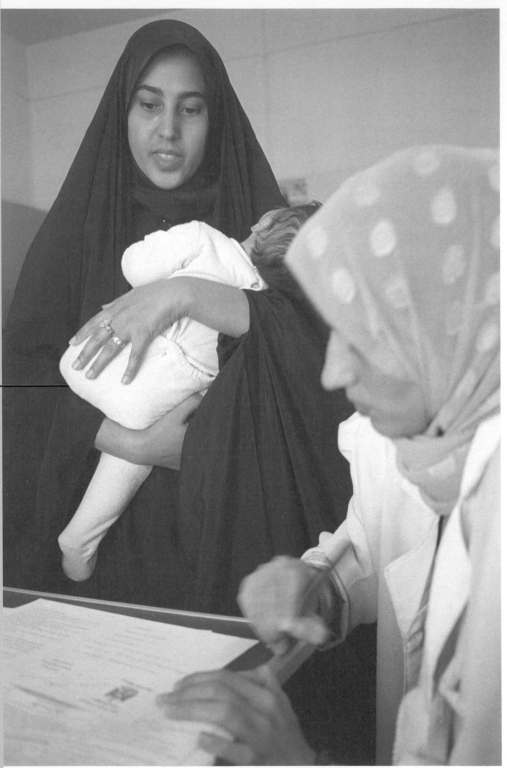

Section Two

Tracking the system

Disaster data: key trends and statistics

Last year saw more disasters reported than any year of the preceding decade. Fortunately, 2002's disasters appeared less deadly than before – 24,500 people were reported killed, compared to the decade's average of 62,000 per year. But they had more impact than ever. A colossal 608 million people were affected – three times the annual average from 1992-2001. Drought in India alone affected 300 million people during 2002. These figures do not include data on those killed or affected by war, conflict-related famine or disease. Reliable global data on such complex emergencies simply do not exist – but mortality studies in Sudan and the Democratic Republic of the Congo present death rates that dwarf those reported in the tables that follow (see Chapter 7).

Disasters continue to target the world's poorest and least developed. Of those killed in 2002, just 6 per cent lived in countries of high human development (HHD). While countries of low human development (LHD) reported the fewest natural disasters during the decade, their death toll is by far the highest. When related to the numbers of reported disasters, an average of 555 people died per disaster in LHD nations, compared to 133 in countries of medium human development (MHD) and 18 people in HHD nations.

While deaths remain low from disasters in highly developed countries, financial costs are very high. Of globally reported disaster damage last year (US$ 27 billion), more than two-thirds occurred in HHD countries. LHD countries reported just 0.15 per cent of total damage. Over the course of the decade, the average cost of damage from each natural disaster in HHD nations was US$ 477 million, compared to US$ 149 million in MHD nations and US$ 61 million in LHD nations. The high financial value attached to infrastructure in developed countries is the main reason for these differences. The enormous financial losses related to infrastructure in LHD countries would be better revealed by a comparison based on losses to gross domestic product (GDP) rather than losses expressed in dollars.

Weather-related disasters continue to rise, from an annual average of 200 between 1993-1997, to 331 per year between 1998-2002. Across the decade, famine remained by far the deadliest disaster, killing at least 275,000 people (nearly half of all reported fatalities) – although this is probably a gross underestimate. Floods, however, affected more people across the globe (140 million per year on average) than all other natural or technological disasters put together.

Comparing the decades 1983-1992 and 1993-2002, reported global deaths from natural and technological disasters have fallen by 38 per cent. However, numbers of people reported affected have risen by 54 per cent over the same period.

In the following tables, some totals may not correspond due to rounding.

Jonathan Walter, editor of the World Disasters Report, *wrote this introduction and table analyses. CRED and USCR contributed to Box 8.1.*

Photo opposite page:
However hard it is to collect, disaster data is vital not only in revealing the scale of current crises but in plotting the underlying trends which can help direct agencies towards those in greatest need.

Christopher Black/International Federation, Iraq.

Box 8.1 Data methodology and definitions

The *World Disasters Report* divides disasters into natural and non-natural disasters. Natural disasters include **hydro-meteorological disasters** (avalanches/landslides; droughts/famines; extreme temperatures; floods; forest/scrub fires; windstorms; and other (insect infestation and waves/surges)) and **geophysical disasters** (earthquakes; volcanic eruptions). Non-natural disasters can be **industrial** (chemical spill, collapse of industrial structures, explosion, fire, gas leak, poisoning, radiation), **miscellaneous** (collapse of domestic/non-industrial structures, explosion, fire) or **transport** (air, rail, road and water-borne accidents).

Tables 1 to 13 in this chapter have been drawn from EM-DAT, the emergencies database maintained by the Centre for Research on the Epidemiology of Disasters (CRED) based at the School of Public Health of the Louvain Catholic University in Brussels (http://www.cred.be). EM-DAT contains essential core data on the occurrence and effects of over 12,000 disasters in the world from 1900 to the present. The database is compiled from various sources, including UN agencies, NGOs, insurance companies, research institutes and press agencies. The entries are constantly reviewed for redundancies, inconsistencies and the completion of missing data.

CRED defines a disaster as a situation or event, which overwhelms local capacity, necessitating a request to national or international level for external assistance. In order for a disaster to be entered in EM-DAT at least one of the following criteria has to be fulfilled: ten or more people reported killed; 100 people reported affected; a call for international assistance; and/or declaration of a state of emergency. The number of people killed includes people confirmed dead, or missing and presumed dead; people affected are those requiring immediate assistance during a period of emergency, i.e., requiring basic survival needs such as food, water, shelter, sanitation and immediate medical assistance. In EM-DAT, the total number of people affected include people reported injured and homeless. The economic impact of a disaster usually consists of direct damage (e.g., to infra-structure, crops, housing) and indirect damage (e.g., loss of revenues, unemployment, market destabilization). EM-DAT's estimates relate only to direct damage.

The data in Tables 14-16 were provided by the US Committee for Refugees (USCR) (http://www.refugees.org), an NGO. The quality of the data in these tables is affected by the less-than-ideal conditions often associated with forced migration. The estimates reproduced in these tables are USCR's preliminary year-end figures for 2002.

Table 14 lists refugees and asylum seekers by country of origin, while Table 15 lists the two groups by host country. Refugees are people who are outside their home country and are unable or unwilling to return to that country because they fear persecution. Asylum seekers are people who claim to be refugees; many are awaiting a determination of their refugee status. While not all asylum seekers are refugees, they are nonetheless entitled to certain protection under international refugee law, at least until they are determined not to be refugees. USCR also includes people granted various forms of humanitarian relief if that relief is based on factors related to the UN refugee definition, as distinct from, for example, relief granted because of natural disaster.

Table 16 concerns internally displaced persons (IDPs). Like refugees and asylum seekers, internally displaced people have fled their homes, but have remained in their home country. No universally accepted definition of IDPs exists. USCR generally considers people who are uprooted within their country because of armed conflict or persecution – and thus would be refugees if they were to cross an international border – to be internally displaced. IDPs often live in war-torn areas and are neither registered nor counted in any systematic way. Estimates of the size of IDP populations are frequently subject to great margins of error. Data in Figures 8.1, 8.2 and 8.3 have been drawn from the OECD's Development Assistance Committee's database. ■

chapter 8

Table 1 Total number of reported disasters, by continent and by year (1993 to 2002)[1]

	1993	1994	1995	1996	1997	1998	1999	2000	2001	2002	Total
Africa	49	58	61	58	56	83	144	196	187	196	1,088
Americas	94	81	97	94	100	112	137	146	128	151	1,140
Asia	221	180	171	176	195	208	240	287	293	291	2,262
Europe	46	69	64	55	60	65	78	122	91	110	760
Oceania	14	17	8	17	15	17	15	13	18	18	152
High human development[2]	110	89	99	88	113	107	114	154	135	145	1,154
Medium human development	247	256	228	233	239	277	361	432	400	447	3,120
Low human development	67	60	74	79	74	101	139	178	182	174	1,128
Total	424	405	401	400	426	485	614	764	717	766	5,402

Source: EM-DAT, CRED, University of Louvain, Belgium

[1] In Tables 1-13, 'disasters' refer to natural and technological disasters only, and do not include wars, conflict-related famines, diseases or epidemics.
[2] In Tables 1-4 and 9-12, the classification of countries as high, medium or low human development is based on the UN Development Programme's Human Development Index (HDI). To classify countries not listed in the HDI, the World Bank's World Development Report was used, classing low income countries as low human development, lower and upper middle income as medium human development and high income as high human development. Islands and territories that are dependencies of a state are classed in the same category as that state.

In 2002, Asia remained the continent most frequently struck by disasters, accounting for 38 per cent of all disasters recorded in EM-DAT. The past three years have seen the number of reported disasters in countries of low human development nearly tripling since the beginning of the decade.

Table 2 Total number of people reported killed by disasters, by continent and by year (1993 to 2002)

	1993	1994	1995	1996	1997	1998	1999	2000	2001	2002	Total
Africa	1,637	3,144	2,962	3,484	4,064	7,006	2,688	5,624	4,436	8,033	43,078
Americas	4,606	2,925	2,622	2,530	3,069	21,865	33,989	1,820	3,450	2,155	79,031
Asia	22,787	13,311	74,925	69,706	71,033	82,373	75,890	11,087	29,121	12,552	462,785
Europe	1,162	2,340	3,366	1,204	1,166	1,429	19,448	1,627	2,196	1,701	35,639
Oceania	120	103	24	111	388	2,227	116	205	9	91	3,394
High human development	1,855	2,404	7,751	1,954	1,754	1,989	2,194	1,713	1,791	1,604	25,009
Medium human development	22,889	15,477	17,281	15,039	18,134	42,613	72,587	12,470	33,084	12,829	262,403
Low human development	5,568	3,942	58,867	60,042	59,832	70,298	57,350	6,180	4,337	10,099	336,515
Total	**30,312**	**21,823**	**83,899**	**77,035**	**79,720**	**114,900**	**132,131**	**20,363**	**39,212**	**24,532**	**623,927**

Source: EM-DAT, CRED, University of Louvain, Belgium

As detailed in Chapter 7, numbers of people reported killed are underestimated, as little reliable data exist on conflict- and famine-related deaths in particular. On the basis of reported data, 2002's death toll was less than half the decade's annual average of 62,000. Countries of high human development account for just 6 per cent of 2002's total. In 2002, three disasters killed more than 1,000 people: an earthquake in Afghanistan in March, a heatwave in India in May and the shipwreck of the *Joola* in Senegal in September.

Table 3 Total number of people reported affected by disasters, by continent and by year (1993 to 2002) in thousands

	1993	1994	1995	1996	1997	1998	1999	2000	2001	2002	Total
Africa	16,500	11,234	9,533	4,282	7,736	10,150	14,362	23,043	18,378	21,695	136,914
Americas	1,970	2,722	1,027	2,380	2,711	17,073	5,008	1,348	11,225	2,030	47,493
Asia	162,254	166,145	225,295	207,163	56,269	315,714	188,605	229,636	140,075	583,065	2,274,220
Europe	600	909	8,220	30	679	621	6,549	2,907	777	1,199	22,491
Oceania	5,158	5,914	2,682	652	730	328	151	7	32	40	15,694
High human development	5,264	6,247	11,361	2,246	1,093	1,870	4,605	981	803	1,398	35,866
Medium human development	147,419	165,962	200,793	196,281	56,064	316,238	194,899	229,090	150,410	590,118	2,247,275
Low human development	33,799	14,715	34,603	15,980	10,968	25,777	15,172	26,870	19,273	16,512	213,670
Total	**186,482**	**186,923**	**246,757**	**214,507**	**68,125**	**343,885**	**214,675**	**256,941**	**170,487**	**608,028**	**2,496,811**

Source: EM-DAT, CRED, University of Louvain, Belgium

As detailed in Chapter 7, numbers of people affected by disaster are unreliable as there is no common definition of an 'affected' person. But on the basis of available data, the numbers affected in 2002 were more than triple the annual average from 1992-2001. Drought in India, which affected 300 million people, accounted for half of 2002's huge total. Meanwhile, floods and storms affected 180 million in China; July floods affected 43 million in Bangladesh and India; and drought in sub-Saharan Africa affected over 17 million.

chapter 8

chapter 8

Table 4 Total amount of disaster estimated damage, by continent and by year (1993 to 2002) in millions of US dollars (2002 prices)

	1993	1994	1995	1996	1997	1998	1999	2000	2001	2002	Total
Africa	11	519	195	127	21	349	784	156	323	128	2,614
Americas	27,444	36,025	26,389	14,135	11,130	19,068	13,942	3,405	10,432	1,956	163,927
Asia	17,236	14,929	183,762	34,182	28,963	31,537	28,799	17,206	16,351	7,123	380,089
Europe	1,929	12,536	14,606	194	10,869	2,743	38,719	8,642	852	15,433	106,344
Oceania	1,767	2,051	1,509	1,073	262	196	921	527	347	2,121	10,774
High human Development	27,641	49,318	195,942	12,881	20,025	15,336	32,358	11,062	9,756	18,150	392,468
Medium human development	20,040	15,823	11,659	33,116	30,959	36,057	50,786	11,891	18,037	8,569	236,937
Low human development	707	740	18,861	3,716	261	2,500	22	6,982	513	41	34,344
Total	**48,387**	**65,881**	**226,462**	**49,713**	**51,245**	**53,893**	**83,166**	**29,936**	**28,306**	**26,760**[1]	**663,749**

Source: EM-DAT, CRED, University of Louvain, Belgium

[1] This total is for natural disasters only, as data on damage from technological disasters during 2002 was unavailable at the time of going to print.

As detailed in Chapter 7, estimations of disaster damage are notoriously unreliable and tend to favour highly insured countries with valuable infrastructure. There are no data on damage for over 80 per cent of all reported disasters. According to available data, 68 per cent of reported damage costs during 2002 occurred in countries of high human development, while countries of low human development reported just 0.15 per cent of the global total.

chapter 8

Table 5 Total number of reported disasters, by type of phenomenon and by year (1993 to 2002)

	1993	1994	1995	1996	1997	1998	1999	2000	2001	2002	Total
Avalanches/landslides	22	8	15	24	13	21	15	29	21	19	187
Droughts/famines	14	9	16	8	17	34	30	47	47	41	263
Earthquakes	14	22	25	11	17	16	33	31	25	35	229
Extreme temperatures	4	10	13	5	13	13	8	31	23	15	135
Floods	82	79	88	70	76	87	112	152	157	172	1,075
Forest/scrub fires	2	13	7	5	15	16	22	30	14	22	146
Volcanic eruptions	6	6	4	5	4	4	5	5	6	7	52
Windstorms	101	66	59	63	67	72	86	100	97	112	823
Other natural disasters[1]	4	1	4	2	3	2	2	4	2	1	25
Subtotal hydro-meteorological disasters	229	186	202	177	204	245	275	393	361	382	2,654
Subtotal geophysical disasters	20	28	29	16	21	20	38	36	31	42	281
Total natural disasters	249	214	231	193	225	265	313	429	392	424	2,935
Industrial accidents	36	34	39	35	35	43	36	50	54	48	410
Miscellaneous accidents	26	30	27	37	30	29	51	47	50	46	373
Transport accidents	113	127	104	135	136	148	214	238	221	248	1,684
Total technological disasters	175	191	170	207	201	220	301	335	325	342	2,467
Total	**424**	**405**	**401**	**400**	**426**	**485**	**614**	**764**	**717**	**766**	**5,402**

Source: EM-DAT, CRED, University of Louvain, Belgium

[1] In Tables 5-12, 'other natural disasters' include insect infestations and waves/surges.

Hydro-meteorological disasters are increasing, from an average of 200 reported per year from 1993-1997, to an annual average of 331 between 1998 and 2002. Meanwhile, technological disasters nearly doubled between 1993 and 2002 – a climb of 66 per cent.

chapter 8

Table 6 Total number of people reported killed by disasters, by type of phenomenon and by year (1993 to 2002)

	1993	1994	1995	1996	1997	1998	1999	2000	2001	2002	Total
Avalanches/landslides	1,548	280	1,497	1,129	801	981	351	1,099	692	1,110	9,488
Droughts/famines[1]	n.a.	n.a.	54,000	54,000	54,520	57,875	54,029	370	199	529	275,522
Earthquakes	10,113	1,242	7,966	584	3,039	7,412	21,870	204	21,355	1,606	75,391
Extreme temperatures	106	416	1,730	300	619	3,225	771	922	1,653	2,807	12,549
Floods	5,930	6,454	7,525	7,309	6,958	9,695	34,366	6,307	4,682	4,335	93,561
Forest/scrub fires	3	84	29	45	32	109	70	47	33	6	458
Volcanic eruptions	99	101	n.a.[2]	4	53	n.a.	n.a.	n.a.	n.a.	254	511
Windstorms	2,965	4,064	3,724	4,380	5,330	24,657	11,899	1,129	1,730	1,093	60,971
Other natural disasters	59	31	n.a.	32	400	2,182	3	1	n.a.	n.a.	2,708
Subtotal hydro-meteorological disasters	10,611	11,329	68,505	67,195	68,660	98,724	101,489	9,875	8,989	9,880	455,257
Subtotal geophysical disasters	10,212	1,343	7,966	588	3,092	7,412	21,870	204	21,355	1,860	75,902
Total natural disasters	20,823	12,672	76,471	67,783	71,752	106,136	123,359	10,079	30,344	11,740	531,159
Industrial accidents	1,244	779	513	674	1,033	1,942	742	1,613	1,271	1,121	10,932
Miscellaneous accidents	1,103	1,719	1,660	1,159	1,277	748	1,330	1,112	1,753	1,869	13,730
Transport accidents	7,142	6,653	5,255	7,419	5,658	6,074	6,700	7,559	5,844	9,802	68,106
Total technological disasters	9,489	9,151	7,428	9,252	7,968	8,764	8,772	10,284	8,868	12,792	92,768
Total	30,312	21,823	83,899	77,035	79,720	114,900	132,131	20,363	39,212	24,532	623,927

Source: EM-DAT, CRED, University of Louvain, Belgium

[1] These figures are probably gross underestimates as most famine victims die from disease rather than hunger and go unreported. Some sources estimate that around 3 million people died from conflict-related famine and disease in Sudan and the Democratic Republic of the Congo alone during the past decade.

[2] In Tables 6-12, n.a. signifies no data available.

Across the decade, famine remains the deadliest disaster, accounting for nearly half of all reported fatalities.

Table 7 Total number of people reported affected by disasters, by type of phenomenon and by year (1993 to 2002) in thousands

	1993	1994	1995	1996	1997	1998	1999	2000	2001	2002	Total
Avalanches/landslides	80	298	1,122	9	34	209	15	208	67	769	2,813
Droughts/famines	19,132	15,515	30,431	5,836	8,016	24,495	38,647	176,477	86,757	328,457	733,763
Earthquakes	270	730	3,029	2,018	634	1,878	3,893	2,458	19,307	548	34,765
Extreme temperatures	3,001	1,108	535	0	615	36	725	28	213	104	6,365
Floods	149,341	127,688	197,504	178,451	44,956	290,179	150,167	62,098	34,030	167,060	1,401,473
Forest/scrub fires	0	3,067	12	6	53	167	19	39	6	25	3,393
Volcanic eruptions	174	236	23	7	7	8	34	119	78	298	984
Windstorms	14,429	38,246	14,051	28,144	13,594	26,784	21,153	15,459	29,975	110,709	312,545
Other natural disasters	n.a.	n.a.	0	0	29	10	1	17	n.a.	2	59
Subtotal hydro-meteorological disasters	*185,983*	*185,923*	*243,655*	*212,446*	*67,297*	*341,881*	*210,727*	*254,326*	*151,048*	*607,125*	*2,460,412*
Subtotal geophysical disasters	*443*	*966*	*3,052*	*2,025*	*641*	*1,885*	*3,928*	*2,577*	*19,386*	*845*	*35,749*
Total natural disasters	186,427	186,889	246,708	214,471	67,939	343,767	214,655	256,903	170,434	607,970	2,496,161
Industrial accidents	8	19	27	16	163	63	3	17	19	1	336
Miscellaneous accidents	45	11	19	18	20	52	12	15	30	52	275
Transport accidents	2	3	3	3	3	4	5	6	3	5	38
Total technological disasters	56	34	50	36	186	119	21	38	53	58	650
Total	**186,482**	**186,923**	**246,757**	**214,507**	**68,125**	**343,885**	**214,675**	**256,941**	**170,487**	**608,028**	**2,496,811**

Source: EM-DAT, CRED, University of Louvain, Belgium

In 2002, 328 million people were affected by drought/famine – more than in any other kind of disaster over the past ten years. Hydro-meteorological disasters accounted for 99.9 per cent of all disaster-affected people in 2002.

Table 8 Total amount of disaster estimated damage, by type of phenomenon and by year (1993 to 2002) in millions of US dollars (2002 prices)

	1993	1994	1995	1996	1997	1998	1999	2000	2001	2002	Total
Avalanches/landslides	885	76	12	n.a.	18	n.a.	n.a.	176	72	2	1240
Droughts/famines	1,376	1,486	6,819	1,376	458	495	7,398	6,587	3,843	3,261	33,100
Earthquakes	1,132	32,089	157,322	606	5,524	417	34,005	149	10,122	93	241,457
Extreme temperatures	n.a.	789	985	n.a.	3,367	4,083	1,080	130	203	n.a.	10,637
Floods	30,427	23,369	30,778	28,387	14,369	31,941	14,376	11,147	3,047	22,101	209,943
Forest/scrub fires	1,245	185	159	1,974	19,065	623	530	1,099	71	92	25,042
Volcanic eruptions	0	486	1	19	9	n.a.	n.a.	n.a.	4	n.a.	519
Windstorms	10,996	6,028	28,766	14,331	8,397	16,136	25,557	10,071	10,933	1,212	132,429
Other natural disasters	n.a.	n.a.	123	n.a.	4	2	0	125	n.a.	n.a.	254
Subtotal hydro-meteorological disasters	44,929	31,932	67,641	46,068	45,679	53,281	48,941	29,336	181,170	26,668	412,645
Subtotal geophysical disasters	1,132	32,574	157,323	625	5,533	417	34,005	149	10,126	93	241,976
Total natural disasters	46,061	64,506	224,964	46,693	51,212	53,698	82,946	29,485	28,296	26,760	654,621
Industrial accidents	91	55	490	1,382	22	142	3	n.a.	10	n.a.	2,194
Miscellaneous accidents	1,442	715	214	1,401	n.a.	21	2	451	n.a.	n.a.	4,246
Transport accidents	793	605	794	237	12	32	214	n.a.	n.a.	n.a.	2,688
Total technological disasters	2,326	1,375	1,498	3,020	33	195	220	451	10	n.a.	9,128
Total	**48,387**	**65,881**	**226,462**	**49,713**	**51,245**	**53,893**	**83,166**	**29,936**	**28,306**	**26,760**[1]	**663,749**

Source: EM-DAT, CRED, University of Louvain, Belgium

[1] This total is for natural disasters only, as data on damage from technological disasters during 2002 was unavailable at the time of going to print.

Estimates of damage from natural disasters should be treated with caution, as the financial value attached to infrastructure in developed nations is much higher than that in developing countries. In 2002, floods accounted for 83 per cent of reported disaster damage. But over the decade, earthquakes have cost the most – Japan's Kobe quake in 1995 resulted in over US$ 150 billion of damage.

Table 9 Total number of reported disasters, by continent and by type of phenomenon (1993 to 2002)

	Africa	Americas	Asia	Europe	Oceania	HHD[1]	MHD	LHD	Total
Avalanches/landslides	13	43	103	22	6	23	139	25	187
Droughts/famines	113	44	84	11	11	19	138	106	263
Earthquakes	10	45	124	38	12	39	166	24	229
Extreme temperatures	6	31	39	54	5	44	72	19	135
Floods	238	239	385	187	26	251	570	254	1,075
Forest/scrub fires	13	62	21	40	10	78	59	9	146
Volcanic eruptions	4	25	15	2	6	12	38	2	52
Windstorms	63	285	328	90	57	343	369	110	823
Other natural disasters	3	5	14	1	2	1	18	6	25
Subtotal hydro-meteorological disasters	449	709	974	405	117	759	1,365	529	2,654
Subtotal geophysical disasters	14	70	139	40	18	51	204	26	281
Total natural disasters	463	779	1,113	445	135	810	1,569	555	2,935
Industrial accidents	39	52	250	67	2	63	302	45	410
Miscellaneous accidents	69	53	194	53	4	77	233	62	373
Transport accidents	517	256	705	195	11	204	1,016	464	1,684
Total technological disasters	625	361	1,149	315	17	344	1,551	571	2,467
Total	**1,088**	**1,140**	**2,262**	**760**	**152**	**1,154**	**3,120**	**1,126**	**5,402**

Source: EM-DAT, CRED, University of Louvain, Belgium

[1] In Tables 9-12, HHD stands for high human development, MHD for medium human development and LHD for low human development.

While LHD countries reported the fewest natural disasters during the decade, their death toll is by far the highest.

chapter 8

chapter 8

Table 10 Total number of people reported killed by disasters, by continent and by type of phenomenon (1993 to 2002)

	Africa	Americas	Asia	Europe	Oceania	HHD	MHD	LHD	Total
Avalanches/landslides	302	2,127	6,094	850	115	432	7,250	1,806	9,488
Droughts/famines¹	4,453	58	270,923	n.a.	88	n.a.	960	274,562	275,522
Earthquakes	225	3,272	51,293	20,525	76	6,080	60,692	8,619	75,391
Extreme temperatures	147	1,979	7,427	2,973	23	2,539	8,188	1,822	12,549
Floods	9,642	35,236	47,009	1,654	20	2,489	77,203	13,869	93,561
Forest/scrub fires	136	104	125	84	9	130	245	83	458
Volcanic eruptions	254	68	180	n.a.	9	39	218	254	511
Windstorms	1,335	23,703	34,923	739	271	3,108	50,873	6,990	60,971
Other natural disasters	n.a.	15	511	n.a.	2,182	n.a.	2,707	1	2,708
Subtotal hydro-meteorological disasters	16,015	63,222	367,012	6,300	2,708	8,698	147,426	299,133	455,257
Subtotal geophysical disasters	479	3,340	51,473	20,525	85	6,119	60,910	8,873	75,902
Total natural disasters	16,494	66,562	418,485	26,825	2,793	14,817	208,336	308,006	531,159
Industrial accidents	2,471	412	7,164	863	22	288	8,058	2,586	10,932
Miscellaneous accidents	2,661	1,919	7,941	1,163	46	1,973	9,440	2,299	13,730
Transport accidents	21,452	10,138	29,195	6,788	533	7,931	36,569	23,606	68,106
Total technological disasters	26,584	12,469	44,300	8,814	601	10,192	54,067	28,491	92,768
Total	**43,078**	**79,031**	**462,785**	**35,639**	**3,394**	**25,009**	**262,403**	**336,497**	**623,927**

Source: EM-DAT, CRED, University of Louvain, Belgium

¹ These figures are probably gross underestimates as most famine victims die from disease rather than hunger and go unreported. Some sources estimate that around 3 million people died from conflict-related famine and disease in Sudan and the Democratic Republic of the Congo alone during the past decade.

Over half of all disaster fatalities from the past decade were in LHD nations. When related to the numbers of reported disasters, an average of 18 people died per disaster in HHD nations, compared to 133 in MHD nations and 555 in LHD nations.

Table 11 Total number of people reported affected by disasters, by continent and by type of phenomenon (1993 to 2002) in thousands

	Africa	Americas	Asia	Europe	Oceania	HHD	MHD	LHD	Total
Avalanches/landslides	4	436	2,358	14	1	13	2,505	295	2,813
Droughts/famines	110,956	15,101	595,363	6,010	6,333	11,250	627,608	94,904	733,763
Earthquakes	117	3,466	29,008	2,124	51	2,344	30,840	1,581	34,765
Extreme temperatures	0	92	893	779	4,601	4,675	1,404	286	6,365
Floods	19,939	9,730	1,364,957	6,700	147	5,579	1,297,415	98,478	1,401,473
Forest/scrub fires	8	145	3,056	123	61	185	3,202	6	3,393
Volcanic eruptions	139	349	323	n.a.	172	35	818	130	984
Windstorms	5,687	18,117	277,780	6,655	4,306	11,637	283,027	17,881	312,545
Other natural disasters	n.a.	3	47	n.a.	10	n.a.	18	41	59
Subtotal hydro-meteorological disasters	136,595	43,624	2,244,454	20,281	15,459	33,340	2,215,180	211,892	2,460,412
Subtotal geophysical disasters	256	3,815	29,331	2,124	222	2,379	31,658	1,711	35,749
Total natural disasters	136,851	47,439	2,273,785	22,405	15,681	35,720	2,246,838	213,603	2,496,161
Industrial accidents	3	39	217	77	0	121	211	4	336
Miscellaneous accidents	50	6	202	5	12	16	205	54	275
Transport accidents	10	8	16	4	0	9	21	9	38
Total technological disasters	63	53	435	86	12	146	437	67	650
Total	136,914	47,493	2,274,220	22,491	15,694	35,866	2,247,275	213,670	2,496,811

Source: EM-DAT, CRED, University of Louvain, Belgium

Over the decade, floods made the most impact in Asia (accounting for 60 per cent of all those affected by natural disasters in Asia); droughts/famines affected the most in Africa (81 per cent); while windstorms accounted for 38 per cent of disaster-affected Americans.

chapter 8

Table 12 Total amount of disaster estimated damage, by continent and by type of phenomenon (1993 to 2002) in millions of US dollars (2002 prices)

	Africa	Americas	Asia	Europe	Oceania	HHD	MHD	LHD	Total
Avalanches/landslides	n.a.	796	419	25	n.a.	287	952	n.a.	1,240
Droughts/famines	424	3,461	13,835	9,455	5,925	15,895	16,837	368	33,100
Earthquakes	151	39,854	173,411	27,724	317	197,615	43,757	85	241,457
Extreme temperatures	1	5,979	3,363	1,091	203	6,574	4,063	n.a.	10,637
Floods	1,109	35,647	122,878	49,433	874	79,132	105,212	25,599	209,943
Forest/scrub fires	4	3,234	21,320	203	281	3,546	21,492	4	25,042
Volcanic eruptions	n.a.	10	1	22	486	31	488	n.a.	519
Windstorms	841	69,584	42,679	16,777	2,548	82,884	41,543	8,001	132,429
Other natural disasters	6	123	0	n.a.	125	125	125	4	254
Subtotal hydro-meteorological disasters	2,385	118,824	204,495	76,984	9,956	188,444	190,224	33,976	412,645
Subtotal geophysical disasters	151	39,864	173,412	27,746	803	197,646	44,245	85	241,976
Total natural disasters	2,535	158,688	377,907	104,731	10,759	386,091	234,469	34,061	654,621
Industrial accidents	10	1,257	425	487	15	579	1,414	201	2,194
Miscellaneous accidents	5	2,939	740	563	n.a.	4,190	52	5	4,246
Transport accidents	64	1,042	1,018	564	n.a.	1,608	1,002	78	2,688
Total technological disasters	79	5,239	2,182	1,613	15	6,377	2,468	283	9,128
Total	**2,614**	**163,927**	**380,089**	**106,344**	**10,774**	**392,468**	**236,937**	**34,344¹**	**663,749**

Source: EM-DAT, CRED, University of Louvain, Belgium

As noted, data on damage estimations are notoriously unreliable. But on available data, HHD nations accounted for 59 per cent of global disaster damage – more than ten times that reported from LHD nations. When related to the numbers of reported disasters, the average cost of damage from each natural disaster in HHD nations was US$ 477 million, compared to US$ 149 million in MHD nations and US$ 61 million in LHD nations.

¹ This total is for natural disasters only, as data on damage from technological disasters during 2002 was unavailable at the time of going to print.

Table 13 Total number of people reported killed and affected by disasters, by country
(1983 to 1992; 1993 to 2002; and 2002)

	Total number of people reported killed (1983-1992)	Total number of people reported affected (1983-1992)	Total number of people reported killed (1993-2002)	Total number of people reported affected (1993-2002)	Total number of people reported killed (2002)	Total number of people reported affected (2002)
Africa	**579,452**	**149,260,227**	**43,078**	**136,913,653**	**8,033**	**21,694,699**
Algeria	233	44,200	1,539	143,183	148	2,364
Angola	307	3,681,042	1,163	181,239	58	35
Benin	64	2,569,000	126	835,283	15	n.a.
Botswana	8	3,758,077	23	144,276	ndr	ndr
Burkina Faso	16	4,085,396	28	164,350	ndr	ndr
Burundi	112	3,600	56	1,151,659	38	8,039
Cameroon	1,847	798,537	721	5,445	ndr	ndr
Canary Is. (ES)	ndr	ndr	23	730	16	430
Cape Verde	29	5,500	18	46,306		30,000
Central African Rep.	31	n.a.	126	80,396	104	768
Chad	3,093	3,682,212	131	1,232,436	ndr	ndr
Comoros	59	115,252	256	n.a.	16	n.a.
Congo, DR of the	722	327,959	1,839[1]	259,911	458	132,580
Congo	154	50	567	126,631	n.a.	48,000
Côte d'Ivoire	99	7,070	406	280	ndr	ndr
Djibouti	10	260,300	146	586,125	1	350
Egypt	1,754	36,913	2,327	170,297	605	2,441
Equatorial Guinea	15	313	2	850	n.a.	500
Eritrea[2]			133	2,727,725	n.a.	39,000
Ethiopia[2]	301,139	41,365,940	883	39,962,871	71	7,121,020
Gabon	72	10,000	44	n.a.	14	n.a.
Gambia	100	n.a.	75	38,750	21	n.a.
Ghana	227	8,800	603	1,170,969	128	2,240
Guinea	648	21,436	356	226,253	35	11
Guinea-Bissau	1	8,328	217	103,222	n.a.	100,000
Kenya	695	3,300,168	1,679	12,633,694	91	308,008
Lesotho	40	850,000	1	833,751	ndr	500,000
Liberia	n.a.	n.a.	80	7,000	60	n.a.
Libya	310	121	103	10	81	10
Madagascar	580	1,848,153	631	3,525,669	23	928,100
Malawi	506	11,437,701	663	14,173,063	540	3,225,784
Mali	148	326,667	3,735	37,257	26	25,026
Mauritania	2,270	3,345,200	179	829,106	30	97,000
Mauritius	161	12,358	8	4,350	3	1,050
Morocco	105	45	1,548	389,952	159	15,112

	Total number of people reported killed (1983-1992)	Total number of people reported affected (1983-1992)	Total number of people reported killed (1993-2002)	Total number of people reported affected (1993-2002)	Total number of people reported killed (2002)	Total number of people reported affected (2002)
Mozambique	105,810	11,928,508	1,681	6,394,978	218	869,685
Namibia	20	250,000	19	538,209	19	345,009
Niger	190	6,210,000	174	3,750,583	4	1,253
Nigeria	1,898	3,307,563	7,815	976,834	1,885	15,406
Réunion (FR)	65	10,261	16	3,700	n.a.	3,100
Rwanda	285	501,678	288	1,297,371	72	25,608
Saint Helena (UK)	ndr	ndr	n.a.	300	ndr	ndr
Sao Tome and Principe	n.a.	93,000	ndr	ndr	ndr	ndr
Senegal	131	1,218,425	2,172	620,486	1,916	179,041
Seychelles	ndr	ndr	5	8,037	n.a.	6,800
Sierra Leone	272	n.a.	865	200,025	ndr	ndr
Somalia	844	633,500	2,725	4,245,589	101	40
South Africa	1,765	5,272,408	2,262	520,794	172	102,890
Sudan	150,593	25,282,029	1,015[1]	8,877,928	175	103,641
Swaziland	553	917,500	30	662,059	n.a.	150,000
Tanzania	409	3,126,624	2,165	8,152,379	431	3,297
Togo	n.a.	450,000	3	231,905	ndr	ndr
Tunisia	88	98,500	61	137	27	48
Uganda	316	949,580	797	1,254,106	192	977
Zambia	429	2,500,000	258	5,334,019	12	1,300,000
Zimbabwe	229	4,600,313	292	12,051,175	68	6,000,036
Americas	**58,168**	**64,179,254**	**79,031**	**47,492,540**	**2,155**	**2,029,745**
Anguilla (UK)	n.a.	n.a.	n.a.	150	ndr	ndr
Antigua and Barbuda	2	83,030	5	76,684	ndr	ndr
Argentina	349	12,467,819	474	727,482	54	13,452
Aruba (NL)	ndr	ndr	ndr	ndr	ndr	ndr
Bahamas	104	1,700	1	1,500	ndr	ndr
Barbados	n.a.	330	n.a.	2,000	n.a.	2,000
Belize	n.a.	n.a.	66	145,170	ndr	ndr
Bermuda (UK)	28	40	18	n.a.	ndr	ndr
Bolivia	458	3,790,334	624	858,026	140	17,246
Brazil	3,761	29,457,752	2,056	11,925,973	228	5,325
Canada	450	78,866	457	575,768	n.a.	933
Cayman Is. (UK)	ndr	ndr	n.a.	300	n.a.	300
Chile	895	2,288,838	531	580,444	238	247,831
Colombia	25,289	833,791	3,076	2,591,148	249	124,538
Costa Rica	109	360,854	135	909,129	10	95,040

	Total number of people reported killed (1983-1992)	Total number of people reported affected (1983-1992)	Total number of people reported killed (1993-2002)	Total number of people reported affected (1993-2002)	Total number of people reported killed (2002)	Total number of people reported affected (2002)
Cuba	820	854,479	301	8,548,851	32	359,044
Dominica	2	10,710	15	3,891	ndr	ndr
Dominican Republic	269	1,193,190	766	1,026,195	28	1,770
Ecuador	1,240	632,991	1,287	454,453	137	204,590
El Salvador	1,237	817,060	1,881	2,098,831	20	620
Falkland Is. (UK)	ndr	ndr	ndr	ndr	ndr	ndr
French Guiana (FR)	ndr	ndr	n.a.	70,000	ndr	ndr
Grenada	n.a.	1,000	n.a.	210	ndr	ndr
Guadeloupe (FR)	5	12,084	24	899	ndr	ndr
Guatemala	386	137,440	1,054	351,598	131	100,260
Guyana	n.a.	281	10	645,400	ndr	ndr
Haiti	566	2,061,686	4,118	1,624,306	40	13,699
Honduras	279	94,137	15,269	3,751,209	11	84,669
Jamaica	119	1,427,640	23	7,872	9	2,500
Martinique (FR)	8	1,500	2	3,610	ndr	ndr
Mexico	11,817	778,205	3,642	2,671,906	191	316,451
Montserrat (UK)	11	12,040	32	13,000	ndr	ndr
Netherlands Antilles (NL)	n.a.	n.a.	17	40,004	ndr	ndr
Nicaragua	416	843,303	3,529	1,770,181	n.a.	29,846
Panama	154	134,903	49	30,470	5	20,300
Paraguay	76	225,575	118	505,194	17	40,105
Peru	3,128	5,058,240	3,055	1,922,264	261	119,254
Puerto Rico (US)	760	2,534	126	115,434	10	n.a.
St Kitts and Nevis	1	1,330	5	12,980	ndr	ndr
St Lucia	45	3,000	4	1,125	ndr	ndr
St-Pierre and Miquelon (F)	ndr	ndr	ndr	ndr	ndr	ndr
St Vincent and the Grenadines	3	1,560	n.a.	100	n.a.	n.a.
Suriname	169	13	10	n.a.	ndr	ndr
Trinidad and Tobago	6	1,020	5	627	ndr	ndr
Turks and Caicos Is. (UK)	n.a.	770	43	n.a.	ndr	ndr
United States	4,641	436,044	5,544	2,670,259	288	170,584
Uruguay	20	24,740	98	27,347	2	4,000
Venezuela	545	38,425	30,550	720,547	54	55,388
Virgin Is. (UK)	n.a.	10,000	n.a.	3	ndr	ndr
Virgin Is. (US)	ndr	ndr	11	10,000	ndr	ndr

	Total number of people reported killed (1983-1992)	Total number of people reported affected (1983-1992)	Total number of people reported killed (1993-2002)	Total number of people reported affected (1993-2002)	Total number of people reported killed (2002)	Total number of people reported affected (2002)
Asia	**326,076**	**1,399,683,589**	**462,785**	**2,274,220,229**	**12,552**	**583,064,708**
Afghanistan	3,295	447,969	10,220	7,091,120	1,359	50,806
Armenia[3]	21	1,300,144	85	319,810	ndr	ndr
Azerbaijan[3]	59	20	595	2,452,696	42	10
Bahrain	10	n.a.	143	n.a.	ndr	ndr
Bangladesh	167,145	245,955,209	9,132	73,368,083	1,232	1,671,640
Bhutan	ndr	ndr	222	1,600	ndr	ndr
Brunei Darussalam	ndr	ndr	ndr	ndr	ndr	ndr
Cambodia	100	900,000	1,123	15,456,614	29	2,120,000
China[4]	21,740	522,477,126	33,650	1,174,824,956	2,715	221,946,548
East Timor[5]			1	2,508	ndr	ndr
Georgia[3]	515	266,791	132	1,238,486	5	18,052
Hong Kong (China)[4]	233	25,248	192	6,820		
India	31,781	523,490,643	77,125	802,063,399	3,185	342,021,333
Indonesia	6,713	1,994,810	6,958	6,650,012	509	150,800
Iran, Islamic Republic of	42,445	1,151,352	5,887	64,487,496	670	351,885
Iraq	796	500	113	808,007	ndr	ndr
Israel	90	660	102	1,897	ndr	ndr
Japan	1,534	3,143,053	6,593	2,833,293	5	101,047
Jordan	34	18,029	112	330,577	5	25
Kazakhstan[3]	ndr	ndr	247	644,216	ndr	ndr
Korea, DPR of	545	20,071	270,678	10,064,811	3	65,844
Korea, Rep. of	1,948	1,109,515	2,377	846,402	276	119,009
Kuwait	ndr	ndr	2	200	ndr	ndr
Kyrgyzstan[3]	58	196,900	228	69,660	n.a.	1,002
Lao PDR	46	1,371,342	193	2,746,025	2	74,500
Lebanon	90	105,575	10	527	n.a.	500
Macau (China)	ndr	ndr	n.a.	3,986	ndr	ndr
Malaysia	505	103,943	769	74,815	12	155
Maldives	n.a.	24,149	10	n.a.	ndr	ndr
Mongolia	93	500,000	222	2,470,062	3	665,000
Myanmar	1,008	525,414	571	462,519	21	50,000
Nepal	2,355	968,233	3,894	1,147,785	633	266,072
Oman	ndr	ndr	53	91	53	91
Pakistan	5,022	19,948,416	6,037	8,989,631	291	192,343

	Total number of people reported killed (1983-1992)	Total number of people reported affected (1983-1992)	Total number of people reported killed (1993-2002)	Total number of people reported affected (1993-2002)	Total number of people reported killed (2002)	Total number of people reported affected (2002)
Palestinian Territory, Occupied[6]			14	20	ndr	ndr
Philippines	24,346	38,225,072	7,131	24,992,188	401	938,074
Qatar	ndr	ndr	ndr	ndr	ndr	
Saudi Arabia	1,884	5,000	964	4,040	116	102
Singapore	27	120	n.a.	1,317	ndr	ndr
Sri Lanka	679	8,645,586	590	4,675,163	25	907,100
Syrian Arab Republic	n.a.	n.a.	322	668,357	113	10,069
Taiwan (China)	909	23,574	3,616	119,308	236	500
Tajikistan[3]	1,601	63,500	309	3,412,794	35	6,305
Thailand	2,829	7,945,306	2,417	29,493,836	218	8,818,457
Turkmenistan[3]	ndr	ndr	51	420	ndr	ndr
United Arab Emirates	112	n.a.	140	139	29	23
Uzbekistan[3]	10	50,400	131	1,123,988	ndr	ndr
Viet Nam	5,277	17,792,879	8,466	29,987,242	276	2,516,716
Yemen[7]	158	397,040	958	283,313	53	700
Yemen, Arab Republic[7]	38	150,000				
Yemen, DPR[7]	25	340,000				
Europe	**42,029**	**6,753,554**	**35,639**	**22,490,687**	**1,701**	**1,198,766**
Albania	196	3,242,801	10	218,384	6	206,884
Andorra	ndr	ndr	ndr	ndr	ndr	ndr
Austria	83	30	263	70,494	10	60,300
Azores (P)	172	n.a.	74	1,215	ndr	ndr
Belarus[3]	ndr	ndr	61	63,468	ndr	ndr
Belgium	259	1,761	60	4,117	3	1,250
Bosnia and Herzegovina[8]	ndr	ndr	60	1,505	ndr	ndr
Bulgaria	94	3,160	44	6,759	n.a.	n.a.
Channel Is. (UK)	ndr	ndr	ndr	ndr	ndr	ndr
Croatia[8]	61	25	87	3,400	11	n.a.
Cyprus	n.a.	n.a.	59	4,307	ndr	ndr
Czech Republic[9]	ndr	ndr	65	302,111	18	200,000
Czechoslovakia[9]	94	95				
Denmark	57	100	8	n.a.	1	n.a.
Estonia[3]			934	170	ndr	ndr
Faroe Is. (DK)	ndr	ndr	ndr	ndr	ndr	ndr
Finland	n.a.	n.a.	11	33	ndr	ndr
France	633	12,490	663	3,876,897	54	2,351

	Total number of people reported killed (1983-1992)	Total number of people reported affected (1983-1992)	Total number of people reported killed (1993-2002)	Total number of people reported affected (1993-2002)	Total number of people reported killed (2002)	Total number of people reported affected (2002)
Germany[10]	66	1,795	360	576,291	117	330,491
German Dem. Rep. [10]	92	n.a.				
Germany, Fed. Rep. [10]	164	4,327				
Gibraltar (UK)	ndr	ndr	ndr	ndr		ndr
Greece	1,265	45,972	485	216,708	41	569
Greenland (DK)	ndr	ndr	ndr	ndr	ndr	ndr
Hungary	20	n.a.	191	147,236	19	1,462
Iceland	4	280	34	282	ndr	ndr
Ireland	364	n.a.	32	4,500	n.a.	300
Isle of Man (UK)	ndr	ndr	ndr	ndr	ndr	ndr
Italy	928	48,636	938	256,960	116	19,634
Latvia[3]	ndr	ndr	21	n.a.	ndr	ndr
Liechtenstein	ndr	ndr	ndr	ndr	ndr	ndr
Lithuania[3]	n.a.	n.a.	68	n.a.	ndr	ndr
Luxembourg	n.a.	n.a.	20	n.a.	20	n.a.
Macedonia, FYR[8]	ndr	ndr	221	13,171	n.a.	1,650
Malta	12	n.a.	283	n.a.	ndr	ndr
Moldova[3]	ndr	ndr	60	2,655,037	1	500
Monaco	ndr	ndr	ndr	ndr	ndr	ndr
Netherlands	80	620	106	265,251	4	n.a.
Norway	236	n.a.	270	6,130	ndr	ndr
Poland	263	939	976	240,768	200	1
Portugal	304	4,687	116	1,602	1	60
Romania	326	21,705	432	241,688	19	5,701
Russian Federation[3]	407	1,966	7,023	2,598,342	674	361,541
San Marino	ndr	ndr	ndr	ndr	ndr	ndr
Serbia Montenegro[8]	1	6,000	128	79,716	11	2,531
Slovakia[9]			73	48,015	n.a.	n.a.
Slovenia[8]	ndr	ndr	n.a.	700	ndr	ndr
Soviet Union[3]	29,644	2,160,202				
Spain	920	570,176	592	6,069,412	27	142
Sweden	36	122	64	162	1	n.a.
Switzerland	68	2,400	111	6,803	4	283
Turkey	3,135	417,367	19,784	1,737,012	185	2,157
Ukraine[2]	89	1,000	567	2,481,153	132	209
United Kingdom	1,456	203,692	285	290,888	26	750
Yugoslavia[8]	500	1,206				
Vatican	ndr	ndr	ndr	ndr	ndr	ndr

	Total number of people reported killed (1983-1992)	Total number of people reported affected (1983-1992)	Total number of people reported killed (1993-2002)	Total number of people reported affected (1993-2002)	Total number of people reported killed (2002)	Total number of people reported affected (2002)
Oceania	**1,117**	**3,158,498**	**3,394**	**15,693,673**	**91**	**39,963**
American Samoa (US)	25	n.a.	ndr	ndr	ndr	ndr
Australia	405	1,773,155	369	13,899,703	2	373
Cook Isl. (NZ)	6	2,000	19	1,644	ndr	ndr
Fiji	73	593,515	80	428,730	ndr	ndr
French Polynesia (FR)	17	5,050	13	511	ndr	ndr
Guam (US)	1	6,044	229	21,635	1	15,144
Kiribati	ndr	ndr	n.a.	84,000	ndr	ndr
Marshall Is.	n.a.	6,000	ndr	ndr	ndr	ndr
Micronesia (Federated States)	5	203	47	30,448	47	1,648
Nauru	ndr	ndr	ndr	ndr	ndr	ndr
New Caledonia (FR)	2	n.a.	n.a.	n.a.	ndr	ndr
New Zealand	23	20,460	4	3,417	n.a.	300
Niue (NZ)	n.a.	200	ndr	ndr	ndr	ndr
Northern Mariana Is. (US)	ndr	ndr	ndr	ndr	ndr	ndr
Palau	ndr	ndr	1	12,004	ndr	ndr
Papua New Guinea	343	147,000	2,555	1,061,351	41	18,644
Samoa	21	285,000	.	n.a.	ndr	ndr
Solomon Is.	134	150,874	4	89,230	n.a.	350
Tokelau (NZ)	n.a.	1,832	ndr	ndr	ndr	ndr
Tonga	1	3,103	n.a.	23,021	ndr	ndr
Tuvalu	n.a.	700	18	150	ndr	ndr
Vanuatu	60	158,862	50	37,809	n.a.	3,504
Wallis and Futuna (FR)	1	4,500	5	20	ndr	ndr
Total	**1,006,842**	**1,623,035,122**	**623,927**	**2,496,810,782**	**24,532**	**608,027,881**

Source: EM-DAT, CRED, University of Louvain, Belgium

[1] As detailed in Chapter 7, this is probably a gross underestimate.

[2] Prior to 1993, Ethiopia was considered one country, after this date, separate countries: Eritrea and Ethiopia.

[3] Prior to 1991 Soviet Union was considered one country, after this date, separate countries. The western former republics of the USSR (Belarus, Estonia, Latvia, Lithuania, Moldova, Russian Federation, Ukraine) are included in Europe; the southern former republics (Armenia, Azerbaijan, Georgia, Kazakhstan, Kyrgyzstan, Tajikistan, Turkmenistan, Uzbekistan) are included in Asia.

[4] Since July 1997, Hong Kong is included in China.

[5] Since May 2002, East Timor is an independent country.

[6] Since September 1993 and the Israel-PLO Declaration of Principles, the Gaza Strip and the West Bank have a Palestinian self-government. Direct negotiations to determine the permanent status of these territories began in September 1999 but are far from a permanent agreement.

[7] Prior to May 1990, Yemen was divided into Arab and People's Democratic Republics, after this date, it is considered one country.

[8] Prior to 1992 Yugoslavia was considered one country, after this date, separate countries: Bosnia and Herzegovina, Croatia, Serbia Montenegro (ex-Federal Republic of Yugoslavia), Slovenia, Macedonia.

[9] Prior to 1993, Czechoslovakia was considered one country, after this date, separate countries: Czech Republic and Slovakia.

[10] Prior to October 1990, Germany was divided into Federal and Democratic Republics, after this date, it is considered one country.

Note: n.a. signifies no data available; ndr signifies no disaster reported.
See Chapter 7 and caveats for more detailed information.

Comparing the decades 1983-1992 and 1993-2002, reported global deaths from natural and technological disasters have fallen by 38 per cent. However, numbers of people reported affected have risen by 54 per cent over the same period.

Table 14 Refugees and asylum seekers by country/territory of origin (1996 to 2002)

	1996	1997	1998	1999	2000	2001	2002
Africa	**3,623,200**	**2,897,000**	**2,880,950**	**3,072,800**	**3,254,300**	**2,923,000**	**3,016,000**
Algeria	–	–	3,000	5,000	–	10,000	10,000
Angola	220,000	223,000	303,300	339,300	400,000	445,000	450,000
Burundi	285,000	248,000	281,000	311,000	421,000	375,000	400,000
Cameroon	–	–	–	–	–	2,000	5,000
Central African Republic	–	–	–	–	–	22,000	20,000
Chad	15,500	12,000	15,000	13,000	53,000	35,000	7,000
Congo, DR of the	116,800	132,000	136,000	229,000	342,000	355,000	350,000
Congo	–	40,000	20,000	25,000	22,000	30,000	25,000
Côte d'Ivoire	–	–	–	–	–	–	20,000
Djibouti	10,000	5,000	3,000	1,000	1,000	–	–
Eritrea	343,100	323,000	323,100	323,100	356,400	305,000	300,000
Ethiopia	58,000	48,000	39,600	53,300	36,200	13,000	15,000
Ghana	10,000	12,000	11,000	10,000	10,000	10,000	10,000
Guinea	–	–	–	–	–	5,000	–
Guinea-Bissau	–	–	11,150	5,300	1,500	–	–
Kenya	–	–	8,000	5,000	–	–	–
Liberia	755,000	475,000	310,000	249,000	196,000	215,000	260,000
Mali	80,000	16,000	3,000	2,000	–	–	3,000
Mauritania	65,000	55,000	30,000	45,000	45,000	50,000	45,000
Namibia	–	–	–	1,000	–	–	1,000
Niger	15,000	10,000	–	–	–	–	–
Nigeria	–	–	–	–	–	10,000	25,000
Rwanda	257,000	43,000	12,000	27,000	52,000	60,000	40,000
Senegal	17,000	17,000	10,000	10,000	10,000	10,000	10,000
Sierra Leone	350,000	297,000	480,000	454,000	419,000	185,000	130,000
Somalia	467,100	486,000	414,600	415,600	370,000	300,000	290,000
Sudan	433,700	353,000	352,200	423,200	392,200	440,000	470,000
Togo	30,000	6,000	3,000	3,000	2,000	–	2,000
Uganda	15,000	10,000	12,000	15,000	20,000	20,000	10,000
Western Sahara	80,000	86,000	100,000	105,000	105,000	110,000	110,000
Zimbabwe	–	–	–	–	–	–	8,000
East Asia and Pacific	**648,200**	**723,000**	**763,200**	**864,100**	**1,056,000**	**1,078,500**	**1,207,800**
Cambodia	34,400	77,000	51,000	15,100	16,400	16,000	16,600
China (Tibet)	128,000	128,000	128,000	130,000	130,000	151,000	177,000
East Timor	–	–	–	120,000	120,000	80,000	28,700
Indonesia	10,000	8,000	8,000	8,000	6,150	5,00	11,500
Korea, DPR of	–	–	–	–	50,000	50,000	100,100
Lao PDR	3,500	14,000	12,100	13,900	400	–	1,300
Myanmar	184,300	215,000	238,100	240,100	380,250	450,000	511,000
Philippines	–	–	45,000	45,000	57,000	57,000	59,300
Viet Nam	288,000	281,000	281,000	292,000	295,800	295,000	302,300

	1996	1997	1998	1999	2000	2001	2002
South and central Asia	**3,184,100**	**2,966,000**	**2,928,700**	**2,906,750**	**3,832,700**	**4,961,500**	**3,923,000**
Afghanistan	2,628,550	2,622,000	2,628,600	2,561,050	3,520,350	4,500,000	3,530,000
Bangladesh	53,000	40,000	-	-	-	-	7,000
Bhutan	121,800	113,000	115,000	125,000	124,000	126,000	127,000
India	13,000	13,000	15,000	15,000	17,000	17,000	38,400
Kazakhstan	-	-	-	-	100	-	1,500
Kyrgyzstan	-	-	-	-	-	-	700
Pakistan	-	-	-	-	-	10,000	12,300
Sri Lanka	100,150	100,000	110,000	110,000	110,000	144,000	153,000
Tajikistan	215,600	32,000	15,100	62,500	59,750	55,000	53,100
Uzbekistan	52,000	46,000	45,000	33,200	1,500	-	-
Middle East	**4,373,100**	**4,304,000**	**4,397,700**	**3,987,050**	**5,426,500**	**4,428,000**	**3,357,800**
Iran	46,100	35,000	30,800	31,200	30,600	34,000	37,800
Iraq	608,500	526,000	555,800	534,450	409,300	300,000	530,000
Lebanon	-	-	-	-	4,400	-	-
Palestinian Territory, Occupied[1]	3,718,500	3,743,000	3,811,100	3,931,400	4,982,100	4,123,000	2,790,000
Syria	-	-	-	-	100	-	-
Europe	**1,875,150**	**1,343,100**	**1,241,300**	**1,238,100**	**755,900**	**674,000**	**641,700**
Albania	-	-	-	-	-	-	9,900
Armenia	197,000	188,000	180,000	188,400	-	9,000	11,900
Azerbaijan	238,000	218,000	218,000	230,000	-	-	4,900
Belarus	-	-	-	-	-	-	4,400
Bosnia and Herzegovina	577,000	342,600	80,350	250,000	234,600	210,000	172,800
Bulgaria	-	-	-	-	-	-	4,800
Croatia	300,000	335,000	329,000	336,000	314,700	272,000	251,000
Czech Republic	-	-	-	-	-	-	3,000
Georgia	105,000	11,000	23,000	2,800	22,400	21,000	25,600
Macedonia	-	-	-	-	-	23,000	5,000
Romania	-	-	-	-	-	-	7,000
Russian Federation	-	-	500	12,350	22,700	18,000	45,000
Serbia and Montenegro	13,700	3,100	136,900	376,400	148,900	60,000	36,000
Slovenia	-	-	-	-	4,400	-	-
Turkey	15,000	11,000	11,300	11,800	12,600	43,000	47,000
Ukraine	-	-	-	-	-	10,000	13,400
Americas and Caribbean[2]	**61,900**	**521,300**	**442,550**	**393,800**	**366,750**	**428,000**	**519,900**
Argentina	-	-	-	-	-	-	400
Brazil	-	-	-	-	-	-	800
Colombia	0	300	600	-	2,300	23,000	58,800
Cuba	850	600	300	850	1,200	3,000	34,200
Dominican Republic	-	-	-	-	-	-	100
Ecuador	-	-	-	-	-	-	300
El Salvador	12,000	12,000	250,150	253,000	235,500	217,000	204,400

	1996	1997	1998	1999	2000	2001	2002
Guatemala	34,650	30,000	251,300	146,000	102,600	129,000	129,600
Haiti	–	–	600	23,000	20,600	25,000	33,200
Mexico	–	–	–	–	–	11,000	37,500
Nicaragua	18,200	19,000	18,000	18,000	3,800	13,000	16,400
Panama	–	–	–	–	–	–	100
Peru	–	–	350	1,700	750	–	3,500
Venezuela	–	–	–	–	–	–	600
Total	**13,769,450**	**12,295,000**	**12,733,150**	**12,511,350**	**14,692,150**	**14,493,000**	**12,667,000**

– indicates zero or near zero.   *Source: US Committee for Refugees*

[1] In light of persistent protection gaps, USCR concludes that the inclusion clause of Article 1D of the UN Refugee Convention brings all Palestinians under the Convention's application. Accordingly, USCR changes its statistical approach by applying the Convention's definition of refugee status – including its cessation – to this population rather than the UN Relief and Works Agency for Palestinian Refugees in the Near East (UNRWA) registration criteria as before. This has three implications: about 1.55 million Palestinians in Jordan who are Jordanian citizens are no longer counted as refugees and the number of Palestinian refugees for which the West Bank and Gaza Strip are listed as a source is reduced by the same amount; about 800,000 Palestinians in Jordan who were displaced from the West Bank by the 1967 war are counted as internally displaced people; and about 75,000 Palestinians not registered with UNRWA in Syria and about 16,000 Palestinans similarly situated in Lebanon are counted as refugees. Some 150,000 Palestinians in Jordan who come from the Gaza Strip and are not eligible for Jordanian citizenship are counted as refugees, as before.

[2] Includes asylum applications pending in the United States; USCR estimates the number of individuals represented per case.

Half of the world's 12.6 million refugees and asylum seekers in 2002 were either Palestinians or Afghans, despite the repatriation of more than 1.5 million Afghans during the year. Numbers of refugees and asylum seekers originating from East Asia and Pacific, and from the Americas and Caribbean rose during 2002. Numbers originating from South and central Asia, and from the Middle East fell; the latter mainly due to a technical reclassification of 1.5 million Palestinian refugees as Jordanian citizens.

(Note: In part because asylum states do not always report country-of-origin data, this table understates the number of refugees and asylum seekers from many countries.)

Table 15 Refugees and asylum seekers by host country/territory (1996 to 2002)

	1996	1997	1998	1999	2000	2001	2002
Africa	**3,682,700**	**2,944,000**	**2,924,000**	**3,147,000**	**3,346,000**	**3,002,000**	**30,014,000**
Algeria	114,000	104,000	84,000	84,000	85,000	85,000	85,000
Angola	9,300	9,000	10,000	15,000	12,000	12,000	12,000
Benin	11,000	3,000	3,000	3,000	4,000	5,000	5,000
Botswana	–	–	–	1,000	3,000	4,000	4,000
Burkina Faso	26,000	2,000	–	–	–	–	1,000
Burundi	12,000	12,000	5,000	2,000	6,000	28,000	40,000
Cameroon	1,000	1,000	3,000	10,000	45,000	32,000	15,000
Central African Rep.	36,400	38,000	47,000	55,000	54,000	49,000	50,000
Chad	–	–	10,000	20,000	20,000	15,000	15,000
Congo, DR of the	455,000	255,000	220,000	235,000	276,000	305,000	220,000
Congo	16,000	21,000	20,000	40,000	126,000	102,000	120,000
Côte d'Ivoire	320,000	202,000	128,000	135,000	94,000	103,000	50,000
Djibouti	22,000	22,000	23,000	23,000	22,000	22,000	23,000
Egypt	46,000	46,000	46,000	47,000	57,000	75,000	80,000
Eritrea	–	3,000	3,000	2,000	1,000	2,000	2,000
Ethiopia	328,000	313,000	251,000	246,000	194,000	114,000	115,000
Gabon	1,000	1,000	1,000	15,000	15,000	20,000	20,000
Gambia	5,000	8,000	13,000	25,000	15,000	15,000	10,000
Ghana	35,000	20,000	15,000	12,000	13,000	12,000	40,000
Guinea	650,000	430,000	514,000	453,000	390,000	190,000	180,000
Guinea-Bissau	15,000	4,000	5,000	5,000	6,000	7,000	7,000
Kenya	186,000	196,000	192,000	254,000	233,000	243,000	215,000
Liberia	100,000	100,000	120,000	90,000	70,000	60,000	60,000
Libya	27,200	27,000	28,000	11,000	11,000	33,000	12,000
Malawi	–	–	–	–	–	6,000	13,000
Mali	15,000	17,000	5,000	7,000	7,000	9,000	3,000
Mauritania	15,000	5,000	20,000	25,000	25,000	25,000	25,000
Mozambique	–	–	–	1,000	2,000	5,000	7,000
Namibia	1,000	1,000	2,000	8,000	20,000	31,000	25,000
Niger	27,000	7,000	3,000	2,000	1,000	1,000	–
Nigeria	8,000	9,000	5,000	7,000	10,000	7,000	7,000
Rwanda	20,000	28,000	36,000	36,000	29,000	35,000	30,000
Senegal	51,000	41,000	30,000	42,000	41,000	43,000	45,000
Sierra Leone	15,000	15,000	10,000	7,000	3,000	15,000	60,000
South Africa	22,500	28,000	29,000	40,000	30,000	22,000	65,000
Sudan	395,000	365,000	360,000	363,000	385,000	307,000	350,000
Swaziland	–	–	–	–	–	1,000	1,000
Tanzania	335,000	295,000	329,000	413,000	543,000	498,000	510,000
Togo	10,000	12,000	11,000	10,000	11,000	11,000	12,000
Tunisia	300	–	–	–	–	–	–

	1996	1997	1998	1999	2000	2001	2002
Uganda	225,000	185,000	185,000	197,000	230,000	174,000	220,000
Zambia	126,000	118,000	157,000	205,000	255,000	270,000	250,000
Zimbabwe	1,000	1,000	1,000	1,000	2,000	9,000	10,000
East Asia and Pacific	**449,600**	**535,100**	**559,200**	**657,300**	**791,700**	**815,700**	**876,200**
Australia	7,400	18,000	15,000	17,000	16,700	21,800	26,000
Cambodia	–	–	200	100	50	1,000	300
China[1]	294,100	281,800	281,800	292,800	350,000	345,000	396,000
Hong Kong[1]	1,300	n.a.	n.a.	n.a.	n.a.	n.a.	–
Indonesia	–	100	100	120,000	120,800	81,300	29,000
Japan	300	300	500	400	3,800	6,400	6,500
Korea, Rep. of	–	–	–	–	350	600	–
Malaysia[2]	5,200	5,200	50,600	45,400	57,400	57,500	59,000
Nauru[2]	–	–	–	–	–	800	500
New Zealand	–	–	–	–	3,100	2,700	1,700
Papua New Guinea	10,000	8,200	8,000	8,000	6,000	5,400	5,100
Philippines	50	100	300	200	200	200	100
Solomon Islands	1,000	800	n.a.	–	–	–	–
Thailand	95,850	205,600	187,700	158,400	217,300	277,000	336,000
Viet Nam	34,400	15,000	15,000	15,000	16,000	16,000	16,000
South and central Asia	**1,794,800**	**1,743,000**	**1,708,700**	**1,689,000**	**2,655,600**	**2,702,800**	**2,139,200**
Afghanistan	18,900	–	–	–	–	–	–
Bangladesh	40,000	40,100	53,100	53,100	121,600	122,000	122,100
India	352,200	323,500	292,100	292,000	290,000	345,800	332,300
Kazakhstan	14,000	14,000	4,100	14,800	20,000	19,500	21,000
Kyrgyzstan	17,000	15,500	15,000	10,900	11,000	9,700	9,200
Nepal	109,800	116,000	118,000	130,000	129,000	131,000	132,000
Pakistan	1,215,700	215,650	1,217,400	1,127,000	2,019,000	2,018,000	1,501,400
Tajikistan	2,200	3,800	5,500	4,700	12,400	4,600	3,700
Turkmenistan	22,000	13,000	500	18,500	14,200	14,000	14,000
Uzbekistan	3,000	1,250	3,000	38,000	38,400	38,000	3,500
Middle East	**5,840,550**	**5,708,000**	**5,814,100**	**5,849,000**	**6,035,300**	**6,830,200**	**5,065,000**
Gaza Strip	716,900	746,000	773,000	798,400	824,600	852,600	893,200
Iran	2,020,000	1,900,000	1,931,000	1,835,000	1,895,000	2,558,000	2,200,000
Iraq	114,400	110,000	104,000	129,400	127,700	128,100	134,000
Israel	–	–	–	400	4,700	4,700	2,500
Jordan[3]	1,362,500	1,413,800	1,463,800	1,518,000	1,580,000	1,643,900	153,000
Kuwait	42,000	90,000	52,000	52,000	52,000	50,000	65,000
Lebanon[3]	355,100	362,300	368,300	378,100	383,200	389,500	409,400
Saudi Arabia	257,850	116,750	128,300	128,600	128,500	128,500	5,200
Syria[3]	384,400	361,000	369,800	379,200	389,000	397,600	482,200
United Arab Emirates	400	500	200	–	–	–	–

	1996	1997	1998	1999	2000	2001	2002
West Bank	532,400	543,000	555,000	569,700	583,000	607,800	639,500
Yemen	54,600	64,900	68,700	60,000	67,600	69,500	81,000
Europe	**2,479,100**	**2,020,300**	**1,728,400**	**1,909,100**	**1,153,300**	**972,800**	**868,300**
Albania	–	–	25,000	5,000	500	400	100
Armenia	150,000	219,150	229,000	240,000	–	11,000	11,000
Austria	80,000	11,400	16,500	16,600	6,100	10,800	30,900
Azerbaijan	249,150	244,100	235,300	222,000	3,600	7,000	11,400
Belarus	10,800	33,500	16,500	2,900	3,200	3,100	3,300
Belgium	18,200	14,100	25,800	42,000	46,400	41,000	32,500
Bosnia and Herzegovina	–	40,000	40,000	60,000	38,200	33,200	28,000
Bulgaria	550	2,400	2,800	2,800	3,000	2,900	1,800
Croatia	167,000	50,000	27,300	24,000	22,500	21,900	8,100
Cyprus	–	–	200	300	300	1,300	1,800
Czech Republic	2,900	700	2,400	1,800	4,800	10,600	6,300
Denmark	24,600	13,000	6,100	8,500	10,300	12,200	4,100
Finland	11,700	1,600	2,300	3,800	2,600	2,100	1,400
France[2]	29,200	16,000	17,400	30,000	26,200	12,400	13,000
Georgia	–	100	300	5,200	7,600	7,900	4,200
Germany	436,400	277,000	198,000	285,000	180,000	116,000	104,000
Greece	5,600	2,100	2,800	7,500	800	6,500	1,800
Hungary	5,400	3,400	3,200	6,000	4,200	2,900	2,500
Iceland	–	–	–	100	50	–	–
Ireland	1,800	4,300	6,900	8,500	7,700	9,500	5,800
Italy	10,600	20,000	6,800	24,900	13,700	9,600	5,100
Lithuania	–	100	100	100	150	300	500
Macedonia, FYR of	5,100	3,500	7,300	17,400	9,000	3,600	2,800
Moldova	–	–	–	–	–	300	–
Netherlands	46,200	64,200	47,000	40,000	29,600	31,000	17,200
Norway	12,700	3,100	2,500	9,500	8,600	13,200	18,000
Poland	3,200	1,200	1,300	1,300	2,300	1,800	1,800
Portugal	200	150	1,400	1,700	1,600	50	–
Romania	600	2,000	900	900	2,100	200	100
Russian Federation	484,000	324,000	161,900	104,300	36,200	28,200	17,500
Serbia and Monenegro	550,000	550,000	480,000	476,000	484,200	400,000	350,500
Slovak Republic	2,000	100	300	400	400	3,100	4,500
Slovenia	10,300	5,300	7,300	5,000	12,000	2,700	–
Spain	7,200	3,300	2,500	4,500	1,100	1,000	600
Sweden	60,500	8,400	16,700	20,200	18,500	18,500	29,800
Switzerland	41,700	34,100	40,000	104,000	62,600	57,900	69,400
Turkey	13,000	5,000	12,000	9,100	9,900	12,600	6,000
Ukraine	8,000	4,900	8,600	5,800	5,500	6,000	3,600
United Kingdom	40,500	58,100	74,000	112,000	87,800	69,800	69,000

	1996	1997	1998	1999	2000	2001	2002
Americas and the Caribbean	**232,800**	**616,000**	**739,950**	**737,000**	**562,100**	**597,000**	**755,700**
Argentina	400	10,700	1,100	3,300	1,000	3,100	2,700
Bahamas	–	50	100	100	100	100	–
Belize	8,700	4,000	3,500	3,000	1,700	–	–
Bolivia	550	300	350	400	–	400	400
Brazil	2,200	2,300	2,400	2,300	2,700	4,050	3,700
Canada	26,100	48,800	46,000	53,000	54,400	70,000	78,500
Chile	200	300	100	300	300	550	400
Colombia	200	200	200	250	250	200	200
Costa Rica	23,150	23,100	23,100	22,900	7,300	10,600	12,800
Cuba	1,650	1,500	1,100	1,000	1,000	1,000	1,000
Dominican Republic	600	600	600	650	500	500	300
Ecuador	200	200	250	350	1,600	4,300	9,100
El Salvador	150	100	100	–	–	–	–
Guatemala	1,200	1,300	800	750	700	700	700
Honduras	–	–	100	–	–	–	–
Jamaica	–	–	50	50	50	–	–
Mexico	34,450	30,000	7,500	8,500	6,500	6,200	4,000
Nicaragua	900	700	150	500	300		
Panama	650	300	1,300	600	1,300	1,500	1,700
Paraguay	–	–	–	–	–	50	–
Peru	300	–	–	700	750	750	900
United States[4]	129,600	491,000	651,000	638,000	481,500	492,500	638,000
Uruguay	–	–	–	150	50	100	100
Venezuela	1,600	300	150	200	100	400	1,100
Total	**15,337,650**	**14,479,550**	**13,566,400**	**13,988,000**	**14,543,700**	**14,921,000**	**12,718,400**

Source: US Committee for Refugees

– indicates zero or near zero.

[1] As of 1997, figures for Hong Kong are included in total for China.

[2] Reliable estimates are not available.

[3] See note 1, Table 14.

[4] Includes asylum applications pending in the United States; USCR estimates the number of individuals represented per case.

The total number of refugees and asylum seekers decreased in 2002. The downward trend was due to many factors, including a technical reclassification of 1.5 million Palestinian refugees as Jordanian citizens, a major repatriation of Afghan refugees and the unwillingness of many states, especially those in the developed world, to accept new refugees and asylum seekers. The number of refugees and asylum seekers hosted by the Americas and Caribbean rose by over one-quarter in 2002, while those hosted by Africa and East Asia remained relatively steady. Numbers hosted by Europe, South and central Asia, and the Middle East all fell, as refugees returned to their homes or were deterred from seeking asylum. During 2002, the Middle East continued to host about 40 per cent of the world's refugees and asylum seekers, with Iran carrying the world's largest caseload of 2.2 million. More than half of the world's refugees and asylum seekers were found in just five countries or territories: Iran, the Gaza Strip and West Bank, Pakistan, the United States and Tanzania.

Table 16 Significant populations of internally displaced people (1996 to 2002)

	1996	1997	1998	1999	2000	2001	2002
Africa	**8,805,000**	**7,590,000**	**8,958,000**	**10,355,000**	**10,527,000**	**10,935,000**	**10,310,000**
Algeria	10,000	n.a.	200,000	100,000	100,000	100,000	100,000
Angola	1,200,000	1,200,000	1,500,000	1,500,000	2,000,000	2,000,000	2,000,000
Burundi	400,000	500,000	500,000	800,000	600,000	600,000	400,000
Central African Rep.	–	–	–	–	–	5,000	10,000
Congo, DR of the	400,000	100,000	300,000	800,000	1,500,000	2,000,000	2,000,000
Congo, PR	–	–	250,000	500,000	30,000	50,000	100,000
Côte d'Ivoire	–	–	–	–	2,000	5,000	300,000
Djibouti	25,000	5,000	–	–	–	–	–
Eritrea	–	–	100,000	250,000	310,000	90,000	75,000
Ethiopia	–	–	150,000	300,000	250,000	100,000	100,000
Ghana	20,000	20,000	20,000	–	–	–	–
Guinea	–	–	–	–	60,000	100,000	20,000
Guinea-Bissau	–	–	200,000	50,000	–	–	–
Kenya	100,000	150,000	200,000	100,000	100,000	200,000	200,000
Liberia	1,000,000	500,000	75,000	50,000	20,000	80,000	100,000
Nigeria	30,000	50,000	3,000	5,000	–	50,000	50,000
Rwanda	–	50,000	500,000	600,000	150,000	–	–
Senegal	–	10,000	10,000	–	5,000	5,000	5,000
Sierra Leone	800,000	500,000	300,000	500,000	700,000	600,000	–
Somalia	250,000	200,000	250,000	350,000	300,000	400,000	350,000
South Africa	500,000	5,000	–	–	–	–	–
Sudan	4,000,000	4,000,000	4,000,000	4,000,000	4,000,000	4,000,000	4,000,000
Uganda	70,000	300,000	400,000	450,000	400,000	500,000	400,000
Zimbabwe						50,000	100,000
East Asia and Pacific	**1,070,000**	**800,000**	**1,150,000**	**1,577,000**	**1,670,000**	**2,265,000**	**1,549,000**
Cambodia	32,000	30,000	22,000	–	–	–	–
East Timor	–	–	–	300,000	–	–	–
Indonesia	–	–	–	440,000	800,000	1,400,000	800,000
Korea, DPR of	–	–	–	–	100,000	100,000	100,000
Myanmar	1,000,000	750,000	1,000,000	600,000	600,000	600,000	600,000
Papua New Guinea	70,000	20,000	6,000	5,000	–	1,000	500
Philippines	–	–	122,000	200,000	140,000	135,000	45,000
Solomon Islands	–	–	–	32,000	30,000	30,000	3,500
Europe	**4,735,000**	**3,695,000**	**3,685,000**	**3,993,000**	**3,539,000**	**2,785,000**	**2,679,000**
Armenia	50,000	70,000	60,000	–	–	50,000	50,000
Azerbaijan	550,000	550,000	576,000	568,000	575,000	572,000	576,000
Bosnia and Herzegovina	1,000,000	800,000	836,000	830,000	518,000	439,000	367,500
Croatia	185,000	110,000	61,000	50,000	34,000	23,000	17,000

	1996	1997	1998	1999	2000	2001	2002
Cyprus	265,000	265,000	265,000	265,000	265,000	265,000	265,000
Georgia	280,000	285,000	275,000	280,000	272,000	264,000	262,000
Macedonia	–	–	–	–	–	21,000	8,500
Russian Federation	400,000	375,000	350,000	800,000	800,000	474,000	370,000
Serbia and Montenegro	–	–	257,000	600,000	475,000	277,000	263,000
Turkey	2,000,000	1,250,000	1,000,000	600,000	600,000	400,000	500,000
Americas and Caribbean	**1,220,000**	**1,624,000**	**1,755,000**	**1,886,000**	**2,176,000**	**2,465,000**	**2,521,000**
Colombia	600,000	1,000,000	1,400,000	1,800,000	2,100,000	2,450,000	2,500,000
Guatemala	200,000	250,000	–	–	–	–	–
Haiti	–	–	–	–	–	–	6,000
Mexico	–	14,000	15,000	16,000	16,000	15,000	15,000
Peru	420,000	360,000	340,000	70,000	60,000	–	–
Middle East	**1,475,000**	**1,475,000**	**1,575,000**	**1,917,000**	**1,700,000**	**1,670,000**	**2,626,000**
Palestinian Territory, Occupied	–	–	–	17,000	–	20,000	26,000
Iraq	900,000	900,000	1,000,000	900,000	700,000	700,000	1,100,000
Israel	–	–	–	200,000	200,000	200,000	250,000
Jordan[1]	–	–	–	–	–	–	800,000
Lebanon	450,000	450,000	450,000	350,000	350,000	250,000	300,000
Syria	125,000	125,000	125,000	450,000	450,000	500,000	150,000
South and central Asia	**2,400,000**	**2,253,500**	**2,130,000**	**1,617,000**	**1,542,000**	**2,402,000**	**1,944,000**
Afghanistan	1,200,000	1,250,000	1,000,000	500,000	375,000	1,000,000	724,000
Bangladesh[2]	–	–	50,000	50,000	60,000	100,000	–
India	250,000	200,000	520,000	507,000	507,000	500,000	650,000
Pakistan	–	–	–	–	–	2,000	–
Sri Lanka	900,000	800,000	560,000	560,000	600,000	800,000	570,000
Tajikistan	50,000	3,500	–	–	–	–	–
Total	**19,705,000**	**17,437,500**	**19,253,000**	**21,345,000**	**21,154,000**	**22,522,000**	**21,629,000**

Source: US Committee for Refugees

– indicates zero or near zero.

[1] See note 1, Table 14.

[2] Reliable estimates are not available.

Approximately 900,000 fewer people were internally displaced at the end of 2002 than at the end of 2001. Large internally displaced populations remained in Sudan (4 million), Colombia (2.5 million), Angola (2 million), the Democratic Republic of the Congo (2 million) and Iraq 1.1 million). These five countries alone account for over half of all IDPs. However, some IDPs were able to return home in Afghanistan, Bosnia and Herzegovina, Guinea, Indonesia, the Philippines, Sierra Leone and Sri Lanka. East Asia and Pacific saw IDP levels drop by one-third in 2002. Almost half of the world's internally displaced people in 2002 were in Africa.

(Estimates of the size of internally displaced populations are frequently subject to great margins of error and are often imprecise.)

Figure 8.1
Source:
CRED/OECD.

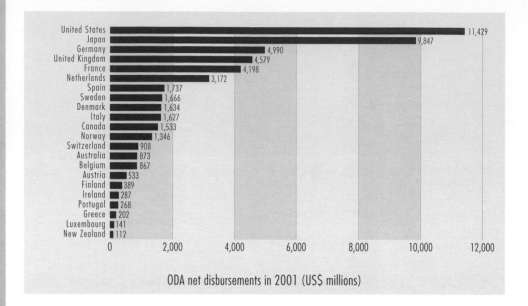

ODA net disbursements in 2001 (US$ millions)

Figure 8.2
Source:
CRED/OECD.

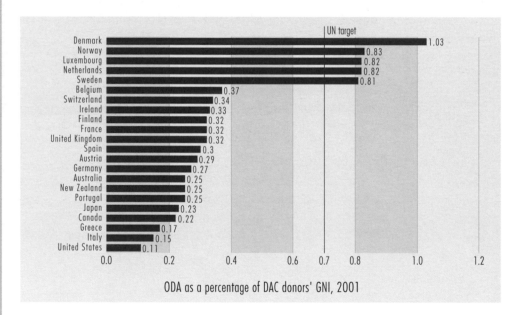

ODA as a percentage of DAC donors' GNI, 2001

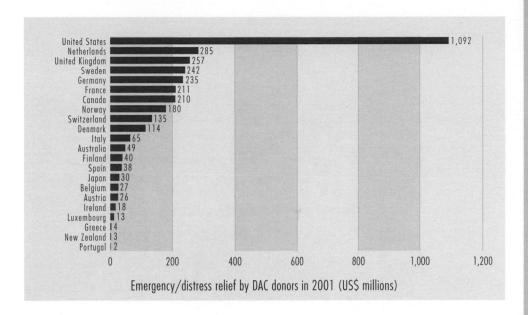

Figure 8.3
Source:
CRED/OECD.

Emergency/distress relief by DAC donors in 2001 (US$ millions)

Notes for Figures 8.1, 8.2 and 8.3

Official development assistance (ODA) from members of the Organisation for Economic Co-operation and Development's Development Assistance Committee (DAC) slipped to US$ 52.3 billion in 2001 (the latest year for which statistics are available), a decrease of some US$ 1.4 billion from aid disbursements in 2000. Expressed as a percentage of donor countries' gross national income (GNI), only five countries (Denmark, Luxembourg, Netherlands, Norway and Sweden) exceeded the UN's 0.7 per cent target. Emergency distress relief fell from 2000's total (US$ 3.6 billion) to US$ 3.3 billion in 2001. As in previous years, the United States was the biggest donor of emergency/distress relief, accounting for one-third of all donations.

chapter 9

Section Two

**Tracking
the system**

Global and local:
the largest
humanitarian
network in the world
links 178 National
Societies.

Daniel Cima/
International Federation,
Argentina.

A network both global and local

Contact details for the members of the International Red Cross and Red Crescent Movement

International Federation of Red Cross and Red Crescent Societies

P.O. Box 372
1211 Geneva 19
Switzerland
Tel. +41 22 730 4222
Fax +41 22 733 0395
Tlx 045 412 133 FRC CH
Tlg. LICROSS GENEVA
E-mail secretariat@ifrc.org
Web http://www.ifrc.org

International Committee of the Red Cross

19 avenue de la Paix
1202 Geneva
Switzerland
Tel. +41 22 734 6001
Fax +41 22 733 2057
Tlx 414 226 CCR CH
Tlg. INTERCROIXROUGE GENEVE
E-mail icrc.gva@gwn.icrc.org
Web http://www.icrc.org

National Red Cross and Red Crescent Societies

National Red Cross and Red Crescent Societies are listed alphabetically by International Organization for Standardization Codes for the Representation of Names of Countries, English spelling.

Details correct as of 1 March 2003. Please forward any corrections to the International Federation's Information Resource Centre in Geneva e-mail: irc@ifrc.org.

Afghan Red Crescent Society

Pul Artel
P.O. Box 3066
Shar-e-Now
Kabul
Afghanistan
Tel. +93 702 80698
Fax +93 229 0097

Albanian Red Cross

Rruga "Muhammet Gjollesha"
Sheshi "Karl Topia"
C.P. 1511
Tirana
Albania
Tel. +355 42 22037
Fax +355 42 25855
Web http://www.kksh.org/

Algerian Red Crescent

15 bis, Boulevard
Mohammed V
Alger 16000
Algeria
Tel. +213 21 633956
Fax +213 21 633690
E-mail cra@algeriainfo.com
Web http://www.cra-dz.org/

Andorra Red Cross

Prat de la Creu 22
Andorra la Vella
Andorra
Tel. +376 825225
Fax +376 828630
E-mail creuroja@creuroja.ad
Web http://www.creuroja.ad

Angola Red Cross

Rua 1° Congresso no 21
Caixa Postal 927
Luanda
Angola
Tel. +244 2 336543
Fax +244 2 372868
E-mail cruzvermelhangola@
     netangola.com

Antigua and Barbuda Red Cross Society

Old Parham Road
P.O. Box 727
St. Johns, Antigua W.I.
Antigua and Barbuda
Tel. +1 268 4620800
Fax +1 268 4609595

Argentine Red Cross

Hipólito Yrigoyen 2068
1089 Buenos Aires
Argentina
Tel. +54 114 9511391
Fax +54 114 9527715
E-mail info@cruzroja.org.ar
Web http://www.cruzroja.org.ar

Armenian Red Cross Society

21 Paronian Street
375015 Yerevan
Armenia
Tel. +374 1 538367
Fax +374 1 583630
E-mail redcross@redcross.am

Australian Red Cross

155 Pelham Street
P.O. Box 196
Carlton South VIC 3053
Australia
Tel. +61 3 93451800
Fax +61 3 93482513
E-mail redcross@nat.
     redcross.org.au
Web http://www.redcross.org.au

Austrian Red Cross

Wiedner Hauptstrasse 32
Postfach 39
1041 Wien
Austria
Tel. +43 1 58900 0
Fax +43 1 58900 199
E-mail oerk@redcross.or.at
Web http://www.roteskreuz.at

Red Crescent Society of Azerbaijan

S. Safarov Street 2
Baku, Nesimi district
PC 370010
Azerbaijan
Tel. +994 12 938481
Fax +994 12 931578
E-mail azerb.redcrescent@azdata.net

The Bahamas Red Cross Society

P.O. Box N-8331
Nassau
Bahamas
Tel. +1 242 3237370
Fax +1 242 3237404
E-mail redcross@bahamas.net.bs

Bahrain Red Crescent Society

P.O. Box 882
Manama
Bahrain
Tel. +973 293171
Fax +973 291797
E-mail hilal@batelco.com.bh
Web http://www.
     batelco.com.bh/brcs/

Bangladesh Red Crescent Society

684-686 Bara Maghbazar
G.P.O. Box 579
Dhaka – 1217
Bangladesh
Tel. +880 2 9330188
Fax +880 2 9352303
E-mail chbdrcs@bdonline.com
Web http://www.bdrcs.org/

The Barbados Red Cross Society

Red Cross House
Jemmotts Lane
Bridgetown
Barbados
Tel. +1 246 4262052
Fax +1 246 4262052
E-mail bdosredcross@caribsurf.com

Belarusian Red Cross

35, Karl Marx Str.
220030 Minsk
Belarus
Tel. +375 17 2272620
Fax +375 17 2272620
E-mail brc@home.by

Belgian Red Cross

Ch. de Vleurgat 98
1050 Bruxelles
Belgium
Tel. +32 2 6454545
Fax +32 2 6460439 French;
     6433406 Flemish
E-mail info@redcross-fr.be
     documentatie@redcross-fl.be
Web http://www.redcross.be

Belize Red Cross Society

1 Gabourel Lane
P.O. Box 413
Belize City
Belize
Tel. +501 2 73319
Fax +501 2 30998
E-mail bzercshq@btl.net

Red Cross of Benin

B.P. No. 1
Porto-Novo
Benin
Tel. +229 212886
Fax +229 214927
Tlx 1131 CRBEN

Bolivian Red Cross

Avenida Simón Bolívar N° 1515
Casilla N° 741
La Paz
Bolivia
Tel. +591 2 202930
Fax +591 2 359102
E-mail cruzrobo@caoba.entelnet
Web http://www.come.to/
     cruzroja.org.bo

The Red Cross Society of Bosnia and Herzegovina

Titova 7
71000 Sarajevo
Bosnia and Herzegovina
Tel. +387 33 269 930
Fax +387 33 200 148
E-mail rcsbihhq@bih.net.ba

Botswana Red Cross Society

135 Independance Avenue
P.O. Box 485
Gaborone
Botswana
Tel. +267 352465
Fax +267 312352
E-mail brcs@info.bw

Brazilian Red Cross

Praça Cruz Vermelha No. 10/12
20230-130 Rio de Janeiro RJ
Brazil
Tel. +55 21 22210658
Fax +55 21 5071538
E-mail cvdobrasil@ig.com.br

Brunei Darussalam Red Crescent Society

P.O. Box 1315
KA1131 Kuala Belait
Brunei Darussalam
Tel. +673 2 339774
Fax +673 2 382797

Bulgarian Red Cross

76, James Boucher Boulevard
1407 Sofia
Bulgaria
Tel. +359 2 650595
Fax +359 2 656937
E-mail secretariat@redcross.bg
Web http://www.redcross.bg

Burkinabe Red Cross Society

01 B.P. 4404
Ouagadougou 01
Burkina Faso
Tel. +226 361340
Fax +226 363121
Tlx LSCR 5438
     BF OUAGADOUGOU

Burundi Red Cross

18, Av. de la Croix-Rouge
B.P. 324
Bujumbura
Burundi
Tel. +257 216246
Fax +257 211101
E-mail croixrou@cbinf.com

Cambodian Red Cross Society

17, Vithei de la Croix-Rouge
Cambodgienne
Phnom-Penh
Cambodia
Tel. +855 23 212876
Fax +855 23 212875
E-mail crc@camnet.com.kh

Cameroon Red Cross Society

Rue Henri Dunant
B.P. 631
Yaoundé
Cameroon
Tel. +237 2224177
Fax +237 2224177
Tlx 0970 8884 KN

The Canadian Red Cross Society

170 Metcalfe Street, Suite 300
Ottawa
Ontario K2P 2P2
Canada
Tel. +1 613 7401900
Fax +1 613 7401911
E-mail cancross@redcross.ca
Web http://www.redcross.ca

Red Cross of Cape Verde

Rua Andrade Corvo
Caixa Postal 119
Praia
Cape Verde
Tel. +238 611701
Fax +238 614174
Tlx 6004 CV CV

Central African Red Cross Society

Avenue Koudoukou Km, 5
B.P. 1428
Bangui
Central African Republic
Tel. +236 612223
Fax +236 613561
E-mail sida_crca@yahoo.fr

Red Cross of Chad

B.P. 449
N'Djamena
Chad
Tel. +235 523434
E-mail crftchad@intnet.td

Chilean Red Cross
Avenida Santa María No. 150
Providencia
Correo 21, Casilla 246 V
Santiago de Chile
Chile
Tel. +56 2 7771448
Fax +56 2 7370270
E-mail cruzroja@rdc.cl

Red Cross Society of China
53 Ganmian Hutong
100010 Beijing
China
Tel. +86 10 65124447
Fax +86 10 65124169
E-mail hq@chineseredcross.
    org.ac.cn
Web http://www.
    chineseredcross.org.cn

Colombian Red Cross Society
Avenida 68 N° 66-31
Apartado Aéreo 11'110
Bogotá D.C.
Colombia
Tel. +57 1 4376339
Fax +57 1 4366365
E-mail mundo@cruzrojacolombiana
Web http://www.
    cruzrojacolombiana.org

Congolese Red Cross
Place de la Paix
B.P. 4145
Brazzaville
Congo
Tel. +242 688 249
Fax +242 828825
E-mail croixrouge_congobzv@
    yahoo.fr

Red Cross of the Democratic Republic of the Congo
41, Avenue de la Justice
Zone de la Gombe
B.P. 1712
Kinshasa I
Congo, D.R. of the
Tel. +243 12 34897
Fax +243 8804551
E-mail: secretariat@crrdc.aton.cd

Costa Rican Red Cross
Calle 14, Avenida 8
Apartado 1025
1000 San José
Costa Rica
Tel. +506 2337033
Fax +506 2237628
E-mail info@cruzroja.or.cr
Web http://www.cruzroja.or.cr

Red Cross Society of Côte d'Ivoire
P.O. Box 1244
Abidjan 01
Côte d'Ivoire
Tel. +225 20321335
Fax +225 20324381
E-mail crci@afnet.net

Croatian Red Cross
Ulica Crvenog kriza 14
10000 Zagreb
Croatia
Tel. +385 1 4655814
Fax +385 1 4655365
E-mail redcross@hck.hr
Web http://www.hck.hr/

Cuban Red Cross
Calle 20#707
C.P. 10300
Cuidad de la Habana
Cuba
Tel. +53 7 228272
Fax +53 7 228272
E-mail crsn@infomed.sld.cu

Czech Red Cross
Thunovska 18
CZ-118 04 Praha 1
Czech Republic
Tel. +420 2 51104111
Fax +420 2 51104261
E-mail cck.zahranicni@iol.cz

Danish Red Cross
Blegdamsvej 27
P.O. Box 2600
DK-2100 Copenhagen Ö
Denmark
Tel. +45 35259200
Fax +45 35259292
E-mail drc@redcross.dk
Web http://www.redcross.dk

Red Crescent Society of Djibouti
B.P. 8
Djibouti
Djibouti
Tel. +253 352270
Fax +253 351451
E-mail crd@intnet.dj

Dominica Red Cross Society
Federation Drive
Goodwill
Dominica
Tel. +1 767 4488280
Fax +1 767 4487708
E-mail redcross@cwdom.dm

Dominican Red Cross
Calle Juan E. Dunant No. 51
Ens. Miraflores
Apartado Postal 1293
Santo Domingo, D.N.
Dominican Republic
Tel. +1 809 6823793
Fax +1 809 6897344
E-mail cruz.roja@codetel.net.do

Ecuadorian Red Cross

Antonio Elizalde E 4-31 y Av.
Colombia esq.
Casilla 1701
2119 Quito
Ecuador
Tel. +593 2 2954587
Fax +593 2 2570424
E-mail difusio@attglobal.net
Web http://www.
    cruzroja-ecuador.org/

Egyptian Red Crescent Society

Abd El Razek Al Sanhoury Street,
Nasr City
7516 Cairo
Egypt
Tel. +20 2 6703979
Fax +20 2 6703967
E-mail erc@brainyl.ie-eg.com

Salvadorean Red Cross Society

17 C. Pte. y Av. Henri Dunant
Apartado Postal 2672
San Salvador
El Salvador
Tel. +503 2227749
Fax +503 2227758
E-mail crsalvador@vianet.com.sv
Web http://www.
    elsalvador.cruzroja.org/

Red Cross of Equatorial Guinea

Alcalde Albilio Balboa 92
Apartado postal 460
Malabo
Equatorial Guinea
Tel. +240 9 3701
Fax +240 9 3701

Estonia Red Cross

Lai Street 17
0001 Tallinn
Estonia
Tel. +372 6411644
Fax +372 6411641
E-mail haide.laanemets@recross.ee

Ethiopian Red Cross Society

Ras Desta Damtew Avenue
P.O. Box 195
Addis Ababa
Ethiopia
Tel. +251 1 519074
Fax +251 1 512643
E-mail ercs@telecom.net.et

Fiji Red Cross Society

22 Gorrie Street
GPO Box 569
Suva
Fiji
Tel. +679 3314133
Fax +679 3303818
E-mail redcross@connect.com.fj

Finnish Red Cross

Tehtaankatu 1 a
P.O. Box 168
FIN-00141 Helsinki
Finland
Tel. +358 9 12931
Fax +358 9 1293326
E-mail forename.
    surname@redcross.fi
Web http://www.redcross.fi

French Red Cross

1, Place Henry-Dunant
F-75384 Paris Cedex 08
France
Tel. +33 1 44431100
Fax +33 1 44431101
E-mail communication@
    croix-rouge.net
Web http://www.croix-rouge.fr

Gabonese Red Cross Society

Place de l'Indépendance
Boîte Postale 2274
Libreville
Gabon
Tel. +241 766159
Fax +241 766160
E-mail gab.cross@
    internetgabon.com

The Gambia Red Cross Society

Kanifing Industrial Area – Banjul
P.O. Box 472
Banjul
Gambia
Tel. +220 392405
Fax +220 394921
E-mail redcrossgam@delphi.com

Red Cross Society of Georgia

15, Krilov St.
380002 Tbilisi
Georgia
Tel. +995 32 961534
Fax +995 32 953304
E-mail georcs@hotmail.com

German Red Cross

Carstennstrasse 58
D-12205 Berlin
Germany
Tel. +49 30 85404-0
Fax +49 30 85404470
E-mail drk@drk.de
Web http://www.rotkreuz.de

Ghana Red Cross Society

Ministries Annex Block A3
Off Liberia Road Extension
P.O. Box 835
Accra
Ghana
Tel. +233 21 662298
Fax +233 21 661491
E-mail grcs@idngh.com

Hellenic Red Cross

Rue Lycavittou 1
Athens 106 72
Greece
Tel. +30 210 3621681
Fax +30 210 3615606
E-mail hrc@netmode.ntua.gr
Web http://www.redcross.gr

Grenada Red Cross Society
Upper Lucas Street
P.O. Box 551
St. George's
Grenada
Tel. +1 473 4401483
Fax +1 473 4401829
E-mail grercs@caribsurf.com

Guatemalan Red Cross
3a Calle 8-40, Zona 1
Guatemala, C.A.
Guatemala
Tel. +502 2 322026
Fax +502 2 324649
E-mail crg@guate.net
Web http://www.
    guatemala.cruzroja.org/

Red Cross Society of Guinea
B.P. 376
Conakry
Guinea
Tel. +224 412310
Fax +224 414255
Tlx 22101

Red Cross Society of Guinea-Bissau
Avenida Unidade Africana, No. 12
C.P. 514-1036 BIX, Codex
Bissau
Guinea-Bissau
Tel. +245 202408
Tlx 251 PCE BI

The Guyana Red Cross Society
P.O. Box 10524
Georgetown
Guyana
Tel. +592 2 65174
Fax +592 2 77099
E-mail redcross@sdnp.org.gy
Web http://www.
    sdnp.org.gy/redcross/

Haitian National Red Cross Society
1, rue Eden
Bicentenaire
CRH, B.P. 1337
Port-Au-Prince
Haiti
Tel. +509 5109813
Fax +509 2231054
E-mail croroha@publi-tronic.com

Honduran Red Cross
7a Calle
entre 1a. y 2a. Avenidas
Comayagüela D.C.
Honduras
Tel. +504 2378876
Fax +504 2380185
E-mail honducruz@datum.hn
Web http://www.
    honduras.cruzroja.org/

Hungarian Red Cross
Magyar Vöröskereszt
1367 Budapest 5, Pf. 121
Hungary
Tel. +36 1 3741338
Fax +36 1 3741312
E-mail intdept@hrc.hu

Icelandic Red Cross
Efstaleiti 9
103 Reykjavik
Iceland
Tel. +354 5704022
Fax +354 5704010
E-mail central@redcross.is
Web http://www.redcross.is/

Indian Red Cross Society
Red Cross Building
1 Red Cross Road
110001 New Delhi
India
Tel. +91 112 3716424
Fax +91 112 3717454
E-mail indcross@vsnl.com
Web http://www.
    indianredcross.org/

Indonesian Red Cross Society
Jl. Jenderal Datot Subroto
Kav. 96
P.O. Box 20
Jakarta
Indonesia
Tel. +62 21 7992325
Fax +62 21 7995188
Tlx 66170 MB PMI IA

Red Crescent Society of the Islamic Republic of Iran
Ostad Nejatolahi Ave.
Tehran
Iran, Islamic Republic of
Tel. +98 21 8849077
Fax +98 21 8849079
E-mail helal@mail.dci.co.ir
Web http://www. redcrescent.ir

Iraqi Red Crescent Society
Al-Mansour
P.O. Box 6143
Baghdad
Iraq
Tel. +964 1 8862191
Fax +964 1 5372519
Tlx 213331 HELAL IK

Irish Red Cross Society
16, Merrion Square
Dublin 2
Ireland
Tel. +353 1 6765135
Fax +353 1 6614461
E-mail redcross@iol.ie
Web http://www.redcross.ie

Italian Red Cross
Via Toscana, 12
I-00187 Roma – RM
Italy
Tel. +39 06 4759399
Fax +39 06 4759223
Web http://www.cri.it/

Jamaica Red Cross

76 Arnold Road
Kingston
Jamaica
Tel. +1 876 98478602
Fax +1 876 9848272
E-mail jrcs@infochan.com

Japanese Red Cross Society

1-3 Shiba Daimon, 1-Chome,
Minato-ku
Tokyo-105-8521
Japan
Tel. +81 3 34377087
Fax +81 3 34358509
E-mail kokusai@jrc.or.jp
Web http://www.jrc.or.jp

Jordan National Red Crescent Society

Madaba Street
P.O. Box 10001
Amman 11151
Jordan
Tel. +962 64 773141
Fax +962 64 750815
E-mail jrc@index.com.jo

Kenya Red Cross Society

Nairobi South "C"
Belle Vue, off Mombasa Road
P.O. Box 40712
Nairobi
Kenya
Tel. +254 2 503781
Fax +254 2 503845
E-mail kenyaredcross@
    kenyaweb.org

Kiribati Red Cross Society

P.O. Box 213
Bikenibeu
Tarawa
Kiribati
Tel. +686 28128
Fax +686 21416
E-mail redcross@tskl.net.ki

Red Cross Society of the Democratic People's Republic of Korea

Ryonwa 1, Central District
Pyongyang
Korea, Democratic People's
Republic of
Tel. +850 2 18333
Fax +850 2 3814644
Tlg. KOREACROSS
    PYONGYANG

The Republic of Korea National Red Cross

32 – 3ka, Namsan-dong
Choong-Ku
Seoul 100 – 043
Korea, Republic of
Tel. +82 2 37053705
Fax +82 2 37053667
E-mail knrc@redcross.or.kr
Web http://www.redcross.or.kr

Kuwait Red Crescent Society

Al-Jahra Strett, Shuweek
P.O. Box 1359
13014 Safat
Kuwait
Tel. +965 4815478
Fax +965 4839114
E-mail krcs@kuwait.net

Red Crescent Society of Kyrgyzstan

10, prospekt Erkindik
720040 Bishkek
Kyrgyzstan
Tel. +996 312 624814
Fax +996 312 662181
E-mail redcross@elcat.kg

Lao Red Cross

Avenue Sethathirath
B.P. 650
Vientiane
Lao People's Democratic Republic
Tel. +856 21 222398
Fax +856 21 212128
Tlx 4491 TE via PTT LAOS

Latvian Red Cross

1, Skolas Street
Riga, LV-1010
Latvia
Tel. +371 7336650
Fax +371 7336651
E-mail secretariat@redcross.lv

Lebanese Red Cross

Rue Spears
Beyrouth
Lebanon
Tel. +961 1 372802
Fax +961 1 378207
E-mail lrc-comm@dm.net.lb
Web http://www.
    dm.net.lb/redcross/

Lesotho Red Cross Society

23 Mabile Road
P.O. Box 366
Maseru 100
Lesotho
Tel. +266 22 313911
Fax +266 22 310166
E-mail lesoff@lesred.co.za

Liberian Red Cross Society

107 Lynch Street
P.O. Box 20-5081
1000 Monrovia 20
Liberia
Tel. +888-330125
Fax +231 330125
E-mail lnrc@Liberia.net

Libyan Red Crescent

P.O. Box 541
Benghazi
Libyan Arab Jamahiriya
Tel. +218 61 9095202
Fax +218 61 9095829
E-mail libyan_redcrescent@
    libyamail.net

Liechtenstein Red Cross

Heiligkreuz 25
FL-9490 Vaduz
Liechtenstein
Tel. +423 2322294
Fax +423 2322240
E-mail info@lieredcross.li

Lithuanian Red Cross Society

Gedimino ave. 3a
2600 Vilnius
Lithuania
Tel. +370 2 628037
Fax +370 2 619923
E-mail international@redcross.lt
Web http://www.redcross.lt

Luxembourg Red Cross

Parc de la Ville
B.P. 404
L – 2014 Luxembourg
Tel. +352 450202
Fax +352 457269
E-mail siege@croix-rouge.lu
Web http://www.croix-rouge.lu/

The Red Cross of The Former Yugoslav Republic of Macedonia

No. 13
Bul. Koco Racin
91000 Skopje
Macedonia, the Former Yugoslav
Republic of
Tel. +389 91 114355
Fax +389 91 230542

Malagasy Red Cross Society

1, rue Patrice Lumumba
Tsavalalana
B.P. 1168
Antananarivo
Madagascar
Tel. +261 20 2222111
Fax +261 20 2266739
E-mail crm@dts.mg

Malawi Red Cross Society

Red Cross House
P.O. Box 30096
Capital City
Lilongwe 3
Malawi
Tel. +265 1 775377
Fax +265 1 775590
E-mail mrcs@eomw.net

Malaysian Red Crescent Society

JKR 32, Jalan Nipah
Off Jalan Ampang
55000 Kuala Lumpur
Malaysia
Tel. +60 3 42578122
Fax +60 3 4533191
E-mail mrcs@po.jaring.my
Web http://www.
    redcrescent.org.my/

Mali Red Cross

Route Koulikoro
B.P. 280
Bamako
Mali
Tel. +223 224569
Fax +223 240414
Tlx 2611 MJ

Malta Red Cross Society

104 St Ursula Street
Valletta VLT 05
Malta
Tel. +356 21222645
Fax +356 21243664
E-mail redcross@waldonet.net.mt
Web http://www.redcross.org.mt/

Mauritanian Red Crescent

Avenue Gamal Abdel Nasser
B.P. 344
Nouakchott
Mauritania
Tel. +222 5251249
Fax +222 5291221
Tlx 5830 CRM

Mauritius Red Cross Society

Ste. Thérèse Street
Curepipe
Mauritius
Tel. +230 6763604
Fax +230 6748855
E-mail redcross@intnet.mu

Mexican Red Cross

Calle Luis Vives 200
Colonia Polanco
México, D.F. 11510
Mexico
Tel. +52 5 3950606
Fax +52 5 3951598
E-mail cruzroja@mexporta.com
Web http://www.
    mexico.cruzroja.org/

Red Cross Society of the Republic of Moldova

67a, Ulitsa Asachi
MD-277028 Chisinau
Moldova, Republic of
Tel. +373 2 729644
Fax +373 2 729700
E-mail moldova-RC@mdl.net

Red Cross of Monaco

27, Boulevard de Suisse
Monte Carlo
Monaco
Tel. +377 97 976800
Fax +377 93 159047
E-mail redcross@monaco.mc
Web http://www.croix-rouge.mc

Mongolian Red Cross Society

Central Post Office
Post Box 537
Ulaanbaatar 13
Mongolia
Tel. +976 1 312578
Fax +976 1 312934
E-mail redcross@magicnet.mn

Moroccan Red Crescent

Palais Mokri
Takaddoum
B.P. 189
Rabat
Morocco
Tel. +212 37 650898
Fax +212 37 653280
E-mail crm@iam.net.ma

Mozambique Red Cross Society

Avenida Agostinho Neto 284
Caixa Postal 2986
Maputo
Mozambique
Tel. +258 1 490943
Fax +258 1 497725
E-mail cvm@mail.tropical.co.mz

Myanmar Red Cross Society

42 Strand Road
Yangon
Myanmar
Tel. +95 1 296552
Fax +95 1 296551
Tlx 21218 BRCROS BM

Namibia Red Cross

Erf 2128, Independence Avenue
Katutura
P.O. Box 346
Windhoek
Namibia
Tel. +264 61 235216
Fax +264 61 228949
E-mail namcross@redcross.org.na

Nepal Red Cross Society

Red Cross Marg
Kalimati
P.O. Box 217
Kathmandu
Nepal
Tel. +977 1 270650
Fax +977 1 271915
E-mail nrcs@nrcs.org
Web http://www.nrcs.org/

The Netherlands Red Cross

Leeghwaterplein 27
P.O. Box 28120
2502 KC The Hague
Netherlands
Tel. +31 70 4455666
Fax +31 70 4455777
E-mail hq@redcross.nl
Web http://www.rodekruis.nl

New Zealand Red Cross

69 Molesworth Street
P.O. Box 12-140
Thorndon
Wellington 6038
New Zealand
Tel. +64 4 4723750
Fax +64 4 4730315
E-mail jcs@redcross.org.nz
Web http://www.redcross.org.nz/

Nicaraguan Red Cross

Reparto Belmonte
Carretera Sur, km 7
Apartado 3279
Managua
Nicaragua
Tel. +505 2 651307
Fax +505 2 651643
E-mail nicacruz@ibw.com.ni
Web http://www.
    nicaragua.cruzroja.org/

Red Cross Society of Niger

B.P. 11386
Niamey
Niger
Tel. +227 733037
Fax +227 732461
E-mail crniger@intnet.ne

Nigerian Red Cross Society

11, Eko Akete Close
South West Ikoyi
P.O. Box 764
Lagos
Nigeria
Tel. +234 1 2695188
Fax +234 1 2691599
E-mail nrcs@wananet.net

Norwegian Red Cross

Hausmannsgate 7
Postbox 1. Gronland
0133 Oslo
Norway
Tel. +47 22054000
Fax +47 22054040
E-mail documentation.
    center@redcross.no
Web http://www.redcross.no/

Pakistan Red Crescent Society

Sector H-8
Islamabad
Pakistan
Tel. +92 51 9257404
Fax +92 51 9257408
E-mail hilal@comsats.net.pk
Web http://www.prcs.org.pk/

Palau Red Cross Society

P.O. Box 6043
Koror 96940
Palau
Tel. +680 4885780
Fax +680 4884540
E-mail palredcross@palaunet.com

Red Cross Society of Panama

Calle Principal
Edificio # 453
Apartado 668
Zona 1
Panama
Tel. +507 3151389
Fax +507 3151401
E-mail cruzroja@pan.gbm.net
Web http://www.
    panama.cruzroja.org/

Papua New Guinea Red Cross Society

Taurama Road
Port Moresby
P.O. Box 6545
Boroko, N.C.D.
Papua New Guinea
Tel. +675 3258577
Fax +675 3259714

Paraguayan Red Cross

Brasil 216 esq. José Berges
Asunción
Paraguay
Tel. +595 21 222797
Fax +595 21 211560
E-mail cruzroja@cruzroja.org.py
Web http://www.cruzroja.org.py/

Peruvian Red Cross

Av. Arequipa No 1285
Lima
Peru
Tel. +51 1 4710701
Fax +51 1 4710701
E-mail cruzrojaperuana@
    terra.com.pe
Web http://www.cruzroja.org.pe

The Philippine National Red Cross

Bonifacio Drive
Port Area
P.O. Box 280
Manila 2803
Philippines
Tel. +63 2 5270866
Fax +63 2 5270857
E-mail secgen_pnrc@email.com

Polish Red Cross

Mokotowska 14
P.O. Box 47
00-950 Warsaw
Poland
Tel. +48 22 3261200
Fax +48 22 6284168
E-mail pck@atomnet.pl
Web http://www.pck.org.pl/

Portuguese Red Cross

Campo Grande, 28-6th
1700-093 Lisboa
Portugal
Tel. +351 21 3905571
Fax +351 21 7822443
E-mail internacional@
    cruzvermelha.org.pt

Qatar Red Crescent Society

P.O. Box 5449
Doha
Qatar
Tel. +974 4 435111
Fax +974 4 439950
E-mail qrcs@qatar.net.qa

Romanian Red Cross

Strada Biserica Amzei, 29
Sector 1
Bucarest
Romania
Tel. +40 21 2129862
Fax +40 21 3128452
E-mail crr@xnet.ro

The Russian Red Cross Society

Tcheryomushkinski Proezd 5
117036 Moscow
Russian Federation
Tel. +7 095 1265731
Fax +7 095 2302867
Tlx 411400 IKPOL SU

Rwandan Red Cross

B.P. 425, Kacyiru
Kigali
Rwanda
Tel. +250 585446
Fax +250 585449
E-mail rrc@rwandate11.com

Saint Kitts and Nevis Red Cross Society

Horsford Road
P.O. Box 62
Basseterre
Saint Kitts and Nevis
Tel. +1 869 4652584
Fax +1 869 4668129
E-mail skbredcr@caribsurf.com

Saint Lucia Red Cross

Vigie
P.O. Box 271
Castries St Lucia, W.I.
Saint Lucia
Tel. +1 758 4525582
Fax +1 758 4537811
E-mail sluredcross@candw.lc

Saint Vincent and the Grenadines Red Cross

Halifax Street
Kingstown
P.O. Box 431
Saint Vincent and the Grenadines
Tel. +1 784 4561888
Fax +1 784 4856210
E-mail svgredcross@caribsurf.com

Samoa Red Cross Society

P.O. Box 1616
Apia
Samoa
Tel. +685 23686
Fax +685 22676
E-mail samoaredcross@samoa.ws

Red Cross of the Republic of San Marino

Via Scialoja, Cailungo
Republic of San Marino 47031
Tel. +37 8 994360
Fax +37 8 994360
E-mail crs@omniway.sm
Web http://www.
    tradecenter.sm/crs/

Sao Tome and Principe Red Cross

Avenida 12 de Julho No.11
B.P. 96
Sao Tome
Sao Tome and Principe
Tel. +239 12 22469
Fax +239 12 22305
E-mail cvstp@sol.stome.telepac.net

Saudi Arabian Red Crescent Society

General Headquarters
Riyadh 11129
Saudi Arabia
Tel. +966 1 4740027
Fax +966 1 4740430
E-mail redcrescent@zajil.ne

Senegalese Red Cross Society

Boulevard F. Roosevelt
B.P. 299
Dakar
Senegal
Tel. +221 8233992
Fax +221 8225369

Yugoslav Red Cross

Simina 19
11000 Belgrade
Serbia and Montenegro
Tel. +381 11 623564
Fax +381 11 622965
E-mail jckbg@jck.org.yu
Web http://www.jck.org/yu

Seychelles Red Cross Society

Place de la République
B.P. 53
Victoria Mahé
Seychelles
Tel. +248 324646
Fax +248 321663
E-mail redcross@seychelles.net
Web http://www.
    seychelles.net/redcross/

Sierra Leone Red Cross Society

6 Liverpool Street
P.O. Box 427
Freetown
Sierra Leone
Tel. +232 22 229845
Fax +232 22 229083
E-mail slrcs@sierratel.sl

Singapore Red Cross Society

Red Cross House
15 Penang Lane
Singapore 238486
Tel. +65 63360269
Fax +65 63374360
E-mail redcross@starhub.net.sg
Web http://www.redcross.org.sg/

Slovak Red Cross

Grösslingova 24
814 46 Bratislava
Slovakia
Tel. +421 7 52923576
Fax +421 7 52923279
E-mail headq@redcross.sk

Slovenian Red Cross

Mirje 19
P.O. Box 236
SI-61000 Ljubljana
Slovenia
Tel. +386 1 2414300
Fax +386 1 2414344
E-mail rdeci.kriz-slo@guest.arnes.si

The Solomon Islands Red Cross

P.O. Box 187
Honiara
Solomon Islands
Tel. +677 22682
Fax +677 25299
E-mail sirc@solomon.com.sb

Somali Red Crescent Society

c/o ICRC Box 73226
Nairobi
Kenya
Tel. +252 1 216049 Mogadishu /
    +254 2 2713785 Nairobi
Fax +252 1 312647 Mogadishu /
    +254 2 2718 862 Nairobi
Web http://www.bishacas.org/

The South African Red Cross Society

1st Floor, Helen Bowden Bldg
Beach Road, Granger Bay
P.O. Box 50696, Waterfront
Cape Town 8002
South Africa
Tel. +27 21 4186640
Fax +27 21 4186644
E-mail sarcs@redcross.org.za
Web http://www.redcross.org.za/

Spanish Red Cross

Rafael Villa, s/n Vuelta Ginés
Navarro
28023 El Plantio
Madrid
Spain
Tel. +34 91 3354444
Fax +34 91 3354455
E-mail informa@cruzroja.es
Web http://www.cruzroja.es/

The Sri Lanka Red Cross Society
307, 2/1 T.B. Jayah Mawatha
P.O. Box 375
Colombo 10
Sri Lanka
Tel. +94 1 678420
Fax +94 1 695434
E-mail slrc@sri.lanka.net

The Sudanese Red Crescent
Al Mak Numir St/Gamhouria St
Plot No 1, Block No. 4 East
P.O. Box 235
Khartoum
Sudan
Tel. +249 11 772011
Fax +249 11 772877
E-mail srcs@sudanmail.net

Suriname Red Cross
Gravenberchstraat 2
Postbus 2919
Paramaribo
Suriname
Tel. +597 498410
Fax +597 464780
E-mail surcross@sr.net

Baphalali Swaziland Red Cross Society
104 Johnstone Street
P.O. Box 377
Mbabane
Swaziland
Tel. +268 4042532
Fax +268 4046108
E-mail bsrcs@redcross.sz

Swedish Red Cross
Hornsgatan 54
Box 17563
SE-118 91 Stockholm
Sweden
Tel. +46 8 4524600
Fax +46 8 4524761
E-mail postmaster@redcross.se
Web http://www.redcross.se/

Swiss Red Cross
Rainmattstrasse 10
Postfach
3001 Bern
Switzerland
Tel. +41 31 3877111
Fax +41 31 3877122
E-mail info@redcross.ch
Web http://www.redcross.ch/

Syrian Arab Red Crescent
Al Malek Aladel Street
Damascus
Syrian Arab Republic
Tel. +963 11 4429662
Fax +963 11 4425677
E-mail SARC@net.sy

Red Crescent Society of Tajikistan
120, Omari Khayom St.
734017 Dushanbe
Tajikistan
Tel. +7 3772 240374
Fax +7 3772 245378
E-mail rcstj@yahoo.com

Tanzania Red Cross National Society
Ali Hassan Mwinyi Road, Plot 294/295
Upanga
P.O. Box 1133
Dar es Salaam
Tanzania, United Republic of
Tel 255 22 2150881
Fax +255 22 2150147
E-mail logistics@raha.com

The Thai Red Cross Society
Terd Prakiat Building
1871 Henry Dunant Road
Bangkok 10330
Thailand
Tel. +66 2 2564037
Fax +66 2 2553064
E-mail wmaster@redcross.or.th
Web http://www. redcross.or.th/

Togolese Red Cross
51, rue Boko Soga
Amoutivé
B.P. 655
Lome
Togo
Tel. +228 212110
Fax +228 215228
E-mail crtogol@syfed.tg.refer.org

Tonga Red Cross Society
P.O. Box 456
South West Pacific
Nuku'Alofa
Tonga
Tel. +676 21360
Fax +676 21508
E-mail redcross@kalianet.to

The Trinidad and Tobago Red Cross Society
7A, Fitz Blackman Drive
Wrightson Road
P.O. Box 357
Port of Spain
Trinidad and Tobago
Tel. +1 868 6278128
Fax +1 868 6278215
E-mail ttrcs@carib-link.net

Tunisian Red Crescent
19, Rue d'Angleterre
Tunis 1000
Tunisia
Tel. +216 71 325572
Fax +216 71 320151
E-mail hilal.ahmar@planet.tn

Turkish Red Crescent Society
Atac Sokak 1 No. 32
Yenisehir, Ankara
Turkey
Tel. +90 312 4302300
Fax +90 312 4300175
E-mail basinyayin@kizilay.org.tr
Web http://www.kizilay.org.tr/

Red Crescent Society of Turkmenistan
48 A. Novoi str.
744000 Ashgabat
Turkmenistan
Tel. +993 12 395511
Fax +993 12 351750
E-mail nrcst@online.tm

The Uganda Red Cross Society
Plot 28/30 Lumumba Avenue
P.O. Box 494
Kampala
Uganda
Tel. +256 41 258701
Fax +256 41 258184
E-mail sgurcs@imul.com

Ukrainian Red Cross Society
30, Pushkinskaya St.
252004 Kiev
Ukraine
Tel. +380 44 2350157
Fax +380 44 2351096
E-mail redcross@ukrpack.net
Web http://www.redcross.org.ua

Red Crescent Society of the United Arab Emirates
P.O. Box 3324
Abu Dhabi
United Arab Emirates
Tel. +9 712 6419000
Fax +9 712 6420101
E-mail hilalrc@emirates.net.ae

British Red Cross
9 Grosvenor Crescent
London SW1X 7EJ
United Kingdom
Tel. +44 207 2355454
Fax +44 207 2456315
E-mail information@r
    edcross.org.uk
Web http://www.redcross.org.uk

American Red Cross
431 18th Street NW, 2nd Floor
Washington, DC 20006
United States
Tel. +1 202 6393400
Fax +1 202 6393595
E-mail postmaster@usa.redcross.org
Web http://www.redcross.org/

Uruguayan Red Cross
Avenida 8 de Octubre, 2990
11600 Montevideo
Uruguay
Tel. +598 2 4802112
Fax +598 2 4800714
E-mail cruzroja@adinet.com.uy
Web http://www.
    uruguay.cruzroja.org/

Red Crescent Society of Uzbekistan
30, Yusuf Hos Hojib St.
700031 Tashkent
Uzbekistan
Tel. +988 712 563741
Fax +988 712 561801
E-mail rcuz@uzpak.uz
Web http://www.redcrescent.uz/

Vanuatu Red Cross Society
P.O. Box 618
Port Vila
Vanuatu
Tel. +678 27418
Fax +678 22599
E-mail redcross@vanuatu.com.vu

Venezuelan Red Cross
Avenida Andrés Bello, 4
Apartado 3185
Caracas 1010
Venezuela
Tel. +58 212 5714380
Fax +58 212 5761042
E-mail dirnacsoc@cantv.net
Web http://www.
    venezuela.cruzroja.org/

Red Cross of Viet Nam
82, Nguyen Du Street
Hanoï
Viet Nam
Tel. +844 8 225157
Fax +844 9 424285
E-mail vnrchq@netnam.org.vn
Web http://www.vnrc.org.vn

Yemen Red Crescent Society
26 September Street
P.O. Box 1257
Sanaa
Yemen
Tel. +967 1 283132 / 283133
Fax +967 1 283131
Tlx 3124 HILAL YE

Zambia Red Cross Society
2837 Los Angeles Boulevard
Longacres
P.O. Box 50001 Ridgeway 15101
Lusaka
Zambia
Tel. +260 1 250607
Fax +260 1 252219
E-mail zrcs@zamnet.zm

Zimbabwe Red Cross Society
98 Cameron Street
P.O. Box 1406
Harare
Zimbabwe
Tel. +263 4 775416
Fax +263 4 751739
E-mail zrcs@harare.iafrica.com

chapter 10

Worldwide support: the International Federation's delegations around the world help National Societies when disaster strikes.

International Federation

Worldwide support

Contact details for regional and country delegations of the International Federation of Red Cross and Red Crescent Societies. Information correct as of 1 March 2003.

International Federation of Red Cross and Red Crescent Societies

P.O. Box 372
1211 Geneva 19
Switzerland
Tel. +41 22 7304222
Fax +41 22 7330395
Tlx 045 412 133 FRC CH
Tlg. LICROSS GENEVA
E-mail secretariat@ifrc.org
Web http://www.ifrc.org

Red Cross/European Union Office

Rue Belliard 65, bte 7
1040 – Brussels
Belgium
Tel. +32 2 2350680
Fax +32 2 2305465
E-mail infoboard@redcross-eu.net

International Federation of Red Cross and Red Crescent Societies at the United Nations

800 Second Avenue
Third floor
New York, NY 10019
United States
Tel. +1 212 3380161
Fax +1 212 3389832

International Federation regional delegations

Yaoundé

Rue Mini-Prix Bastos
BP 11507
Yaoundé
Cameroon
Tel. +237 2217437
Fax +237 2217439
E-mail ifrccm04@ifrc.org

Beijing

Apt. 4-2-5-1 Building 4, Entrance 2, Floor 5, Apt.1
Jianguomenwai Diplomatic Compound
Chaoyang District
Beijing 100600
China
Tel. +8610 65327162
Fax +8610 65327166
E-mail ifrccn10@ifrc.org

Abidjan

II Plateaux Polyclinique-
Lot no. 14 - Îlot 4
Villa Duplex
04 PO Box 2090
Abidjan, 04
Côte d'Ivoire
Tel. +225 22404450
Fax +225 22404459
E-mail ifrcci13@ifrc.org

Suva

77 Cakobau Road
P.O. Box 2507
Government Building
Suva
Fiji
Tel. +679 3311855
Fax +679 3311406
E-mail ifrcfj01@ifrc.org

Budapest

Zolyomi Lepcso Ut 22
1124 Budapest
Hungary
Tel. +361 2483300
Fax +361 2483322
E-mail ifrchu01@ifrc.org

New Delhi

C-1/35 Safdarjung Development Area
New Delhi 110 016
India
Tel. +9111 26858671
Fax +9111 26857567
E-mail ifrcin01@ifrc.org

Amman
Al Shmeisani
Maroof Al Rasafi Street
Building No. 19
P.O. Box 830511 / Zahran
Amman
Jordan
Tel. +962 6 5681060
Fax +962 6 5694556
E-mail ifrcjo01@ifrc.org

Almaty
86, Kunaeva Street
480100 Almaty
Kazakhstan
Tel. +732 72 918838
Fax +732 72 914267
E-mail ifrckz01@ifrc.org

Nairobi
Woodlands Road (off State House
Road)
P.O. Box 41275
Nairobi
Kenya
Tel. +2542 2714255
Fax +2542 2718415
E-mail ifrcke01@ifrc.org

Panama
Edificio No. 804
Clayton, Ancon
Panama
Tel. +507 317 1300
Fax +507 317 1304
E-mail ifrcpa50@ifrc.org

Lima
Los Naranjos 351
San Isidro, Lima
Peru
Tel. +511 2219006
Fax +511 4413607
E-mail ifrcpe07@ifrc.org

Bangkok
213/4 Sukhumvit 21 Road
North Klongtoey
Wattana
Bangkok 10110
Thailand
Tel. +662 6616933
Fax +662 6616937
E-mail ifrcth23@ifrc.org

Ankara
Cemal Nadir Sokak, No. 9
Cankaya, Ankara 06680
Turkey
Tel 90312 441 42 92
Fax +90312 441 3866

Harare
4, Bates Street
Milton Park
Harare
Zimbabwe
Tel. +2634 705166
Fax +2634 708784
E-mail ifrczw01@ifrc.org

International Federation country delegations

Afghanistan
Estgah Dawa Khana,
Shash Darak
Kabul
Afghanistan
Tel. +873 3822 80530
Fax +873 3822 80534
E-mail kabuldel@wireless.ifrc.org

Albania
c/o Albanian Red Cross
Rruga "Muhamet Gjollesha"
Sheshi "Karl Topia"
P.O. Box 1511
Tirana
Albania
Tel. +355 4256708
Fax +355 4227966
E-mail irfca102@ifrc.org

Angola
Caixa Postal 3324
Rua 1 Congresso de MPLA 26/27
Luanda
Angola
Tel. +2442 372868
Fax +2442 372868
E-mail ifrcao01@ifrc.org

Armenia
Gevorg Chaush St. 50/1
Yerevan 375088
Armenia
Tel. +3741 354649
Fax +3741 395731
E-mail ifrcam03@ifrc.org

Azerbaijan
S. Safarov Street 2
Baku, Nesimi District
PC 370010
Azerbaijan
Tel. +99412 925792
Fax +99412 971889
E-mail baku02@ifrc.org

Bangladesh
c/o Bangladesh Red Crescent
Society
684-686 Bara Magh Bazar
Dhaka - 1217
Bangladesh
Tel. +8802 8315401
Fax +8802 9341631
E-mail ifrcbd@citecho.net

Belarus
Ulitsa Mayakovkosgo 14
Minsk 220006
Belarus
Tel. +375172 217273
Fax +375172 219060
E-mail ifrcby01@ifrc.org

Burundi
Avenue des Etats-Unis 3674A
B.P. 324
Bujumbura
Burundi
Tel. +257 229524
Fax +257 229408

Cambodia
17 Deo, Street Croix-Rouge
Central Post Office/P.O. Box 620
Phnom Penh
Cambodia
Tel. +855 23 210162
Fax +855 23 210163
E-mail ifrckh01@ifrc.org

Colombia
c/o Colombian Red Cross
Avenida 68 N° 66-31
Bogotá
Colombia
Tel. +571 4299329
Fax +571 4299328
E-mail ifrcbogota@
        sncruzroja.org.co

Congo, Democratic Republic of the
21 Avenue Flamboyant
Place de Sefoutiers
Gombe
Kinshasa
Congo, Democratic Republic of the
Tel. +871 763050365
Fax +871 763050366
E-mail hod@ficr.aton.cd

East Timor
Bidau-Santana Rua de
        Cristo Rei s/n
Dili
East Timor
Tel. +670 390 322778
Fax +670 390 322778
E-mail ifrc_east_timor01@ifrc.org

El Salvador
c/o Salvadorean Red Cross Society
17 calle Poniente y Av. Henry
Dunant
Centro de Gobierno, San Salvador
El Salvador
Tel. +503 2222166
Fax +503 2811932
E-mail ifrcsv11@ifrc.org

Eritrea
c/o Red Cross Society of Eritrea
Andnet Street
P.O. Box 575
Asmara
Eritrea
Tel. +2911 150550
Fax +2911 151859
E-mail ifrc@eol.com.er

Ethiopia
Ras Destra Damtew Avenue
P.O. Box 195
Addis Ababa
Ethiopia
Tel. +2511 514571
Fax +2511 512888
E-mail ifrcet04@ifrc.org

Georgia
54, Chavchavadze Ave., Apt. 18
380079 Tbilisi
Georgia
Tel. +99532 922248
Fax +99532 226136
E-mail ifrcge01@ifrc.org

Guatemala
c/o Guatemala Red Cross
3A Calle 8-40, Zona 1
Guatemala, Guatemala
Tel. +502 2532809
Fax +502 2380091
E-mail fedecng@intelnet.net.gt

Guinea
Coleah, route du Niger
(derrière la station Shell)
Près de l'Ambassade de Yougoslavie
B.P. No 376
Conakry
Guinea
Tel. +224 413825
Fax +224 414255
E-mail ifrc.gn01@ifrc.org

Honduras
Colonia Florencia Sur,
Segunda avenida, casa No. 3702
Boulevar Suyapa
Tegucigalpa
Apartado postal No. 15031
Honduras
Tel. +504 2320707
Fax +504 2320710

Indonesia
c/o Indonesian Red Cross Society
P.O. Box 2009
Jakarta
Indonesia
Tel. +6221 79191841
Fax +6221 79180905
E-mail ifrcid07@ifrc.org

Iraq
c/o Iraqi Red Crescent Society
P.O. Box 6143
Baghdad
Iraq
Tel. +964 1 5370042
Fax +964 1 5372547

Democratic People's Republic of Korea

c/o Red Cross Society of the DPR Korea
Ryonwa 1, Central District
Pyongyang
Korea, Democratic People's Republic of
Tel. +8502 3814350
Fax +8502 3813490
E-mail ifrckp02@ifrc.org

Lao People's Democratic Republic

c/o Lao Red Cross
P.O. Box 2948
Setthatirath Road, Xiengnhune
Vientiane
Lao People's Democratic Republic
Tel. +856 21215762
Fax +856 21215935
E-mail laoifrc@laotel.com

Lebanon

N. Dagher Building
Mar Tacla
Beirut
Lebanon
Tel. +9611 424851
Fax +9615 459658
E-mail ifrclb01@ifrc.org

Mongolia

c/o Red Cross Society of Mongolia
Central Post Office
Post Box 537
Ulaanbaatar
Mongolia
Tel +97611 321684
Fax +97611 321684
E-mail ifrcmn01@ifrc.org

Myanmar

c/o Myanmar Red Cross Society
42 Strand Road
Yangon
Myanmar
Tel. +951 297877
Fax +951 297877
E-mail ifrc@mptmail.net.mm

Nicaragua

c/o Nicaraguan Red Cross
Reparto Belmonte, Carretera Sur
Apartado Postal P-48 Las Piedrecitas
Managua
Nicaragua
Tel. +505 2650186
Fax +505 2652069

Nigeria

c/o Nigerian Red Cross Society
11, Eko Akete Close
Off St. Gregory's Road
South West Ikoyi
P.O. Box 764
Lagos
Nigeria
Tel. +2341 2695228
Fax +2341 2695229
E-mail: ifrcng02@ifrc.org

Pakistan

c/o Pakistan Red Crescent Society
National Headquarters
Sector H-8
Islamabad
Pakistan
Tel. +9251 9257122
Fax +9251 4430745
E-mail ifrcpk01@ifrc.org

Papua New Guinea

Taurama Road
Port Moresby
P.O. Box 6545
Boroko
Papua New Guinea
Tel. +675 3112277
Fax +675 3230731
E-mail ifrcpg01@ifrc.org

Russian Federation

c/o Russian Red Cross Society
Tcheryomushkinski Proezd 5
117036 Moscow
Russian Federation
Tel. +7502 9375267
Fax +7502 9375263
E-mail moscow@ifrc.org

Rwanda

c/o Rwandan Red Cross
B.P. 425, Nyamiranbo
Kigali
Rwanda
Tel. +250 585446
Fax +250 585448
E-mail ifrcrw01@ifrc.org

Serbia and Montenegro

Simina Ulica Broj 21
11000 Belgrade
Serbia and Montenegro
Tel. +381 11 3282202
Fax +381 11 3281791
E-mail telecom@ifrc.org.yu

Sierra Leone

c/o Sierra Leone Red Cross Society
6, Liverpool Street
P.O. Box 427
Freetown
Sierra Leone
Tel. +23222 227772
Fax +23222 228180
E-mail ifrcsl01@ifrc.org

Somalia

c/o Regional Delegation Nairobi
Woodlands Road, off State House Road
P.O. Box 41275
Nairobi
Kenya
Tel. +254 2 2715249
Fax +254 2 2729070
E-mail ifrcso01@ifrc.org

South Africa

c/o South African Red Cross
1st Floor, Helen Bowden Bldg
Beach Road, Granger Bay
P.O. Box 50696, Waterfront
Cape Town 8002
South Africa
Tel. +27 21 4186640

Sri Lanka

3rd floor, 307 T B Jayah Mawatha
LK Colombo
Sri Lanka
Tel. +9474 7155977
Fax +9474 571275
E-mail ifrclk01@srilanka.net

Sudan

Al Mak Nimir Street/Gamhouria
Street
Plot No 1, Block No 4
P.O. Box 10697
East Khartoum
Sudan
Tel. +24911 771033
Fax +24911 770484

Tajikistan

c/o Tajikistan Red Crescent Society
120, Omar Khayom St.
734017 Dushanbe
Tajikistan
Tel. +992372 245981
Fax +992372 248520
E-mail ifrcdsb@ifrc.org

Tanzania

Ali Hassan Mwinyi Road
Plot No. 294/295
P.O. Box 1133
Dar es Salaam
Tanzania, United Republic of
Tel. +255 22 21116514
Fax +255 21117308
E-mail ifrctz01@ifrc.org

Uganda

c/o Uganda Red Cross Society
18/30 Lumumba Road
P.O. Box 494
Kampala
Uganda
Tel. +25641 348437
Fax +25641 258184
E-mail ifrc@imul.com

Viet Nam

15 Thien Quang Street
Hanoï
Viet Nam
Tel. +844 9422983
Fax +844 9422987
E-mail ifrc@hn.vnn.vn

Zambia

c/o Zambia Red Cross
2837 Los Angeles Boulevard
P.O. Box 50001
Ridgeway 15101
Lusaka
Zambia
Tel. +2601 250607
Fax +2601 2522219
E-mail ifrczmb03@ifrc.org

Index